Plantagenet Princesses

Also by Douglas Boyd

Histories:

April Queen, Eleanor of Aquitaine

Voices from the Dark Years

The French Foreign Legion

The Kremlin Conspiracy: 1,000 Years of Russian Expansionism

Normandy in the Time of Darkness: Life and Death in the Channel Ports 1940–45

Blood in the Snow, Blood on the Grass: Treachery and Massacre, France 1944

De Gaulle: The Man who Defied Six US Presidents

Lionheart: The True Story of England's Crusader King

The Other First World War: The Blood-soaked Russian Fronts 1914–22

Daughters of the KGB: Moscow's Cold War Spies, Sleepers and Assassins

Agente – Female Spies in World Wars, Cold Wars and Civil Wars

The Solitary Spy

Red October: The Revolution that Changed the World

Lockerbie: The Truth

Moscow Rules

Normandy's Nightmare War

In preparation:

The Plantagenet Princes

Novels:

The Eagle and the Snake

The Honour and the Glory

The Truth and the Lies

The Virgin and the Fool

The Fiddler and the Ferret

The Spirit and the Flesh

Plantagenet Princesses

The Daughters of Eleanor of Aquitaine and Henry II

Douglas Boyd

PEN & SWORD HISTORY

First published in Great Britain in 2020 by
Pen & Sword History
An imprint of
Pen & Sword Books Ltd
Yorkshire – Philadelphia

ISBN 978 1 52674 310 7

A CIP catalogue record for this book is
available from the British Library.

Printed and bound in the UK by TJ International Ltd,
Padstow, Cornwall.

Pen & Sword Books Limited incorporates the imprints of Atlas,
Archaeology, Aviation, Discovery, Family History, Fiction, History,
Maritime, Military, Military Classics, Politics, Select, Transport,
True Crime, Air World, Frontline Publishing, Leo Cooper, Remember
When, Seaforth Publishing, The Praetorian Press, Wharncliffe
Local History, Wharncliffe Transport, Wharncliffe True Crime
and White Owl.

For a complete list of Pen & Sword titles please contact

PEN & SWORD BOOKS LIMITED
47 Church Street, Barnsley, South Yorkshire, S70 2AS, England
E-mail: enquiries@pen-and-sword.co.uk
Website: www.pen-and-sword.co.uk

Or

PEN AND SWORD BOOKS
1950 Lawrence Rd, Havertown, PA 19083, USA
E-mail: Uspen-and-sword@casematepublishers.com
Website: www.penandswordbooks.com

Contents

Chapter 1

Eleanor of Aquitaine, Founder of the Dynasty

Perhaps surprisingly to non-medievalists, the early Middle Ages saw a number of women exercise great power. In the ninth century, the Lombard queen Angilberga was given the honorific *consors regni*. In the tenth century the Byzantine princess Theophano, married to Holy Roman Emperor Otto II, ruled the Empire after his death as regent for her son Otto III and, in England the Lady Aethelflaed both ruled Mercia and led its army into battle. In the eleventh century, Gisela, wife of Salian Emperor Konrad II, reigned with him as *consors imperii*. Early in the twelfth century, Adelaide of Savona governed Sicily as regent until her son Roger II came of age. In Visigothic Spain, Petronila of Aragon and Urraca of León-Castile were both queens regnant.

Another of these strong and powerful women was the daughter of England's King Henry I named Matilda or Maud. After the death in May 1125 of her first husband, the Holy Roman Emperor Heinrich V, she returned to the land of her birth at the age of 23 but kept the title of Empress for the rest of her life. Her father was a son of William the Conqueror and succeeded to the throne on the allegedly accidental death of his brother William Rufus in 1100. Having lost his legitimate 18-year-old son William Adelin and several of his illegitimate sons in the disastrous sinking of the White Ship off Barfleur in 1120, he named his only surviving legitimate child Matilda as his heir to the English crown and the Duchy of Normandy, forcing the Anglo-Norman barons of the island realm to swear allegiance to her.

At the time, nobody called sons and daughters of royalty by the title 'prince' or 'princess'; for example, William Adelin was known as *guilelmus filius regis* – William, the king's son or *guilelmus filius Henrici* with everybody knowing which Henry was being referred to. So, strictly speaking, the title of this book is a misnomer, but a convenient one for modern readers. Frustratingly, the only extant images of most of these women are the wax imprints of their seals that legitimised documents, and these give little impression of the person even in colour photographs – and none in monochrome.

When Henry I died in December 1135, his nephew Stephen of Blois was among the first to hear the news in Boulogne. Breaking the oath he had sworn to recognise Matilda as the legitimate successor, he immediately took ship from there to England. He seized the treasury with the help of his brother, Bishop Henry of Winchester, bribed the citizens of London to support his claim and persuaded William de Corbeil, Archbishop of Canterbury, to officiate at a coronation ceremony before the end of the year. Speed had won him the throne, allied to the dislike of many Anglo-Norman barons for the idea of being ruled by a woman – although Matilda Empress was far from a shrinking violet, being described in the eulogy later pronounced by Bishop Arnulf of Lisieux as 'an exceptional woman, devoid of womanliness'.[1] High praise indeed! Married for the second time to the lusty Count Geoffrey the Fair of Anjou, who was ten years her junior, the 'unwomanly' empress nevertheless more than fulfilled her duty to give him a male heir by bearing him three sons.

The Plantagenet dynasty takes its name from Geoffrey the Fair's custom of sporting a sprig of bright yellow flowering broom (in French, *genêt*) in his helmet as a highly visible rallying point to his supporters during battle and in *mêlées*, those violent free-for-all skirmishes at a tournament, confronting two teams of armed and mounted knights, where prisoners could be taken and held for ransom, and wounds and deaths were common. The earliest Plantagenets were from Geoffrey's county of Anjou in France, and therefore known as the Angevins, who ruled England 1154–1216. After the loss of the county of Anjou, came the Plantagenets proper, ruling 1216–1399, followed by the cadet branches, usually referred to as the houses of Lancaster and York, which ruled 1399–1485.

Following the difficult birth of her third son, christened Henry after his regal grandfather, Matilda Empress decided – as had Henry I's queen Matilda of Scotland after two births – to cease sexual relations with her husband, leaving him, as a chronicler once said, to take his pleasures elsewhere. Matilda's efforts to claim her legitimate inheritance on the death of Henry I were hampered by her last pregnancy. In the castle of Argentan in Normandy she produced the third son, christened William, at the end of July 1136, by which time Stephen of Blois had already been acclaimed king by the citizens of London. It was not until September 1139 that an offer of support from her half-brother Robert of Gloucester emboldened Matilda to cross the Channel and claim her throne with a mixed force of Angevin[2] and Norman knights and nobles, the latter wavering somewhat in their support because, if Stephen won the confrontation, they stood to lose their estates in England. For the next decade Matilda lived the precarious life of a female warlord in France and England. There was little contact with her sons until after her famous escape from Oxford castle, wrapped in a white cloak during a snowstorm in December 1140 which was thought by Stephen's force besieging the castle too severe for any man, let alone a woman, to venture out of doors. Clambering down the unguarded riverbank, Matilda and a few companions walked through the blizzard on the ice of the Thames to Wallingford and made their escape.

After her next major defeat by Stephen's forces at Winchester in 1141, she retreated to Devizes in Wiltshire, styling herself ambiguously as *domina anglorum* or 'Lady of the English'. Her eldest son, 9-year-old Henry Plantagenet, was sent to England to be brought up in Robert of Gloucester's household with the aim of making him the warrior-statesman capable of realising Matilda's frustrated political ambitions. Seven years later Matilda fled the country and retired to the Norman capital of Rouen a bitter and frustrated woman, leaving young Henry Plantagenet in England as figurehead for her forces in the bloody civil war, known as 'the anarchy', that ravaged England 1139–1153.

Here we run into a complication of medieval history. When Matilda died and her remains were taken to Rouen cathedral, her epitaph there read, and still reads: *Ci-gît la fille, femme et mère d'Henri*, which translates as Here lies the daughter, wife and mother of Henry. A witty epitaph for the daughter of England's King Henry I, wife of German Emperor Heinrich V and mother of England's King Henry II. So many males were christened using a handful of names rendered in English as William, Henry, Robert, Geoffrey and so on that eponymous individuals had often to be distinguished by sobriquets like Fat Louis, Henry the Proud, Geoffrey the Fair and William the Bastard or toponyms, as in Robert of Gloucester or Stephen of Blois. Similarly, so many female children were named Matilda or Maud, Eleanor or various forms of Mary and Margaret that use of the name alone can be confusing.

When Empress Matilda's eldest son Henry married Duchess Eleanor[3] of Aquitaine, his wife was an equally extraordinary woman. Her father Duke William X died on pilgrimage to the shrine in the Galician town of Santiago de Compostela at Easter 1137. As the older of his two surviving children, both girls, Eleanor inherited at the age of 15 the county of Poitou and duchy of Aquitaine – a vast slice of southwest France. Because many young noblewomen were carried off for their dowries and married against their will, the duke's death was hushed up by his companions when they returned to Bordeaux, for fear that some unruly vassal or neighbour might force Eleanor into marriage and become the new duke of Aquitaine by *fait accompli*. Physically beautiful, highly intelligent, literate in, and speaking, several languages, Eleanor was described by one who knew her well as *avenante, vaillante et courtoise* – or approachable, courageous and courtly.[4]

In searching for a suitable match, her guardian, the politically shrewd archbishop of Bordeaux Geoffroi de Lauroux set his sights high, arranging for her to marry the 17-year-old French crown prince Louis of the house of Capet. During the weeks it took Prince Louis to gather a suitable *mesnie* of nobles and knights to make the 300-mile journey from the royal domain around Paris to Bordeaux, Eleanor and her younger sister Aelith, also known as Petronilla, were effectively under house arrest for their own protection, closely guarded so that no intruder could snatch either of them away and foil the archbishop's plan. By the standards of the time, their quarters in the ducal palace of l'Ombreyra were luxurious indeed.

Society was then divided into three estates. In Latin, they were *oratores, bellatores et laboratores*: those who prayed, those who fought and those who laboured to support the totally unproductive knightly classes. It has been calculated that twenty-three entire families of serfs were required to support one modest knight and his household, and correspondingly more for grander knights and nobles. Outside the city of Bordeaux the serfs laboured from dawn to dusk in the fields. In summer, the men stripped to their *brais* – a cross between loincloth and underpants and

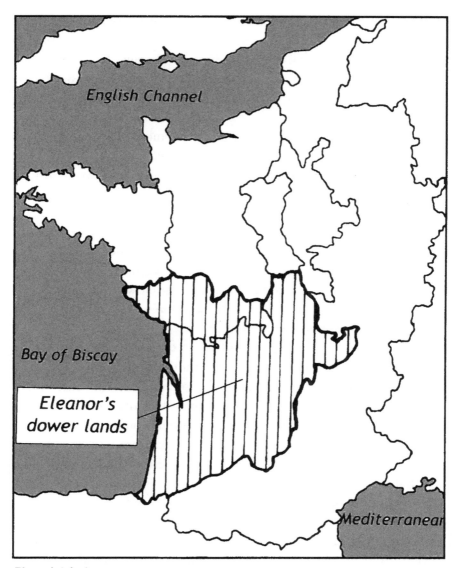

Eleanor's inheritance.

the women laboured alongside them with their skirts hitched up, to free their legs. They also cleared the vast forests of the region to make more productive land for their masters. So much land was cleared and so many new settlements established on it that even today twenty-five per cent of all place names in southwest France date from this period.

Eleanor and her sister Aelith wore ankle-length dresses of the finest cloth, some of silk trimmed with fur. The fashionable sleeves were so long they reached the floor and had to be knotted up out of the way much of the time. Their feet were protected from the cold flagstones of the palace by slippers of *vair*, the fur from the soft under-belly of squirrels – which became mistranslated as the homophone *verre* or glass in the fairy tale of Cinderella. Their arms and hands were embellished with bracelets and rings which, like their earrings, were set with precious stones. They also used cosmetics like eye shadow and rouge, and wore their hair long and loose, not confined in a wimple.

Such glamour horrified the most famous monk in France. Abbé Bernard at the Benedictine abbey of Clairvaux, who had a gift for words, deplored 'the beauty that is put on in the morning and laid aside at night.'[5] So, perhaps Eleanor dressed down to meet her bridegroom, when he finally arrived, for Prince Louis had been raised in the cloister until obliged by his elder brother's accidental death to abandon a religious career. The very disparate bride and groom were married in Bordeaux's Cathedral of St André on 25 July 1137. Louis and his entourage did not impress the locals, his monkish demeanour earning him the label *colhon* – a word in the Occitan language of southern France meaning 'testicle' or 'a stupid man'. It seems likely that a fight broke out on the wedding day between the Frankish northerners and the proud Aquitaine nobility, for the bride and groom fled before the wedding feast ended, riding on relays of horses for eighty miles to reach the safety of the castle of Taillebourg before nightfall.

On the death two weeks later of his long-suffering father Louis VI, once known as Battling Louis, but for years called just Fat Louis, Eleanor became the 15-year-old queen consort of France, for her new husband had already been crowned in accordance with Capetian custom, to ensure there was no break in the succession. Her official coronation came later. Raised in the pleasure-loving ducal court of Aquitaine to enjoy music, poetry and dance, accustomed since girlhood to flirting with sons of important vassals and courtly troubadours – some noble, some penniless – and free to ride the length and breadth of the duchy as the heir to her father Duke William X, she understandably chafed at the restrictions imposed at Louis' court in Paris as proper conduct for a Frankish queen by her devout and forceful mother-in-law Adelaide de Maurienne. Instead of complying, Eleanor did everything in her power to thwart the dowager queen until finally driving her away from court to reside in one of her dower castles in Champagne.

As pliant as his mother was dominant, Louis VII had been raised for high office in the Church until his older brother broke his spine when thrown by his mount stumbling over a pig snuffling through the garbage in a Parisian street. The fatal injury compelled his younger brother, who would have made a good abbot, to act the part of monarch in the turbulence of the twelfth century – a position he occupied from duty and for which he had little liking. Once back in Paris after the trip to Bordeaux, Louis returned to the cloister, where he felt at ease, fasting with the other monks and sharing their all-night vigils. This was not how Eleanor had imagined married life would be. Accidental succession to a title was the only thing the royal couple had in common, and their relationship is summed up in Eleanor's frequent complaint, 'I thought I had married a king, and found I had wed a monk.'[6]

For a while she used her excess energy in introducing southern comforts into the rude Capetian palace on the Ile de la Cité. Heating there was by charcoal embers in braziers, producing dangerous carbon monoxide, until she had a chimney installed in her quarters. Similarly, she had the narrow windows, through which came all the clamour of the citizenry and the stench of tanneries and sewage, glazed for warmth and quiet – and precious wall-hangings brought from Aquitaine and Poitou. For her entertainment, scandalising the religious members of Louis' court, she brought troubadours to recite poetry and sing songs for her pleasure. As to her queenly duty to provide a male heir for Louis, that was made more difficult by his preference for spending more nights in vigil on his knees at an altar than in her bed.

Eleanor's first surviving daughter Princess Marie was the incarnation of her failure to fulfil the queenly duty, as was the previous stillbirth. In between births, her domination of the monkish monarch led him far from the religious paths for which he had been trained – into warfare and worse.[7] Trying to live up to her expectations of a warrior husband, on one occasion he personally hacked off the feet of a recalcitrant vassal, so that he would be unable to mount a horse, the king's feeble build requiring many strokes of his sword to cut through bone and sinew. His worst excess under Eleanor's influence at the siege of Vitry-en-Perthois, during his 1143 invasion of Champagne, came when 1,300 men, women and children were burned alive after the town was fired by his troops. Seeking sanctuary in the church, virtually the entire population died when its blazing roof fell in on them. For this, Louis was excommunicated and denied all the comforts of confession, the sacrament and the rituals of the Mass that he adored.

When Louis sought the remission of his sin by taking the cross in the Second Crusade,[8] there was no way Eleanor intended to miss the greatest adventure of her lifetime. Knowing that her personal wealth and the manpower of her vassals were essential to the crusade, she ignored the interdiction of Pope Eugenius III on women[9] accompanying their menfolk, who had taken a vow of chastity. Gathering a personal court of noble ladies to go with her meant that the long baggage train of ox-drawn carts transporting their clothes, food, bedding and rich pavilions for the night, had to set off before the crusading army, to avoid causing a huge traffic jam. For part of the outward journey the queen and her ladies rode bare-breasted to taunt Louis' flagging and exhausted troops in the Anatolian mountains, suffering by day and night injury and death from harassing hit-and-run Seljuk Turks.

Meanwhile, back in France the wives of the crusader knights and barons were governing their possessions, never knowing whether their menfolk would return. Once in the Holy Land, excluded from access to Louis' daily councils with his religious advisers, Eleanor turned her back on them all, preferring to live in the sophisticated court of her uncle Raymond of Toulouse, the Count of Antioch known for his exotic lifestyle and extramarital dalliances. When the crusade fizzled out after costing thousands of crusaders' lives – more from disease than in combat – she was abducted from Antioch by the Templar eunuch Thierry Galeran and forcibly removed from the Holy Land. Both on land and at sea, she resisted Louis' authority every inch of the way back to France – which seemed proof to gossiping tongues that her relationship with Raymond had been carnal. Adultery by a queen of France counted as high treason, never mind the close family connection between Raymond and herself.

Breaking the journey, Eleanor was obliged to pay a courtesy visit with Louis to the papal court at Tusculum, where Eugenius' secretary John of Salisbury recorded her skilful presentation in Latin of her case for an annulment of the marriage to Louis on the grounds of their consanguinity. In this, she cited the authority of the future saint Bernard of Clairvaux, whom the Pope himself consulted on points of canon law. But Eugenius would have none of it. Smiling but firm, he ruled to her horror that her marriage to Louis was legitimate and threatened with anathema anyone rash enough to refer in future to the matter of the royal couple's consanguinity. Taking no notice of this woman desperate to escape from a frustrating marriage that bound her to a man more drawn to the altar than her bed, Eugenius gave instructions that a double bed be prepared in his palace for the royal spouses and spread with his own bedcovers. What Eleanor did to contain her fury at being treated by Eugenius like a wayward child, is not recorded.

The next stop for Louis on the royal progress back to Paris was in Rome, the city from which Eugenius was exiled by its rebellious citizens. Squalid and reduced to less than a quarter of its Imperial size by the barbarian invasions, the city once labelled 'eternal', was a sad mockery of its former glory. As a devout pilgrim, Louis was welcomed at the gates by a deputation of senators representing the commune that had killed the previous pope trying to assert his pontifical rights only six years before. Guided by the senators, the pilgrim king toured the holy sites accompanied by a claque chanting, *'Beatus qui in nomine domini venit.'* Blessed is he that comes in the name of the Lord. Blessed? Despite Eugenius' attempt to mend the rift by forcing Louis and Eleanor to sleep together for a few nights, Louis can have been under no illusion that she felt for him anything except contempt. They agreed on just one thing: it was unwise to linger in Rome at this time of year, when *la mal'aria* – literally 'the bad air' from the mosquito-infested swamps around the city – was blamed for killing off many visitors, although the natives appeared to have developed some resistance to the *plasmodium falciparum* parasite carried by those mosquitoes.

Resuming the interrupted journey back to France pregnant, Eleanor was furious with the Pope and equally furious with the indecisive husband whose seed she carried in her womb, yet who failed in every respect to meet her expectations. In Aquitaine, her husband would have been a warrior-poet, like her grandfather, the troubadour Duke William IX, who had carried on his shield the portrait of his mistress, the married Countess of Châtellerault rightly known as La Dangerosa. This was in return, he said, for her bearing him on her body in bed.

Back in Paris, on giving birth to a second daughter, whom she christened Aelith after her own sister, Eleanor realised that the repeated failures to provide Louis with a son could be the key to unlock the marital prison to which Eugenius sought to confine her. Had this child been male, her enemies – and she had made many at Louis' court in Paris during the fifteen years' marriage – might have come to overlook her scandalous conduct before and during the crusade. Although Louis was never hostile to her, his bishops were determined to rid the court of 'the whore of Aquitaine'. The divorce that was later described by John of Salisbury as Louis' repudiation of an adulterous wife, was negotiated at Beaugency, midway between Orleans and Blois.

Although present, 30-year-old Eleanor was not permitted to speak, but listened in silence to the legal arguments of Louis' bishops and hers, who were led by Geoffroi de Lauroux, the archbishop of Bordeaux who had arranged the marriage to Louis fifteen years earlier. In defiance of Eugenius' threat of anathema made at Tusculum, the grounds used for separating the disparate couple lay in their known consanguinity.[10] The marital bonds severed at long last, Eleanor rode with her small cortège of household knights back to the safety of her own possessions in what was no regal progress elegantly mounted on a side-saddle. It was a hell-for-leather race with her riding astride, in which she twice narrowly avoided ambushes by young nobles intent on carrying off such a rich prize.

Once safely inside the walls of her palace in Poitiers, the capital of her county of Poitou, her first priority was to wed a strong enough second husband to protect her domains by force of arms, if necessary. Adjacent to the northern frontier of Poitou lay the territory of Anjou, ruled by 19-year-old Count Henry fitz Empress, who was also Duke of Normandy. The *fitz* prefix was a corruption of the Latin *filius*, meaning 'son of', for the mother of this battle-hardened young warrior was Matilda Empress. Eleanor had met him before the crusade at Louis' court on the Ile de la Cité, where she discussed with Geoffrey the Fair the possibility of marrying Henry to her daughter Princess Marie in order to guarantee a powerful dynasty on the throne of France, should Louis die in Outremer without a male heir, but that discussion came to naught. On the 200-mile ride home from Beaugency in the heat of early September, father and son stripped off to cool down in the river Loir near their own city of Le Mans. Shortly afterward, Duke Geoffrey went down with a high fever – probably from swallowing contaminated river water. When he died three days later, the gossips on the Ile de la Cité accused Eleanor of sleeping with him and saw in the manner and timing of his death the hand of God striking down an adulterer.

But Geoffrey's three sons were alive and thriving and, although Henry Plantagenet was ten years her junior, there had been a similar difference in ages when Matilda Empress married his father. In Eleanor, Henry saw a powerful, elegant and beautiful woman in her prime, a lover of fashion, literate in several languages and schooled in the harsh politics of twelfth-century Europe. Ambitious to reclaim the English realm Matilda had lost, he knew Eleanor's immense wealth and territory allied to his own could tip the balance in his favour. Confident that he could get her pregnant with a son, despite Louis' failure to do so, he also calculated that, if she had failed to produce a son for him by the time of her menopause, he could, like Louis, invoke their consanguinity as grounds for divorce, put her away in a convent and take a younger wife with many more childbearing years ahead of her. When, after she had borne him sons and daughter, he initiated that plan, it was only Eleanor's unflagging strength of will throughout fifteen years as his prisoner which foiled it.

There were no stars in Eleanor's eyes, either. She had at that moment no intention of being other then a dutiful wife and consort and was confident that she would never say of him, as she had of Louis, 'He spent more nights on his knees at the altar than in my bed.' With his powerful chest and shoulders, Henry walked with a horseman's swagger, already slightly bandy-legged due to all the hours spent in the saddle each day. Betraying his Viking ancestry, his face was freckled, his eyes grey and his reddish hair was cut unfashionably short because long hair became tangled by rubbing against the arming cap worn inside a metal helmet. His nickname, Henry Curtmantle, referred to his habit of wearing a very

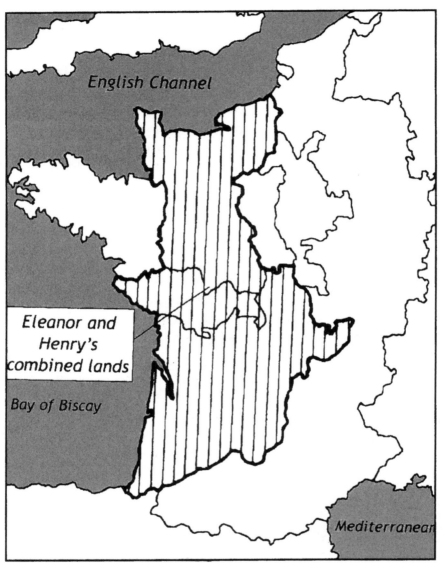

Eleanor's and Henry's combined possessions on 19 May 1152.

short cloak that gave little protection from the weather but made it easy
to mount and dismount speedily. It was well-known that, like his Viking
ancestors, he went literally berserk, if frustrated or defied, foaming at the
mouth, falling to the floor and rolling in the soiled reeds and refuse of an
audience hall, groaning like an animal in agony.

Feudal custom required them to seek the permission of their feudal overlord King Louis before marrying, but they ignored that formality and were married on 18 May 1152 in Poitiers Cathedral, neither party worrying that their consanguinity was one degree closer than Eleanor's had been with Louis. Whatever feelings they may have had for one another initially, the marriage was a political union that united her duchy of Aquitaine and county of Poitou with Henry's adjacent counties of Anjou, Maine and Touraine, plus the important duchy of Normandy. United by their marriage, this was a continuous swathe of territory that ran from the Spanish border to the English Channel and constituted nearly half of Louis' kingdom.

Chapter 2

Poems of Love and Bloodshed

The immediate consequence of the May wedding was a war, into which Louis was pressured by his barons, among whom was King Stephen of England, who was also a vassal of Louis as count of Mortain and Boulogne. Stephen saw this civil war as the best way to weaken the chief competitor of his son Eustace of Blois for the English throne when he died. Louis' brother Robert of Dreux, forgiven for attempting a coup d'état while Louis and Eleanor were in Outremer, joined in. Count Thibault of Blois, who had just been betrothed to Eleanor's second daughter, two-year-old Aelith, also took the king's side, as did Henry's younger brother, Geoffrey Plantagenet. Both of these men had failed in their attempts to kidnap Eleanor on the flight from Beaugency. Count Henry of Champagne, just married to Eleanor's elder daughter Marie, also supported Louis. When Princess Aelith was betrothed to Count Thibaut V of Blois, both Eleanor's daughters were the property of her enemies.

One of Louis VII's worst failings as king lay in his inability to think ill of anyone. It took him a while to realise that all the vassals in his coalition were not so much dutifully obeying their liege lord when called upon for knight service as hoping to grab plunder or claim a slice of Henry's and Eleanor's domains. They launched their invasion just after Midsummer Day in the belief that Henry was preoccupied with preparations to invade England. As later events were to prove, he was adept at making enemies think he was doing one thing when he was actually doing another. Riding horses into the ground and laying waste the land as he travelled, he invaded Robert of Dreux's territory, the speed and violence of his campaign so horrifying Louis with the reality of the war unleashed in his name that he fell ill with a fever and retreated as soon as the Church called for a truce. Still furious, Henry rode back to Anjou, which his brother Geoffrey had attempted to raise against him, and captured Montsoreau castle, garrisoned by Geoffrey's supporters. The youngest of Matilda's three sons, named William, had kept a low profile, having wisely decided to hitch his wagon to Henry's star.

Far from weakening Henry's position as Stephen of Blois had hoped, Louis' failed invasion actually achieved the reverse in forcing Eleanor's new husband to show his military prowess, thus warning his vassals and neighbours not to try and take advantage of his absence when he did eventually invade England. The short-lived war in France obliged Henry to delay that invasion until the following year, when he was far better prepared, but it also confirmed Eleanor's choice of her new husband as being of the stuff of her male ancestors in Aquitaine. The ducal couple spent the summer and autumn of 1152 in a grand feudal progress through her lands with their household knights and courtiers, to make the point to her vassals and vavasours that they owed homage to a powerful new duke. Henry also used the trip to assess the castles and fortified towns of Gascony both militarily and fiscally and assure himself that his administrators who had replaced Louis' appointees were up to the job of taxing the notoriously independent barons of Aquitaine.

Indifferent to food, Henry contented himself while travelling with gruel or bread and expected his companions to do the same. His curiosity was insatiable, whether focussed on trying out a horse, a hawk, a dog or a weapon, or examining with his own hands a jewel or piece of material offered by a merchant. Enjoying the company of the few lay and religious vassals and foreign ambassadors with the intellect to amuse him, he dismissed them from his entourage the moment they could no longer be of service or entertainment value. That first journey which Eleanor shared fits the description by chronicler Peter of Blois of his own travels with Henry's court a few years later:

> If the King announces that he will not be travelling on a certain day, he is sure to be off at first light, forcing his men to rush around like madmen, rousing the pack horses and crashing the carts into one another. If he says he will be setting out early to a certain destination, he is sure to sleep to noon. The loaded pack horses and carts stand waiting, the outriders snooze, everyone mutters and ponders. At last an enquiry is sent to the court prostitutes to see about the king's

travel plans, for this kind of court follower often knows the palace secrets.[1]

That was a euphemism for saying how Henry spent many nights. Yet there was nothing haphazard about his apparently erratic hyperactivity, which later enabled him to govern the enormous spread of territory on both sides of the English Channel, later known as the Angevin Empire, using methods of communication that had not changed in a thousand years. While confusing everyone else, Henry knew exactly what he was about, but was too paranoid to tell anyone.

Another chronicler, Arnulf of Lisieux described the relationship between the courtiers travelling with Henry thus:

Friendship among those who are summoned to give the king counsel and undertake his business is one of the rarest things. Anxious ambition dominates their minds; each of them fears to be outstripped by the endeavours of the others, and so is born envy, which necessarily turns immediately into hatred.[2]

The chronicler Walter Map, although not so greatly respected by modern historians as he was, called greed the main motivation of the court, where laughter was vanquished by care, and Peter of Blois said that court life was death to the soul.

During the long ride through Eleanor's domains, of which he was duke by marriage, Henry was affable enough in giving alms to religious establishments and confirming treaties. Yet, when thwarted by a religious or lay vassal, he reacted violently, as when tearing down the newly built walls of Limoges and its bridge across the river Vienne as a reminder to his new vassals and vavasours not to try and take advantage of his absence in the invasion of England planned for the following year. Those plans were also the reason he took an interest in the tuna and whale fisheries along the Gascon and Poitevin littoral, of which the vessels could be useful in transporting hundreds of men and horses across the Channel with him.

A different wife might have retired from their hectic progress to the civilised comforts of the comital palace at Poitiers or the ducal palace at Bordeaux, but the woman who had defied the pope to ride across the Anatolian mountains on the Second Crusade was tougher than that and also determined to establish her own position in the marriage from the outset, although rapidly realising she would never have over her new husband a fraction of the influence that she had enjoyed over Louis.

The tour of inspection was abruptly cut short after receipt of encouraging intelligence from Matilda's partisans in England. After hastening north to gather his forces, on 8 January 1153 Henry defied the winter storms by setting sail from Barfleur with a small fleet of twenty-six vessels, leaving Eleanor pregnant in France. England was a country whose native inhabitants still spoke low German dialects like Anglo-Saxon, but Henry could speak Norman-French, the language of the ruling aristocracy, descended from the barons and knights of William the Conqueror's army in 1066, who had taken English noblewomen as wives in order to claim their lands. He was also fluent in Latin, the language in which legislation and charters were recorded, and had some English, acquired when living in Robert of Gloucester's household.

Landing in England again on 9 January 1153 with an army of around 3,000 men, Henry found that being the most powerful man in France was not enough to oust King Stephen, despite widespread dissatisfaction with the raping and looting of the undisciplined Flemish mercenaries employed to keep the usurper king's unstable regime in power. Henry settled down to a long campaign, considering that he had little to fear from a rebellion in his French domains with Matilda in control of Normandy and Eleanor acting as regent for his other domains. The two women kept their distance. A pious autocrat, Matilda accepted the political necessity for her son's marriage, but had no welcome for a daughter-in-law fresh from another man's bed and within the prohibited degrees of consanguinity. Nor was Eleanor inclined to curry favour from such a mother-in-law. Leaving her uncle Raoul de Faye to govern Aquitaine, she moved to the capital of Henry's county of Anjou. In Rouen, all was sobriety and pious observance at the Empress' court; in Angers, men at Eleanor's court were required to prove their valour, but also to speak eloquently, dress well and have fashionably cut hair when in her presence.

Louis had banished from his court Eleanor's *trouvères* and other entertainers, whom he accused of distracting men's minds from their faith.[3] They and others flocked to Eleanor's new court, where she and her intimates were treated to the best of contemporary European poetry and music.[4] It was certainly about this time – and it may well have been there – that the code of courtly love originated, for at Angers men were set convoluted tasks by the ladies of the court who sat in sometimes cruel judgement on their suitability. This was a reversal of the convention that every woman of whatever rank owed deference to her father, brothers and husband simply because they were male. In the words of a poem by an anonymous *trobairitz* – for ladies also wrote romantic poetry:

> ... *domna deu a son drut far onor*
> *com ad amic mas non com a senhor.*

> ... the lady must honour her lover
> like a friend, but not as her master[5]

Since Eleanor's troubadours were writing to please a demanding, autocratic patroness, some have taken this to mean that their verses represent a normally hidden side of her personality that yearned for the joy of abandoning herself to the caress of an adoring lover – a dream that no noblewoman, let alone a queen or princess, could afford to indulge. One of the many disservices in Hollywood's depictions of the Middle Ages is the image of an itinerant *jonglar* or minstrel strolling from castle to castle with a lute slung over his shoulder, inventing the songs to entertain each host. The troubadours[6] who *composed* the songs and poetry were mostly of knightly families, although Guilhem Figuera was a tailor's son and Bernat de Ventadorn's parents were a sergeant-at-arms and a kitchen maid working in the bakery of the castle of Ventadorn. The only codification of what came to be called courtly love was Andreas Cappelanus' treatise *De Amore*,[7] according to which when a man catches sight of his beloved, his heart beats faster. The author wrote this work at the command of Eleanor's daughter Marie de Champagne; opinions differ as to whether it was a cynical comment on courtly behaviour or genuine advice to a young pupil of Andrew the Chaplain. At Eleanor's court, Bernat de Ventadorn put it poetically:

> *Quant ieu la vey, be m'es parven*
> *als huelhs, al vis, a la color –*
> *quar aissi tremble de paor*
> *cum fa la fuelha contre'l ven.*

> When I see her, what's in my mind shows
> in my eyes and my pale cheek.
> What is this fear that makes me weak,
> trembling like a leaf in the wind?

At some point during Eleanor's journey through the Limousin with her new husband, Bernat attached himself to her household after being banished from Ventadorn for becoming too close an admirer of its countess, Marguerite de Turenne. Five years younger than Eleanor, he was endowed with a fine voice, poetic talent and handsome good looks, gaining her patronage, if not her heart. In his poem *Quand vei la lauseta mover de joì sas alas contre'l rai*, he likens his visibly pregnant mistress to a swallow, its wings joyously silhouetted against the sun as it soars so impossibly high above him in station:

> *Ailàs tant cujava saber d'amor et tant petit en sai!*
> *Car ieu d'amar no'm posc téner celui*[8] *dont ja pro non arai.*
> *Anc non aguí de mi poder, ni no fui meus de l'or' en çai*
> *que'm lesset en sos òlhs veser en un miralh que mìut mi plai.*

> Alas, I who thought much to know of loving, yet know so little! /
> I cannot help but love her, though she will never be mine. / Before
> her I am powerless and really not myself at all / since the moment
> she met my gaze in a mirror and put me in her thrall.

Henry cared little for rhymes and rhymers, and less still for the love poems of troubadours like Bernat but when rumours of Eleanor's admirer reached him in England, Bernat was summoned thither. If he did 'sing songs for his supper' while with Henry's comfortless court, they would have been from the very different body of troubadour compositions vaunting warfare and other manly pursuits that were composed by, among others, Bertran de Born, the troublesome lord of Hautefort castle.[9]

Tournaments then were not the organised ritual of later years, with two mounted knights thundering towards each other with lances poised, separated by a stout wooden barrier. That was dangerous enough, but the *mêlée*, which was a swirling mass of armed and armoured men and mounts, usually started in a town square with two teams of knights charging straight at each other. They could roam for miles across the fields and orchards causing much damage to crops as pursuers chased after wealthy knights, to take them for ransom. To be unhorsed often meant death beneath the hooves of the horses, as one of Eleanor's sons was to find out. Bertran de Born gloried in the whole scene:

> *Bela m'es pressa de blezos*
> *Coberts de teintz vermelhs e blaus*
> *D'entresens e de gonfanos*
> *De diversas colors tretaus*
> *Tendas e traps e rics pavilhos tendre*
> *Lanzas frassar, escutz trancar e fendre*
> *Elmes brunitz, et colps donar e prendre ...*

The *mêlée* with its thousand charms: / shields vermilion and azure, / standards, banners, coats of arms / painted in every bright colour, / the pavilions, the stands, the tents, / shattered lances, shields split and bent, / blows given, taken, helmets dented ...

The violence of the *mêlée* was justified as training for war, but Henry banned them in England because he saw these assemblies of several hundred, and sometimes thousands, of armed men as a possible cloak for a rebellion. Defying Henry's orders, Bernat returned to Angers and was abandoned there when Eleanor's court moved on. Something of his despair may be deduced from his decision to enter a monastery and afterwards use his voice only to sing the offices.

On 17 August 1154 in Normandy, her relief redoubled by the knowledge that she had erased forever the stigma of having produced only daughters for Louis, Eleanor gave birth to a son. Learning of this in Paris, Louis saw it quash the faint chance of either of his daughters inheriting the duchy of Aquitaine through their mother. Within a few days of the birth, she was resuming her normal life, her baby put out to a wet-nurse and her own breasts tightly bound to inhibit the swelling natural in lactation. Christening the boy-child William, after her father and grandfather and all the other Williams among her ancestors, Eleanor honoured him with the courtesy title Count of Poitou[10] without asking Henry's advice. Since the counts of Poitou were by tradition also dukes of Aquitaine, the infant seemed to have a glorious future ahead of him, possibly including the throne of England. But this was not to be.

Never had Eleanor felt more secure, having every reason to believe that she had forfeited none of her independence in return for her new status. Many minor events bear this out. When issuing charters at this time, she included no mention of Henry indicating his assent. When Pope Anastasius IV confirmed by a papal bull the privileges of the foundation of Notre Dame de Saintes on 29 October of that same year, the list of donors includes Louis of France, Eleanor and Aelith, but of Henry there is no mention. Even that wily churchman Geoffroi de Lauroux, forever sniffing the winds of change, went on record by stating in a charter of 25 September 1153 that Aquitaine acknowledged only the authority of its duchess.[11]

A few days after the birth of William, Eleanor received news that King Stephen's son Eustace of Boulogne had choked to death during a meal near Bury St Edmunds on the day after her confinement. Worn out with strife, and hoping to avoid another civil war, the grieving King of England formally accepted Henry fitz Empress as his legal successor after protracted negotiations that dragged on into mid-November. At Christmas of that year Archbishop Thibault of Canterbury enshrined the arrangement in a treaty witnessed at Westminster by fourteen bishops and eleven earls of the realm. It was a wonderful stroke of luck for Eleanor's ambitious young husband because Stephen of Blois was in his late fifties and thus an old man by the standards of the time. So, Henry looked certain to be one of the two most powerful monarchs in Europe within a few years. The other was the German emperor.

Returning to France in high spirits, Henry summoned his wife and infant son to Rouen, where they moved into the palace built by his grandfather. Henry made peace with Louis. In consideration of a thousand silver marks as a 'fine' or gift, Louis ceased to include 'Duke of Aquitaine' among his titles, which he had been doing since the divorce on the strength of the specious argument that Eleanor had become duchess by virtue of her marriage to him as successor to Louis the Fat. In Bordeaux during September 1154, Geoffroi de Lauroux sniffed the political winds again and proclaimed that the master of Aquitaine was henceforth Henry of Anjou.[18]

Under the obligations of homage for his domains in France, Henry owed military service to King Louis when called upon. After recovering from some unspecified but severe illness, which may have been an attack of the malaria then endemic in Europe, he rode at the head of a large body of men to help Louis pacify the ever-restless Vexin – a contentious territory between Normandy and the royal possessions. It was during this time that messengers from Archbishop Thibault in Canterbury arrived a few days after Stephen's death on 25 October to announce that the Duke and Duchess of Aquitaine and Normandy could now add 'King and Queen of England' to all their other titles.

Seemingly stunned by Eleanor's rapid rise in the world since their divorce, Louis left Paris on pilgrimage to Compostela. He did not ask her and Henry for the safe conduct through their lands to which he was doubly entitled, both as a pilgrim and as the liege to whom they owed homage for their possessions in France, but travelled by a longer roundabout route, via Montpellier, Barcelona and Aragon, which had the advantage of giving him the opportunity to visit the Christian courts of northern Spain, searching for a new wife.[12]

With no intention of letting the twenty-year anarchy of Stephen's reign continue a day longer than necessary, Henry wanted to claim the English throne rapidly and show the Anglo–Norman magnates from the outset that things were going to be very different from now on. In two weeks he had assembled a reasonable force to do this. With a small retinue of personal servants, Eleanor joined him at Barfleur. There, surrounded by Frankish nobles and prelates who had witnessed or heard of her humiliation after the abduction from Antioch, she confronted them in triumph, requiring from each man the proper deference due to the mother of their overlord's son, seven months' pregnant with another child by him. As though to remind Henry that his power was only temporal, November gales blew in from the Atlantic day and night, making it impossible to put to sea. They were stormbound in Barfleur until 7 December when, determined to celebrate Christmas wearing the crown of England, Henry ignored the lesson of the White Ship sinking in that very place and embarked himself, Eleanor and the infant prince William on a grey sea under a leaden sky in a vessel almost identical: clinker-built with high bow and stern, rigged with a lateen sail that should enable them to cross against the westerly winds and swell.

The weather was still so bad that, even with sails reefed, the convoy was scattered before nightfall, after which the usual station-keeping devices of horn lanterns and bugle calls were useless. For more than twenty-four hours, the ships were buffeted by wind and tide until widely separated. Henry and Eleanor first set foot on the soil of their new kingdom in the New Forest near Lyndhurst. Their first call was at Winchester to secure the royal treasury, commandeering fresh horses on the way and gradually acquiring a cortège of Anglo-Norman prelates and nobles, drawn to Henry's banner by the news of his apparently miraculous arrival, borne on the wings of the storm. From Winchester they progressed to London without a hand lifted or a sword drawn in protest, thanks to Archbishop Thibault of Canterbury who had assembled the bishops of the realm to acclaim their new monarch. The traditional setting for coronations was Westminster Abbey, a few miles up-river from the city of London, where a ford was the main crossing point before the Romans built the first bridge connecting the road from Dover directly with the city. Because the adjoining palace had been vandalised by Stephen's mercenaries during the civil war and was uninhabitable, Henry and Eleanor set up court south of the River Thames in Bermondsey – then an island surrounded by marshes. On the Sunday before Christmas they were crowned King and Queen of England in a curious mixture of pomp and squalor at Westminster Abbey.

The common people were miserably poor after all the fighting, but there was no shortage of food for the Anglo-Norman nobles at the coronation feast. If the venison and game birds being served were fresh, the beef and pork had been salted for winter consumption when the animals not required for breeding were slaughtered in November. As a result, dried herbs, pepper and other imported spices were used heavily in stuffings, sauces and marinades to disguise the residual saltiness in the meat after its soaking in water, and to cover the unpalatable taste of bad meat. There were omelettes, stews, pies and fish in abundance. To cleanse the palate there was a wide range of sweet desserts – fruit stewed and candied, also jellies, tarts, waffles and wafers. While Henry's native subjects preferred to drown their sorrows in mild ale, less likely to be polluted than the water in their wells because fermentation killed many bacteria, their Anglo-Norman masters preferred wine – from France, of course, although there were vineyards in England as far north as Ely at the time.

The waferers, who made and served the thin pastries eaten at the end of the meal with sweet white dessert wine, were also the cabaret. There were tumblers of both sexes, storytellers, conjurers and jugglers, farters, singers and musicians playing bowed and plucked stringed instruments, harps, lyres, flutes of various kinds, shawms, bagpipes and other instruments. Chrétien de Troyes, a contemporary poet employed at the court of Marie de Champagne, describes a wedding at which young girls sang and danced. Jesters, whose original function had been retelling the *res gestae* or great deeds of past heroes, were now jokers whose irreverent humour was indulged so long as their wits were faster than those of the victims they mocked, enabling them to keep the majority of the audience on their side.

The coronation festivities over, Eleanor at the age of 32 was the crowned consort of the man who ruled from the Scottish border to the frontier of Spain. Mother of his son and heir, and aware how great a part her wealth and possessions had played in his rise to this position of power, she had every reason to feel secure in her marriage to Henry as she awaited the birth of his next child.[13]

Chapter 3

Founding a Dynasty

London at the time was all things to all men. In the preface to his biography of Thomas Becket, *descriptio nobilissimae civitatis londoniae*, the cleric William fitz Stephen lauded it as a 'most noble city', but the chronicler Walter Map averred it was a haunt of pimps and whores. The city was thirteen times the size of Paris, having more than 100 stone-built parish churches and monasteries within the walls. Most private homes were timber-framed with lath and plaster infill and the thatched roofs that caused the rapid spread of many fires before such roofing was banned after the great fire of 1212 killed about 3,000 Londoners.

Less than a century after William the Bastard conquered the country and imposed the knights who had crossed the Channel with him as the new aristocracy, class was determined by the language one spoke: the Anglo–Norman French of the rulers was already evolving away from the language of northern France, but the labouring class continued to speak the Germanic Anglo–Saxon of their forebears. In London itself, money was the motor of society, so many natives learned enough French to trade with their overlords in local produce for consumption and imported goods like wine and fine cloth, including silk that had come all the way from southern Italy. Each trade clustered in one area, and we still use the names Bread Street, Fish Street, Ironmonger Lane, Poultry Avenue and others for urban thoroughfares that then were hives of retail commerce.[1] London Wall, built by the Romans and long since fallen into disrepair along the river, was pierced by seven double gateways that could be closed by stout oaken doors at night or when danger threatened. Most imported goods arrived by river, the vessels transporting them halting at the ramshackle wooden London Bridge, which had been partially rebuilt many times since the original Roman one.

The bridge was also a customs station and barrier to invading fleets, which had to serve until 1209, when at last Henry's stone-built bridge that had taken thirty-three years to build was completed, the main problem during the construction being the dangerous swirling tides up- and down-river twice daily. With its nineteen arches and a drawbridge permitting the passage of tall-masted vessels, the new bridge was regarded as a marvel of the age. Three years later a fire that started on the south bank swept across the wooden superstructure, causing many casualties and much damage.

Upstream was a dock constructed under Henry I's consort Matilda and known as Queenhythe, which Eleanor exploited to import wine from her possessions in southwest France. Known as Vintry, this was also the site of the royal bonded warehouses, where all wine entering the country was assessed for taxation purposes. Revenue was a big problem for Henry because commerce had suffered greatly during the civil war and feudal dues had not been paid to the Exchequer. It was largely to sort out this economic tangle that 30-year-old Thomas Becket was employed by Henry on the recommendations of Archbishop Theobald. Tall, well-built and dark-haired, Becket was an ambitious workaholic, whose first important task was to restore the palace of Westminster as a more fitting setting for Henry's itinerant court when at London. Despite working his labour force around the clock, this was not completed on 28 February, when Eleanor gave birth in Bermondsey to a second son and named him Henry after his absent father, who was in the north, where dissident barons learned swiftly that the liberties they had taken during the anarchy, such as building adulterine castles, not paying taxes and refusing the obligation of knight service, would in future be defied at their peril, no matter how far they lived from London.

Roughly half of the country through which he travelled on roads that had not been maintained for 1,000 years was owned by the 200 related Anglo-Norman families and the rest by the Crown and the Church, a situation very different from France, where King Louis directly owned very little territory. The forests that covered much of England in the twelfth century were infested with outlaws, mostly serfs who had been driven away from the lands they had cultivated by one side or other in the civil war. Their fields had reverted to scrubland and the orchards to woodland, which produced no revenue and hence no taxes for the Exchequer, so Henry forced vassals and vavasours to bring the land back into production or suffer the consequence. He also restored a semblance of the rule of law, which had fallen into abeyance during Stephen's reign, and appointed justices to enforce his laws and punish transgressors.

Eleanor saw little of her husband during these incessant travels, discovering when she moved into the refurbished palace of Westminster at Whitsun that her household was to include Henry's bastard son Geoffrey by his Saxon mistress Ykenai – a not unusual arrangement. She had known well her own half-brothers William and Joscelin by her father's second wife Emma de Limoges and Henry's grandfather King Henry I had imposed his bastards on his wife's household. What Eleanor thought of Becket is not on record, but his arrival on the scene marked the weakening of her initial influence over the king.

There was no privacy in her life, whether at Westminster or other palaces while on tour. In September 1155, she moved her court to Winchester, to be nearer Henry, who was hunting in the New Forest with Becket and planning an invasion of Ireland, which presented no threat and would have produced little in the way of taxes. A surprise visitor was the Empress Matilda, bringing the news that her second son Geoffrey was preparing to seize by force the land his father had left him, but which Henry had denied him because it comprised Anjou, Maine and Touraine. A wedge of land that was vulnerable to attack from neighbouring Berry, the property of relatives of Stephen of Blois, it would, if lost, have cut Henry's empire in two. On 10 January 1156 Henry re-crossed the Channel, leaving Eleanor pregnant again and the country in the care of Becket and the appointed justiciars – officials charged with applying the law in the king's absence. After paying a belated homage to Louis for his continental possessions, in Rouen he listened to his brother Geoffrey's reminder of the oath Henry had sworn to observe Geoffrey the Fair's bequest – and ignored it. Waiting for the end of Lent because launching a war during it would have set the entire Church against him, he attacked Geoffrey's castles at Chinon, Mirebeau and Loudun, taking the first two and leaving Geoffrey with only Loudun. Compensation for Chinon and Mirebeau was agreed at 1,000 English pounds and 2,000 pounds Angevin – not all of which was ever paid.[2]

Meanwhile, Eleanor was not idle, but travelled widely, issuing charters and making bequests. Medieval records of the Exchequer, the pipe rolls record payments to her, her sons, her sister Aelith and William X's two sons by Emma de Limoges. In June 1156 she gave birth at Winchester[3] to a daughter christened by Archbishop Thibault at Holy Trinity Church in Aldgate with the name of Matilda, in honour of the Empress. Then came tragedy. Prince William, or Count William of Poitou, as he was titled, died before his fourth birthday and was buried by Abbot Reginald of Reading in the grounds of the still incomplete abbey church there,[4] beside his great-grandfather Henry I. Eleanor crossed the Channel with the two surviving children to join the king at Poitiers. Henry had not forgiven the recalcitrant citizens of Limoges and returned there at the beginning of November to tear down their newly built castle, taking hostage Viscount Aymar and replacing him with two Norman vassals, who had no local connections. Present in the ducal *mesnie* was Becket, who described himself in a charter recorded in the cartulary of La Sauve Majeure Abbey near Bordeaux as 'Thomas of London', which sounded so much classier than 'Becket'.[5]

The Christmas court of 1156 was held in Bordeaux, after which the cortège split up to travel north, Henry departing first with his entourage and Eleanor following. It was about this time that Henry permitted his brother Geoffrey to accept the title of Count of Britanny, to keep him from fomenting more trouble in Anjou. Eleanor returned to England before Henry in February 1157. They must have met up somewhere on the journey north because she was once again pregnant and gave birth on 8 September in Henry I's palace outside Oxford to the son christened Richard, who would become her most famous offspring. Like his dead brother, the new-born was honoured with the titles Count of Poitou and Duke of Aquitaine. Just over a year after the birth of Prince Richard, on 23 September while acting as joint regent of England for the king, who was in France, Eleanor produced her fourth boy-child, named Geoffrey after his uncle who had just died in Brittany, aged 24.

The Christmas court of 1158 was held in Cherbourg, with Eleanor crossing from England to be present. Before the next Christmas court, Henry and some Aquitaine allies tried to wrest back control of the county of Toulouse, which had been part of Aquitaine until mortgaged to provide the funds for Eleanor's grandfather to go on the First Crusade and never redeemed. Henry urgently needed to plunder the English treasury to recoup his current losses and sent Eleanor to brave the risks of the necessary cross-Channel trips in midwinter. Once in England, she rode to Winchester, secured the bullion, escorted it back to Henry in Normandy and returned without him to England, where she was to be his regent for three years, with help from his justiciar Robert de Beaumont, Earl of Leicester and Richard de Luci, both of whom had long experience of government. Hers was a powerful position, which she enjoyed to the full. The pipe rolls record her expenditure while travelling extensively in southern England with her court of ladies-in-waiting, household knights and servants to ensure that the several palaces she frequented met her requirements. At Westminster, she also recreated the ambiance of her court at Poitiers, importing musicians, troubadours and other entertainers and requiring courtiers of both sexes to dress, behave and speak to her liking. This did not go down well with the Church; in the summer of 1160 the Archbishop of Canterbury Thibault of Bec[6] pleaded with Henry to return to the island kingdom and put a stop to all this frivolity.

The reverse happened. In September Eleanor was summoned to Normandy, bringing the princes and Princess Matilda with her. The pipe rolls record a payment of seven pounds for her use of the royal ship.[7] The summons was no gesture of a fond father: Henry intended getting in first if Louis VII's very pregnant consort Constance produced a son, in which case he would immediately betroth 4-year-old Matilda to the infant prince. The plan was foiled by Queen Constance of Castile dying in childbirth on 4 October, after producing yet another daughter for Louis. Instead, Henry betrothed 5-year-old Prince Henry to Louis' 3-year-old daughter Marguerite. It was quite normal for under-age princesses to be sent to live in their new family's care, but Louis plainly did not want a child of his second marriage to be brought up by the first wife who had dishonoured and divorced him, so he made it clearly understood that the child was to be brought up until of marriageable age not in Eleanor's household, but in the home of Roger of Neubourg, the pious justiciar of Normandy. Grabbing control of Marguerite's dowry – the disputed territory of the Vexin with its three castles – Henry installed supposedly neutral Templar castellans to hold all three fortresses, then ignored the marriage contract and had the two children snatched away from Louis' reach and married in England on 5 November 1160. Furious at the deceit, Louis assembled a force of knights and soldiery from Champagne and Blois – neither of which county had any love for the house of Anjou – to punish this betrayal. As usual, Henry struck first before Advent ended campaigning until the end of Lent. During the Christmas court of 1160, held in Le Mans, Henry was planning the next move in the 4-dimensional chess game.

After the Easter court in Falaise, he ordered Becket to take Prince Henry and the infant Marguerite back to Britain, so that Louis had no chance of recovering his daughter. At Whitsun in Winchester, Becket obediently convened the barons and bishops to do homage to the 7-year-old prince, to be known as Henry the Young King. The event was rapidly overshadowed by the furore in the Church at the news that Becket had been appointed by the king Archbishop of Canterbury, disregarding the wishes of the monks there.

In September of 1162 Eleanor gave birth for the ninth time, to a girl christened Eleanor. In thanksgiving, she and Henry generously subsidised the construction of Poitiers Cathedral, adjacent to her quarters in the Maubergeonne Tower of the comital palace, which now houses the law courts and is still an impressive building. Henry wanted to hold his Christmas court in England, to impress on the Anglo-Norman barons that he was back and personally in charge, but the elements were against him. It was not until 25 January 1163 that he and Eleanor crossed the still troubled seas of the Channel, where Henry punished Becket for his intransigence since being consecrated Archbishop by depriving him of the sources of his personal wealth and removing Henry the Young King and his child bride from Becket's household. Eleanor's powers as regent were also curbed, reducing her to the level of arranging a suitably grand eighth birthday party for Henry the Young King.

With the benefit of hindsight, this was the beginning of the end between Eleanor and her second husband. The Christmas court of 1163 was held in the luxurious palace Becket had built for himself at Berkhamsted when he was chancellor, where Henry worked with Becket's former staff to reduce the power of the Church, whose head in England was engaging in a trial of strength, in which Pope Alexander III gave him no support. With the power struggle between the two men dragging on and Becket fleeing the country to save his life, the year of 1164 ended with the Christmas court at Marlborough, where Henry went berserk with fury and ruled that *anyone* remotely related to Becket was to be exiled. As a result some 400 innocent men, women and children were forcibly transported to Flanders and abandoned there with just the clothes they wore.

In April 1165 King Henry II's court in Rouen welcomed the archbishop of Cologne Rainald von Dassel, a trusted envoy of the German Emperor Friedrich Barbarossa. That shrewd observer of courtly behaviour Empress Matilda, who well remembered the German court, observed his arrogant manners and reminded her son the king of the danger of giving a bishop or archbishop too much power – a warning he had ignored, with disastrous results. Archbishop Rainald had come to play a part in the dispute between the Holy Roman Emperor Frederick Barbarossa and Pope Alexander III. To strengthen his hand against the pope, Barbarossa wanted to ally himself with the powerful king of England and ruler of much of France by uniting their houses. The Emperor's 1-year-old eponymous son was betrothed to Princess Eleanor but died five years later before the wedding had been arranged. Barbarossa's cousin and ally in the subjugation of northern Italy was his most powerful vassal, Heinrich der Löwe – Henry the Lion, Duke of Saxony and Bavaria. When Rainald arranged Heinrich's betrothal to 9-year-old Princess Matilda, the intended groom was twenty-seven years older than her and had just divorced his first wife Clementia von Zähringen, employing the usual grounds of consanguinity. The true reason was that it was unlikely, for whatever reason, that she would give him another heir after the death of their only son, an infant who was accidentally allowed to fall off a table onto the stone floor.

The spring of 1165 was spent by Eleanor and her children, with the exception of the Young King, moving from palace to palace in England. She was again pregnant when summoned to Rouen after Easter with 8-year-old Richard and his sister Matilda. With the ageing Empress Matilda no longer the powerful force she had been when younger, it was Eleanor's turn to enjoy an upturn in her fortunes, being left in charge of the continental possessions when the King recrossed the Channel to lead a violent campaign against the Welsh princes with the reluctant support of the Anglo-Norman barons. His fury with them and the Welsh at this point is made clear by the decision to blind and castrate all male prisoners and slit the noses and cut off the ears of the female captives.[8] Punishment like this was not unique in medieval warfare.[9]

Chapter 4

A Grand Design?

In Angers, Queen Eleanor revived her elegant court yet again, unhindered by her tenth pregnancy. On the Ile de la Cité also, maternity was in fashion. On 22 August Louis at last had a son and heir to the throne of France. Gerald de Barri – Welsh name Gerallt Gymro and later best known as the chronicler Giraldus Cambrensis – was then a young student of the *trivium* in Paris. Woken at midnight by the ringing of all the church bells, he stuck his head out of the window and learned from some women passing by in the street that France had at last a prince who might one day put the Count of Anjou back in his place. Baptised Philippe Auguste, the infant prince was also known as 'Dieudonné' – the gift of God. When the news reached Henry in Wales, he realised that his plan to claim the throne of France through the marriage of the Young King and Marguerite was now unlikely to succeed. This was an intrinsic problem with infant and child betrothals.

At the time, Eleanor was seven months pregnant and produced a third daughter for Henry in October 1165, christening her Joanna. While all the princesses of the marriage lived adventurous lives, Joanna was to know literally the ultimate highs and lows of regal life, being imprisoned by her first husband – who spent his nights in his harem of beautiful European and Saracen girls – and nearly killed when leading her absent second husband's knights against a dissident vassal.

At Christmas 1165 Henry held his Christmas court in Oxford with Eleanor holding her own in Angers. Whether or not Henry's current mistress, the daughter of Walter de Clifford, a Marcher lord performing knight service for him in Wales, was present, is not recorded. Rosamund Clifford has gone down in history as Fair Rosamund, but no one can say whether Henry cared more for her than his many other mistresses. It is improbable that she could have rejected his advances and there is no reason to think she merited the various Latin puns on her name. 'Rosamunda' from *rosa mundi* or 'rose of the world' was twisted to *rosa immunda* or 'unclean rose' and to *rosa immundi* or 'rose of filth or unchastity'. After being discarded by her royal lover, she entered the abbey convent at Godstow near Oxford, where she had been schooled, and there died before her thirtieth birthday. The legend of 'Ellinor the furious queen' poisoning her in the lovers' bower at Woodstock is a later invention, and there is no evidence that Eleanor, whose father and grandfather had also kept mistresses, would have regarded Henry's adulteries as more than the normal foibles of a high-ranking nobleman, or seen his female partners as other than useful vessels for his lust.

He was now thirty-three but showing signs of wear and tear from the relentless pace of the almost ceaseless warfare that had constituted his adult life. For six months before returning to France on 16 March 1166 he had been ill in England. At some point a horse kicked him and broke a leg, which caused him to limp, but whether complications from that were the problem, is not known. He also suffered from frequent attacks of malaria, as did many Europeans in those times. Health improving in the Norman spring, he forced Count Conan IV of Brittany to abdicate in favour of his daughter Constance and betrothed her to 8-year-old Prince Geoffrey.

When they met again at Angers for the Easter court of 1166, Henry's queen was approaching the menopause but became pregnant yet again, perhaps in the hope of keeping some kind of personal relationship with him; she was under no illusion that she would have any influence on Henry once her childbearing years were over. The eleventh pregnancy availing her nothing, she was informed that he had issued a summons from Caen for all her vassals in Aquitaine and Poitou to attend his Christmas court at Poitiers, where he required them to swear allegiance to the Young King as duke of Aquitaine. Eleanor was furious at this peremptory dispossession of her favourite son, Richard. Taking him back to England with Princess Matilda, she spent a troubled Christmas at Oxford, and there on 27 December gave birth to another son, christened John in honour of St John the Baptist, whose feast day it was. At approximately the same time and roughly 365 miles to the south Henry was compelling her vassals to acknowledge the Young King as their duke. Her fury at this calculated insult may have coloured her view of the new-born prince, whom she never liked, and regarded as 'the runt of the litter'.

Henry's investing the Young King as duke of Aquitaine so angered the barons of the duchy as to provoke yet another war, of which Louis took advantage to invade Normandy. When, through the Church, a truce was arranged in August 1167 to last until the following Easter, Henry marched into Brittany to subdue a number of Breton lords who refused to recognise Geoffrey as their Count, but that campaign was cut short by the news that his mother, Empress Matilda, had died on 10 September, aged 65. In poor health once again, Henry attended her funeral with a frigid Eleanor by his side. With his mother dead, Becket a sworn enemy and Eleanor irreconcilably alienated, he had isolated himself from any close adviser.

So, what is one to make of Eleanor's prolonged childbearing for Henry? After the three pregnancies that produced princesses Marie and Aelith for Louis, she gave her second husband three daughters and five sons, one of whom died in childhood – and this in a time when many women of all classes died in childbed. Had Eleanor been a submissive and not very intelligent young woman, or one of the child brides married to a man old enough to be her father, one might think she had no choice. But she was trained by her father, after the death of her brother William Aigret when she was 7 or 8 years old, to rule the turbulent barons of Aquitaine. When she married for the second time at the age of 30, she was also a stateswoman of fifteen years' experience at Louis' court. Admittedly, Louis had not been a worthy opponent, but rather putty in her hands. But she had resisted his mother, the dowager queen, and Louis' bishops and archbishops, who had administered the kingdom for Louis the Fat and had every intention of doing the same for his son. She had even defied the Pope by ignoring the ban on women accompanying the Second Crusade and had had the courage to demand of the leader of all Christendom – which was a very powerful *political* post – that he set her free from the marriage to Louis.

Senior churchmen were then the equivalents of high-powered modern lawyers and top politicians. Working always in Latin, the cleverest moved from country to country, climbing up a ladder leading, not to Heaven, but to great temporal power. A mistress of contemporary debate, Eleanor had held her own with the best of them. And she had not so much been raised to greatness by her marriage to Henry as used her own wealth and possessions to enrich his coffers and give him the political leverage to increase to near certainty his chances of becoming king of England when Stephen was still on the throne.

Why did such a consort as independently rich, powerful and intelligent as her need to keep producing children? There were many arguments against this. William the Norman had at least nine children by his marriage to Matilda of Flanders. After his death, they squabbled lethally over their several entitlements. Too many siblings were known to fight over the rich pickings after a ruler's death. For that reason alone, many royal wives limited their families. One of them was Henry's own mother: Matilda Empress grudgingly bore three sons before refusing to sleep with Geoffrey the Fair any longer. Henry's maternal grandmother, Scottish Edith-Matilda had dutifully produced a son and a daughter in the first three years of her marriage to King Henry I, and then occupied herself with good works like kissing lepers on the lips and washing the feet of the poor. Her refusal to share her husband's bed and leaving him to find his pleasures elsewhere, which he did frequently, produced more bastards than begotten by any other English monarch, according to the chronicler William of Malmesbury.[1] According to another chronicler, Herman of Tournai, the wife of Count Robert II of Flanders 'practised womanly arts' after producing three sons in three years because she feared that more sons would fight among themselves for the succession to the county, as had the children of William the Norman. Various contraceptive devices and practices were known about and condemned by the Church, but the fact that the punishments existed proves the devices and practices existed.[2] There was also an involuntary contraception – although probably not for noblewomen – in the diet of the lower classes so deficient in iron as to cause anaemia and amenorrhea.

In Eleanor's case, there was no need for 'womanly arts'. Henry kept mistresses and regularly used the whores who travelled everywhere with his court. It seems very unlikely from what we know of her character from the age of 15 – when she inherited the duchy – to her menopause, that she would insist on sharing his bed and getting repeatedly pregnant in order to wheedle out of him the promise of some favour. In any case, as she well knew, Henry's promises were rarely fulfilled.

So what was in her mind?

If strong princes and kings were supposed to fight in defence of their territory, and to expand it, the value of princesses was their use as marriage pawns to form alliances with other powerful states. Eleanor had a sense of political geography far in advance of her time, when most male nobles and royalty saw strategy in terms of attacking their immediate neighbours. She had travelled widely and knew from personal experience the enormous spread of England and France, plus what is now Germany and Italy, as well as the Norman Kingdom of Sicily, Central Europe, the Balkans, Cyprus, the Byzantine Empire and the Holy Land. She had also met and talked with lay and religious leaders from many other countries. For her, foreign lands were not a vague Never-Never Land left blank on maps for centuries to come or marked with mythical beasts and vague legends like *hic sunt leoni* – here there are lions. To Eleanor, each foreign kingdom was a more or less valuable territory that could be united into an empire as powerful as Rome in its heyday by alliances formed by the four living princes and three princesses. Which seems to indicate that she had what the Greeks called *megali idea* – a grand design.

In this context, Henry's appointment of his clever chancellor Thomas Becket to the supreme office of the Church in England can be seen as preparation for his winning move in the continental chess game, shown on the map below as *6. Becket to Pope.* This was before the papacy became almost an Italian monopoly and shortly after the primacy of the only English pope ever elected: Adrian IV was born Nicholas Breakspear and received much of his education at Becket's old school, under the Augustinian canons of Merton Priory. Henry's sustained fury against Becket as archbishop may well have been caused not just by Becket's intransigence at Canterbury – an archbishop could possibly be replaced or moved – but by him throwing away *the winning move* in a carefully calculated game of continental chess.

It is possible that Henry worked out the grand design for himself or under Empress Matilda's tuition, but far more probable that Queen Eleanor was its architect, giving her a powerful political reason for all those pregnancies.

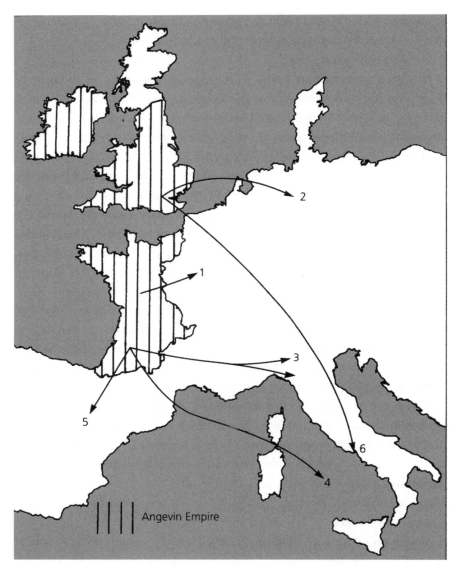

1. *Young Henry marries Princess Marguerite of France*
2. *Princess Matilda marries Henry the Lion of Saxony*
3. *Prince John marries Alix de Maurienne, gaining the crown of Lombardy*
4. *Princess Joanna marries William II of Sicily*
5. *Princess Eleanor marries Alfonso of Castile*
6. *Becket to Pope*

Chapter 5

Eleanor's Bid for Freedom

W hen Marguerite of France was not crowned together with the Young King on 14 July 1170, this was an insult to her and her father Louis VII in Paris – especially since Henry had manoeuvred Louis into handing over another daughter by his second queen in January of the previous year. Henry's ploy was to betroth her to Prince Richard, which looked to Louis at the time like a good match. The girl was 8-year-old Alais,[1] whose initial attraction for Henry was her dowry of the Berry, a county that lay between Aquitaine and the duchy of Burgundy. Alais was to be sadly used and abused in the game of kings, but never married to Richard. To further bewilder King Louis, Henry II showed what appeared to be good faith by having Young Henry re-crowned and Marguerite crowned with him on 27 August 1172. However, the lingering consequences of the dispute with Becket meant that this ceremony could not be at Canterbury, and instead took place in Winchester cathedral, Archbishop Rotrou of Rouen officiating. When Marguerite became pregnant, she went back to Paris and there gave birth prematurely to a son christened William on 19 June 1177, who died three days later. Marguerite had no further children. It was speculated at the time that the difficult delivery of her short-lived son had rendered her barren.

Eleanor of Aquitaine had her own agenda at this time: freeing herself from King Henry's domination. To this end, she returned to England and collected all her personal possessions, which, with her retinue, filled seven cargo ships for the crossing to Normandy. Once on land, her progress on the 300-mile journey to Poitiers could hardly be kept a secret. Travelling with her were the ladies- and maids-in-waiting of her personal court with their personal servants. They and the household knights mounted on their palfreys were followed by a long train, guarded by men-at-arms, of pack- and cart horses which limited the speed of the court's progress to the distance they could cover in a day. This was at most twelve or fifteen miles and less in bad weather, so ill-tended were the roads along which they travelled. At the core of the entourage rode Eleanor and her ladies, attended in those labour-intensive times by her chaplain and the servants in charge of the chapel accoutrements, plus the staff of the pantry, or bread supply, the larder, kitchen and great kitchen and the buttery (or bottlery). Extremely important was the marshalsea, whose grooms were responsible for the stabling and feeding on the journey of all the palfreys, pack horses and the destriers of the knights, led by their squires. With 200 or more mounts and draught animals, the feed required was a significant burden for their hosts at each night's stop. It was not just the human bellies that had to be filled, and human thirst satisfied.

Although Eleanor's entourage was not as extensive as Henry's, it was similar in composition. So many people died of poor kitchen hygiene that the cook was always important, ruling over the man of the cook, the usher of the kitchen, the man of the usher, the scullions responsible for all the pans, dishes and plates. Then came the napier,[2] who was in charge of the household linen. Everyone had to be paid, in money and/or kind. Her chancellor received each day five shillings, plus one good-quality and one coarse wheaten loaves, four gallons of fine wine and four of ordinary wine for himself and his staff, plus one large candle and forty candle ends. A chamberlain received two shillings, one ordinary wheaten loaf, four gallons of ordinary wine, one small candle and twenty-four candle ends. And so on down to the humblest members of her train, who received just their daily food and occasional replacement items of clothing.

Eleanor's convoy presented to the eyes of the serfs labouring in the fields the spectacle of a very long baggage train following the grand lords and ladies. Important for everyone's comfort were the *herberjurs* or billeting officers busily coming and going as they arranged shelter for the next several nights for the important members of the court. Lesser folk had to bed down in barns or peasant hovels, or on carts that had been unloaded for the night.

At least one complication of Henry's travelling logistics was not present. Two of his four bakers were sent ahead each day to the next night's planned stop, but since he often changed his itinerary on the spur of the moment after the advance bakers had departed with their carts bearing equipment, grain and flour for the day, they often they ended up in one place with an abundance of bread, while the household was miles distant gnawing on anything to still the pangs of hunger. Even for Eleanor's less complicated court, also needed were the accoutrements like spare bridles, halters, saddles, saddle bags, saddle cloths and horse shoes, with a farrier and his apprentice to re-shoe horses when necessary.[3]

Her desire not to cause unnecessary delays before she was safely home in Poitiers avoided any long stays on the journey, to the relief of her hosts. Later, King John's court moved on average every two or three days, one of the reasons being that there so many officials and hangers-on that they could literally eat their temporary hosts 'out of house and home'. An abbot honoured with the king's visit would see six months' supplies for his community consumed in a couple of days and heave a sigh of relief when the court moved on.

The atmosphere of the 1177 Christmas court in Argentan must have been electric, with Henry aware that his queen had redeployed her court to Poitou, of which she was the hereditary countess and therefore a vassal of Louis VII, who would not hesitate to defend her, if need be. On the one hand, Henry was relieved to be rid of a wife who could bear no more legitimate children yet refused to retire to a nunnery; on the other, his paranoia must have caused him to wonder what she would do next. He could hardly invoke their consanguinity to enable him to take another, younger wife. Nor, while still widely blamed for the death of Becket, could he risk arranging Eleanor's death and re-marry.

Only after crossing the Loire, marking the northern boundary of Poitou, could she relax the pace and spend several days at the extraordinary foundation of Fontevraud, of which she was a benefactress. This was more than just an abbey; it was a complete town of monks and nuns, numbering as many as 10,000 inhabitants, all ruled by the abbess. Its founder, Robert d'Arbrissel was a charismatic itinerant preacher-monk charged by Pope Urban II in 1096 to establish what became a complex of four monasteries in a valley known as *fons ebraldi* in Latin, just south of the river Loire. Le Grand Moustier was for nuns, La Madeleine for repentant prostitutes, St Jean de l'habit for male religious and St Lazare for lepers. The last is now a very comfortable hotel, where guests dine elegantly in the converted cloisters. D'Arbrissel was an unorthodox monk, insisting on sleeping chastely among the women as an exercise in controlling his carnal lust,[4] rather like Mahatma Gandhi at his *ashram* in the twentieth century. Celibacy was at the time not uncommon between couples, both of whom had taken vows of chastity. When d'Arbrissel departed to resume preaching elsewhere, he decreed that the whole complex be ruled by an elderly widow, reasoning that post-menopausal women were more stable than men and also possibly thinking that the cessation of their menses made them quasi-men.

Under Henry II and Eleanor of Aquitaine, Fontevraud became the necropolis of the Plantagenets. Henry and Richard were buried there and Eleanor spent her last years there before joining them beneath the flagstones of the nave. Both Princess Joanna and Prince John were sent there for much of their childhood. Prince John's older brother, Henry the Young King, was likewise sent away by his parents – in his case to live in the household of his father's powerful and clever chancellor Thomas Becket. Before the terrible schism between him and the king, Becket's house in London was the smart place to be seen and daily contact with the great and good was a form of education in courtly behaviour for the boy prince being prepared for kingship. While there, he formed an attachment with his surrogate father during the absence from England of his biological parents, whom he hardly knew. This caused a great rift between the Young King and his father after King Henry made Becket Archbishop of Canterbury. In the falling out of these two powerful and arrogant men, the Young King sided with Becket and blamed his father for Becket's death.[5]

With the growth of cities and the rise of an enfranchised merchant class living in them, a similar practice was adopted by the bourgeoisie, whose sons were sent away young to learn the business in the household of an associate of their father. Lower down the social scale, the growing artisan classes sent boys away as apprentices – literally, learners – to acquire the skills of a trade. At the bottom of the social scale in peasant homes children were regarded as cost-free pairs of hands, looking after the livestock or caring for young siblings unless required under the terms of the family's tenancy to serve as unpaid maidservants, stable boys and scullions in the house of their parents' overlord.

England's King Henry I had arranged his daughter Matilda's match because the German Empire was then the most prestigious power in continental Europe, and, situated to the east of France, would make a powerful ally in time of need. It is an illustration of the precarity of twelfth-century royalty that Emperor Heinrich V needed the dowry of 10,000 marks or £6,666 to pay for travelling in suitable style to Rome for his coronation by the Pope. After the wedding at Worms in 1114, although still only a girl of twelve, the youthful Matilda was given a seal with which to issue her own charters and became a public figure with her own identity. Unfortunately, Heinrich V's high-handedness had alienated many of his lay vassals; more seriously, he had infuriated the senior churchmen responsible for the considerable amount of Church property in the German Empire, which led to his excommunication by Pope Paschal II. Determined to show who was the stronger, in early 1116 Heinrich V set off across the Alps with his young bride and a considerable retinue to put the pope in his place, on the way spending the better part of a year imposing his rule over northern Italy, which was then not a single state but a collection of principalities and kingdoms, each of which had to be separately subdued. In 1167 a number of these banded together in the *Liga lombarda* or Lombard League expressly to resist German domination.

After the year in northern Italy, the imperial couple led their followers south to Rome. Prudently, Pope Paschal II avoided a direct confrontation by fleeing; it was an ambitious papal envoy, later to become the antipope Gregory VIII, who crowned Heinrich V and 'English Matilda' in St Peter's Basilica as Emperor and Empress of the German Empire, also known as the Holy Roman Empire. For this and other reasons, it was never completely clear whether 'English Matilda' had the right to style herself 'empress', but she did, and insisted on everyone else doing the same for the rest of her life. It says much for her character and force of personality that when Heinrich returned to Germany in 1118 to suppress new challenges to his authority there, he left his teenaged wife as regent to govern northern Italy in his name for almost two years. In 1119 she headed north again for a reunion with her husband in Lotharingia[6], a rump of the Carolingian Empire where, at the Diet of Worms in 1122 Heinrich V conceded to the Church the right to invest bishops, the 'investiture contest' having been at the heart of his differences with Rome.

Suffering from what may have been prostate cancer, Emperor Heinrich V died in May 1125 at Utrecht when Empress Matilda was twenty-three. Although she had not borne him any children in the eleven years of their marriage, her production of three sons in her second marriage to Count Geoffrey the Fair of Anjou proved that this was not her fault, and Heinrich V had also sired three children by his first wife, so it is possible that the cancer interfered with his ability to get her pregnant. After his death, the lack of a son and heir, which could have permitted Matilda to rule the Empire as regent until the child's majority, caused her to abandon her considerable property in Germany and return to Normandy with her more valuable personal possessions – including a couple of Heinrich V's bejewelled crowns.

When the Saracen leader Salah-ed-Din, known to Europeans as Saladin, captured Jerusalem on 2 October 1187, Bishop Joscius of Tyre travelled to Europe, preaching a new crusade to recover the Holy City. Henry II promised Joscius that he would take the cross, although he had no intention of doing so, his bluff compelling Philippe Auguste, now king of France, to do the same. While the two kings were amassing the necessary taxes, knights and barons eager to earn remission of the sins committed in their violent lives, began departing individually for the East in a frenzy of military fervour. Few considered it a sin to kill Saracens, although Radulphus Niger, the courageous future canon of Lincoln cathedral, raised a lone voice declaring that Muslims, although not believers in the Holy Trinity, had the right to life.[7] In France meanwhile, in defiance of the crusaders' oath to be as a brother to all others who had taken the cross, a war ground on between Henry II and Philippe Auguste, who was supported by the princes Richard and John fighting their own father. It ended with Henry's death on 6 July 1189. In his first meeting with Philippe at the traditional meeting place under an ancient elm tree near Gisors castle, Richard showed that he had no gratitude for French support in the war with Henry, now lying dead in Fontevraud. He refused to hand back the Vexin, using as his spurious reason that he would, after his return from the Third Crusade, marry Alais, to make that much abused woman his consort as queen of England. Meanwhile, since both he and Philippe had sworn an oath to go on the crusade, they were supposed to behave as brothers.

Alais was one of a complex of elements exercising Queen Eleanor's mind after Henry's death. It was vital that Richard father a son, or even a daughter, in case he did not return from the crusade because her only other living son Prince John was considered – not only by her – as totally unsuited to become king of England. Alais was known to be fertile, having borne children to Henry, but Richard said he would have no truck with marrying his late father's mistress. And Eleanor, notwithstanding that this French princess had been brought up with her own children, bore her no love, or even liking. She also concurred with Richard's reasoning that Alais could not be returned to France because that would mean returning her dowry of the Vexin, which was unthinkable. So, she must stay a prisoner.

Both Richard and Philippe Auguste did depart on the crusade, but not in the spirit of brotherly love that was supposed to exist between the lords and knights departing for Jerusalem. Matters came to a head between the two kings when their armies were overwintering at the port-city of Messina on Sicily, rather than risking the Mediterranean winter storms on the journey to the Holy Land. At some time in November 1190 Count Philippe of Flanders, a vassal of Philippe Auguste who was related to Richard, set up a compromise deal under which Richard would keep the Vexin, but return Alais when he came back from the crusade, plus 10,000 marks which Philippe Auguste could use as her dowry to marry her off to whomever he wished. Richard accepted the deal, for the good reason that he had heard his mother was on her way to Sicily, escorting Berengaria of Navarre, whom he would have to marry at the end of Lent in 1191, like it or not.

But Richard's was not the only hand moving pieces on this chessboard. When he was being held to ransom in Germany after the crusade,[8] Prince John was conspiring with Philippe Auguste, who pretended to legitimise his claim to be duke of Normandy, in return for which John said he would divorce his wife Isabel of Gloucester and marry in her stead poor Alais, then languishing in the Norman fortress of Rouen. Nothing came of this. In 1195, she was still there, but had to be moved from castle to castle as the latest war between Richard and Philippe Auguste ebbed and flowed across Normandy. Alais was then 34 years old – an age by which most women of the time were dead. Under the Treaty of Louviers in January 1196, Philippe Auguste handed back to Richard all the Norman territory he had recently captured, receiving in return his half-sister Alais and her dowry of the Vexin with its castles. Since being traded by her father Louis VII to Henry II twenty-four years before, this Capetian princess had never known liberty, was despised by the Plantagenets who had kept her in a gilded cage and was a total stranger to her blood relatives in Paris. Philippe married her off to Guillaume IV de Ponthieu, the county lying strategically between Richard's ally Baldwin of Flanders and Normandy. Alais bore him a daughter named Marie in April 1199. On the death in 1221 of Guillaume IV this daughter became *suo jure* countess of Ponthieu, marrying Simon of Dammartin. Their daughter Jeanne re-enters our history later as the second wife of King Fernando III of Castile.

Chapter 6

Matilda and the Lion

S hortly after the funeral of her mother-in-law Matilda Empress, Eleanor escorted her eldest daughter back to England, to prepare for her marriage to the second most powerful man in Germany, Heinrich der Löwe – Henry the Lion – the ambitious duke of Saxony and Bavaria. To ensure that his new bride Princess Matilda arrived at his court in fitting style to show the might and wealth of Henry's realm, a trousseau costing £63 was commissioned for her. Including a set of scarlet velvet-covered saddles with gilt fittings for her palfreys, the total cost of all the arrangements was about £4,500, which was equivalent to one quarter of the annual income of the island realm. By feudal custom, this was raised by an extra tax on Henry's vassals, known as an *auxilium*.

As was also customary, the Saxon duke sent an embassy of his noble vassals, led by Bishop Baldwin of Utrecht – then in Saxony, although now Dutch – to accompany this bride on her journey to Germany. To show his wealth, Henry II presented them with entirely new wardrobes of costly garments and, since representatives of the Byzantine emperor and the Swedish king were also in England at the time, they too benefitted with complete new outfits.

To satisfy herself that all was going as well as she could make it, Queen Eleanor escorted her 11-year-old daughter to Southampton,[1] together with the noble Saxon embassy. There Princess Matilda boarded Duke Heinrich's own sleek galley with a crew of ninety men operating thirty rows of oars, sent by him to convey her safely in a convoy of fifteen vessels across the lawless North Sea to Saxony. Little is known about the other vessels in the convoy, but since the north German ports were the heartland of the future Hanseatic league with its perpetual traffic of merchants' *cogges* or cogs, they were probably roundships of this type, only partly decked in and bearing a single square-cut sail on the one mast. Lacking any proper keel, they rolled sickeningly in even a moderate swell. Also travelling with Matilda was a party of important Anglo–Norman barons, known to her from their frequent presence at the English court, and who would remain with her until the wedding, to lessen the strangeness of her new surroundings. Some sources say that Eleanor travelled with them to Germany, but it is more likely that she left the convoy at its first port of call in Normandy and returned straightaway to England, as she had other matters on her mind

Princess Matilda's voyage retraced the journey of her eponymous paternal grandmother, Matilda, daughter of King Henry I, around the time of her eighth birthday in February 1110 en route to marry the 24-year-old German King/Emperor Heinrich V. These betrothals of young girls have to be put into context. Life was hard. People of all ages dropped dead all the time from causes that today would be countered by modern medicine or surgery. There was no place for cosseted 'mummy's boys' or 'daddy's girls'. Noble mothers rarely bonded with their babies in breast-feeding, which was done by wet-nurses until children were 2 years old or possibly older, to avoid any possibility of tuberculosis from imbibing cow's milk – a connection that was already known even in this time with little understanding of infection. Although breast milk was thought to be menstrual blood mysteriously converted in the breast, the choice of a wet-nurse had its own corpus of teaching, with contributions from many Latin, Greek and Persian teachers. She should be neither thin nor fat, aged between 25 and 30 and of impeccable health. Her psychological stability, the shape of her breasts and the period since the last time she gave birth – preferably of a son and not longer than two months before – must all be considered. Her diet, too, must be regulated, as it was thought to affect the quality of the milk, which could be tested by placing some drops on a piece of glass. The nurse must not rock the child too vigorously, as this could cause the milk in its stomach to curdle. She must not have intercourse during breast-feeding. The list went on ...[2]

Many children became emotionally attached for life to their wet-nurse, whose duties included all their toilet needs, dressing them and preparing their food when old enough to take solids, even masticating meat and placing it in the child's mouth until he or she was able to chew. Throughout the early years she would stay close, comforting and caring when and if childhood ailments were suffered. The wet-nurse was, in short, the source of all that complex of affection and caring which today is labelled 'maternal'. King Richard visited and cared for his nurse as the woman for whom he felt most affection, in much the same way that many middle-class Englishmen in the twentieth century felt more affection for the nannies who brought them up until they were sent away to boarding school than for their real mothers. Thirty-three years after his birth at Oxford, Richard allotted the annual rent of £7.10s from a house at Rowdon, between Chippenham and Bath *hodierne nutrice* meaning, to Hodierna [my] wet-nurse. It has to be noted that some noble ladies considered their breast milk to be superior for transmitting their intelligence and piety to their offspring. One such was the mother of Bernard of Clairvaux. Countess Ida of Boulogne also insisted on personally nursing her sons, of whom two became heroes of the First Crusade while the third – who had *once* been comforted in his mother's absence by another woman's breast – never rose higher than Count of Boulogne.[3]

With no, or very little, mother-child bonding in infancy, noble boys of tender age were routinely sent away to live in the households of people they had never met, usually of a higher station in life than their own parents, where the young lads served as pages and perhaps later as squires, or military servants travelling with their knightly masters to tournaments before in turn becoming knights in their lords' households. Noble girls, similarly, were sent away to become maids of honour and later ladies-in-waiting, learning the skills of managing domestic staff and large estates from their mistresses. They were also taught chess, embroidery and how to play musical instruments; how to dress elegantly; to hunt and hawk; and the art of good conversation. All these skills constituted a training for successful marriages, and certainly in the case of royalty, produced many women who were both politicians and diplomats. For both sexes, the practice of fostering out inculcated lifelong obligations that knitted relationships where no kinship existed.

Half a century after her grandmother had travelled to Germany, Princess Matilda's ship en route to Saxony ploughed its way across the North Sea with the other vessels transporting her numerous ladies- and maids-in-waiting and her personal staff of servants including clerks, her confessor, a doctor and one or more cooks – all of whom were destined to remain with her in Saxony. The common language of all these persons was

Anglo–Norman French, for few of them will have spoken the languages of the native English during whatever time they had spent in England. Well guarded by men-at-arms aboard one of the ships was Matilda's substantial dowry of gold and silver bullion and coin, valued at more than £4,000, her father's *auxilium* tax having raised £3,000. Duke Heinrich intended to use this treasure to pay for a pilgrimage to the Holy Land, to cleanse his soul of guilt for all the blood he had shed in several wars. The bride's personal possessions included her large wardrobe of clothes to impress the Saxon courtiers, cosmetics, golden dishes, pots and pans for her use and valuable carpets and wall hangings to embellish her quarters. All this was under the care of trusted London merchant Edward Blund as her steward. There were also valuable presents for important lay and religious persons in Saxony.

The most unhappy passengers in the convoy must have been the palfreys and the thirty-four packhorses Matilda was bringing to transport the considerable volume of her personal belongings after making landfall. One wonders why, since there were packhorses a-plenty in Saxony. The Bayeux tapestry shows the manner in which the Norman knights' horses were hoisted aboard William the Conqueror's ships in slings for the invasion of Britain and then placed in padded stalls to avoid injury from the ships' movements. For the short Channel crossing, that was tolerable. For the longer voyage to Saxony there was a problem because horses unable to move about for more than a day require several days of rest afterwards to cure their 'Monday morning sickness', so Matilda's palfreys and packhorses would have had to be rested for several days after landing. Had the weather been even slightly stormy, their condition would have been worse because horses cannot vomit to relieve the nausea and distress of seasickness.

It must have been a great relief for both biped and quadruped passengers when landfall was made. Princess Matilda being familiar with the story of her grandmother's adventures and misadventures in Germany, it must have been with some misgivings that she stepped ashore, to be welcomed by important members of the Church and the Saxon aristocracy as 'Prinzessin Mechtilde' – a third name to add to 'Mathilde' and 'Maud', by which she was known respectively in France and England. She was placed under the guardianship of Archbishop Bruno of Trier, whose responsibility it was to ensure her education in German language, politics, history and manners that would equip the young Plantagenet princess to behave appropriately as a German duchess.

On 1 February 1168, still four months short of her twelfth birthday, Princess Matilda was married in Minden Cathedral to Duke Heinrich der Löwe in the presence of a congregation of Saxon and allied nobility. Officiating was the suffragan Bishop Werner von Bückeburg, because the groom was in a state of conflict with the archbishops of Bremen and Magdeburg. There was no exchange of rings, but in medieval German custom the wedding was completed by a second ceremony, the exchange of bread and wine at a wedding meal in the groom's rude palace at Brunswick, symbolising the establishment of a shared home.

Few child-brides can have had a greater culture shock than Matilda. Accustomed to the elegance of her mother's courts in France and England and to the constant comings and goings of lay and religious vassals and important administrators at her father's peripatetic court on both sides of the Channel, she found the ducal court at Brunswick more like a military camp. Duke Heinrich preferred the company of knightly warriors, more interested in weapons, horses and tales of bravery and bloodshed than in poetry and song. But she made her mark in this military society as the daughter of culture-loving Queen Eleanor, whose gracious beauty was praised by the Minnesinger, or German troubadours. Firstly, she commissioned a translation of the Song of Roland by a monk named Konrad, who dedicated it when finished in 1170 to 'Herzog Heinrich', mentioning his descent from Karl der Grosse – Charlemagne, the original founder of the Empire. Under Mathilda's civilising patronage, about this time the poet Eilhart von Oberg produced at Heinrich's court the first German version of the legend of Tristan and Isolde, apparently taken from a French original.

Matilda's influence was later responsible for the production of the 266-page book of illuminated gospels for the Virgin Mary's altar she sponsored in Brunswick Cathedral, which is now preserved in the Herzog August Bibliothek at Wolfenbüttel in Lower Saxony.[4] One of the fifty full-page illustrations in glorious colour depicts Matilda's wedding to Duke Heinrich, showing the groom on his knees, to bring his head down to the level of the 12-year-old bride standing beside him. The words written there are: *This golden page shows the reader that the devout duke Heinrich and his wife with all their hearts placed the love of Christ above all else.*[5]

After the coming to power of Adolf Hitler's Nazionalsozialistische Deutsche Arbeiterpartei in 1933, the new German government, intent on proving the Teutonic identity of the nation, ordered the opening of the two sarcophagi in the crypt of Brunswick cathedral that were reputed to contain the remains of Henry the Lion and Matilda. Because it would have been traditional for the wife to be on the right side of her husband – although Matilda was usually depicted as being on her husband's left side – there was a confusion of the two sets of remains which were interpreted as showing a very tall woman and a man too short to be a German hero. Immediately, plans to make the crypt into an investiture venue of the kind where SS and other recruits were sworn in, were abandoned. Since it is not difficult to distinguish between adult male and female skeletons, one wonders whether the 'confusion' of the two bodies was a deliberate device of the cathedral chapter to avoid the crypt becoming a cult site for Nazi ceremonies. In 1974 the sarcophagi were re-opened and Heinrich's bones were measured and calculated to give a height of 1.90 metres, or around 6 feet 2 inches. Proofs of identity included considerable damage to the bones of his left foot, which corresponded with the contemporary report of a bad fall from his horse. In the other sarcophagus were the remains of a small woman with dark hair and a congenital hip deformity– and of a small child! It would be interesting if modern DNA testing were allowed to check the relationship of Matilda and the infant.

In 1172, when she was fifteen, Matilda's first recorded child was born. This was a girl christened Richenza[6] in honour of German Empress Richenza of Nordheim, the powerful grandmother of Heinrich, to whose tenacity and political acumen he owed his election as Duke of Saxony. There was scant privacy for the 15-year-old girl undergoing her first labour. As was customary for noble and royal births, she was delivered of the child in the presence of a number of men who were senior churchmen and important lay vassals. They could later testify in any dispute that they had seen with their own eyes that the child was indeed 'the fruit of her womb' and therefore of her husband. The baby was removed from Matilda's arms immediately after the birth, washed, swaddled and put to a wet-nurse; the young mother's breasts were tightly bound so that they would stay small and high, as was the fashion for noblewomen, slightly bulging over the square neckline of their dresses.

Heinrich was not present. Having departed after getting his young wife pregnant, he was busily spending much of Matilda's dowry on a pilgrimage to Jerusalem with an entourage of 500 or more vassals, clerics, knights and followers – far too small for the journey to be labelled a crusade and in any case without any professed military aim. Picking up more pilgrims on the way, they travelled through Hungary, suffering a shipwreck at the confluence of the river Morava and the Danube and raids by bandits once in Byzantine territory, to arrive at Constantinople on Good Friday of 1172. There, since this group of a few hundred travellers was patently not a threat, Heinrich was welcomed with great pomp by Emperor Manuel I Komnenos. As part of the 'entertainment' a debate was arranged between the bishops in Heinrich's party and some senior Greek clergy over the interpretation of the scriptures. If this seems strange today, it was completely in keeping with similar public debates in the schools at Paris. From the Byzantine capital, the Saxons travelled by sea to the Holy Land, where King Amalric or Amaury of Jerusalem received them in state, with visits laid on to the Church of the Holy Sepulchure, to Judean Bethlehem – the alleged birthplace of Christ – and to Nazareth in Galilee where His family had actually lived. At every stop, Heinrich dispensed generous donations to the monks, as he did also to the military orders of the Templars and Hospitallers.

The German sources concur that *kaum etwas ist bekannt* – little is known – about Matilda's activities during her husband's absence on pilgrimage. But since it was largely her money which paid for the conversion of his Dankwarderode castle into something approaching a palace and the embellishment of the adjacent Cathedral of St Blaise, it seems likely that she used the time he was away to put in hand and oversee the considerable construction programme required.

Meanwhile, in the Holy Land people were dying. Most casualties on the crusades were from disease, not combat, and this party of pilgrims suffered losses too, Bishop Konrad of Lübeck dying at Tyre on the first, overland, stage of the return journey. From there, Heinrich chose not to use a safe-conduct from the Armenian ruler of Cilicia – now southern Turkey. Instead, the party sailed on ships provided by Bohemund III of the Latin kingdom of Antioch – modern Antakya – to Tarsus, birthplace of the apostle Paul. From there, a body of Seljuk troops escorted the Saxons to Ikonium – modern Konya. Sultan Kilij Arslan II received them courteously and had them escorted in safety by the shortest route from there to the Bosphorus. Crossing over to Constantinople on the European side, they retraced the outward route through Byzantium and Hungary, arriving back in Saxony in time for Christmas or just after.

On his return, Duke Heinrich wasted no time getting his teenage wife pregnant again. Her second child, born in the following autumn, was the son for which her husband had been praying. Christened Heinrich, like his father, he was named Palatine Count Heinrich V of the Rhine in 1195. In all, the young duchess would bear her husband seven children, and was known among the Saxons as *die Fromme* – the virtuous lady, who was a faithful wife and generous giver of alms to the poor and sick. A second son was born in 1177 and christened Otto.

Matilda's son Otto was to have an adventurous life, just failing to become king of England after ruling Aquitaine disastrously for several years. It is thought by some historians that he was the Lionheart's deathbed choice to succeed him on the throne of England. There is, at any rate, considerable mystery about the Lionheart's testament, dictated in secrecy at Châlus in the presence of Queen Eleanor while he was dying of gangrene there in April 1199.[7] For several days after the decomposing body of her son was brought to the abbey of Fontevraud for burial, she did not disclose the terms of his will for the succession, despite considerable pressure to do so.

There were three principal possibilities. Prince John was the only surviving brother of the dead king, but nothing in his past life indicated that he would be a good king, capable of holding together the empire[8] that his parents had accumulated and defending it against King Philippe Auguste. Even worse, he was guilty of high treason in attempting with Philippe to bribe the German Emperor after the crusade to keep Richard in prison indefinitely. The late Prince Geoffrey was survived by a son, Arthur of Brittany, who had been named by Richard as his successor in the treaty of Messina signed in March 1191, while Richard was on Sicily during the Third Crusade. Arthur being a nephew of Richard by a brother who was senior to John, it was a way of blocking John's succession. The third contender was Matilda's son Otto of Brunswick, who was the late king's favourite nephew. To plead his cause, Otto's sister Richenza/Matilda, then married to Count Geoffrey of Le Perche, came to Fontevraud in person. Her failure to gain him the English crown was of little moment, since he had been elected German king in 1198 and became German Emperor Otto IV in 1209. After mulling it over until she could no longer put off the decision, Eleanor made what she considered the best of a poor choice by herself naming John Lackland king of England. Richard's chaplain, who had written down the dying monarch's actual last words regarding the succession, was richly rewarded for his silence.

Soon after the birth of Otto, Matilda must have become pregnant again, giving birth to a son christened Lothar in the same twelvemonth. The rapid succession of her early pregnancies may have resulted in some gynaecological problem, for two more daughters – Eleonore born in 1178 and Ingiborg in 1180 – died in infancy after premature births, and a son was stillborn in 1182 and buried without christening. Was his the tiny corpse found in Matilda's sarcophagus? In 1184 while the family was in exile in England, Matilda gave birth to another living son, named William of Winchester for his place of birth and later made Lord of Lüneburg. [9]

The reason why the family was in England for the last birth was Duke Heinrich's refusal in 1180 to perform his feudal duty to join Barbarossa's attempt to subdue the increasingly powerful Lombard League of northern Italian states. When subsequently the German imperial forces were defeated by the League supported by the forces of Pope Alexander III at the battle of Legnano, Heinrich believed that he would be elected Emperor, but was instead sentenced by Barbarossa to exile for seven years, his four counties with their sixty-seven castles and forty towns confiscated and assigned to the Emperor's favourites.[10] The entire family except 7- or 8-year-old Lothar, who stayed in Brunswick seemingly as a hostage for the family's good behaviour while abroad, sought refuge in Normandy, effectively as refugees.

When Matilda, Duke Heinrich and an entourage of 200 noble vassals, household knights and servants[11] arrived to seek asylum at Henry II's court in the Norman town of Caen in Autumn of 1181, Queen Eleanor was still under house arrest in England, as she had been since raising her sons in rebellion against Henry II in 1173. Instead of a warm welcome from him, the Saxons received a brush-off. Mean as ever about hospitality,[12] Matilda's father paid for most of the hangers-on to return to Germany as being cheaper than feeding, clothing and accommodating them throughout the exile, for they had not been banished, but had chosen to accompany their duke, to show loyalty or perhaps for the adventure.

To sweeten the pill of expelling so many of Duke Heinrich's followers, Henry gave him the funds to make a pilgrimage to Santiago de Compostela and placed the palace of Argentan in Normandy at Matilda's disposal. It was at Argentan that she met Bertrand de Born, the Occitan troubadour favoured by Richard and best known for his celebration in verse of knightly prowess. Bertran dedicated two of his love songs to a heroine he named Elena, meaning Helen of Troy. They included the words:

> *Et ont óm plus n'ostaria garnisons,*
> *plus en seria envejós,*
> *que la nuech fai parer dia la gola*
> *e qui'n vesia plus en jos.*
> *tots lo mond en gençaria …*

> When her last garment's on the floor,
> I'll want her all the more.
> The sight of her neck changes night to day
> and to see her lower down
> would indeed pleasure any man …

If he had not named the pseudonymous Elena, this would have passed as just another courtly fantasy, but Bertran was never discreet and typically complained that he would have died of boredom at Argentan …

> *ma'l gentils còrs amorós e la douça chara pia*
> *e la bonha companhia e'l respons de la Sassia'm defendia*

> … but for the desireable body and sweet, kindly face
> and the good company and wit of my Saxon lady …

… who could only be Matilda.

At the Plantagenet court, such explicit poetic tribute was acceptable, but one wonders whether the time she had spent in Germany caused any embarrassment for Matilda at the Christmas court held in Caen after the return of Henry the Lion, back from his pilgrimage. Her daughter Richenza became known as Mathilde, like her mother, because her originally Icelandic name sounded outlandish to French ears. Henry the Young King was present, having been lured away from King Philippe Auguste's court in Paris by his father upping his allowance to £100 a day plus £10 a day for his wife Marguerite, a half-sister of Philippe Auguste. Sweetening the pill even more, King Henry undertook to pay the expenses of 100 household knights to guarantee the Young King a fittingly imposing retinue. Meeting in Caen, both Richard and the Young King were determined to spoil whatever joy might be had that Christmas, fighting with each other except when uniting against their father to argue they had the right to hold their own plenary courts, an idea which he rejected outright.

In spring of 1184 Duchess Matilda travelled with her father to England, spending Easter at Becket's confiscated luxurious palace of Berkhamsted before going to Winchester for the birth of William/Wilhelm. After much pleading by the Saxon ducal couple, Henry II allowed Queen Eleanor to join them there. It was the first time Eleanor had seen this daughter in sixteen years. The pipe rolls record the expenditure of more than £28 for scarlet dresses, grey fur and embroidered cushions, enabling Eleanor to appear suitably regal after eleven years' imprisonment. Purchase of rewards for her maid Amaria, who shared the imprisonment at Old Sarum and elsewhere, were also recorded. Was it due in some way to Eleanor's presence – such as a choice of midwife – that Matilda successfully gave birth to a full-term son in April or June 1184? The boy known as William of Winchester was to become the progenitor of the dukes of Brunswick and thereby an ancestor of England's Hanoverian King George I.

The next Christmas court, held at Windsor, was a fraught occasion, even by the standards of Henry II's family gatherings, which he used to set his sons against each other by making conflicting promises to them. For the first time in years, Queen Eleanor was also present, a 63-year-old woman still very much sound in mind and limb despite all those years of confinement. Where Duchess Matilda and Heinrich der Löwe and their children stood in the manoeuvrings of Henry II and the princes Henry, Richard, Geoffrey and John, is unclear.

The chronicler Benedict of Peterborough recorded the betrothal in 1184 of *willelmus rex scotiæ*, that is King William the Lion of Scotland and *matildem filiam matildis ducissae saxoniæ* – who was Matilda's 12-year-old daughter Richenza, but the marriage never took place as Pope Lucius III refused a dispensation from the impediment of consanguinity that so bedevilled the closely interrelated medieval European nobility.[13] Benedict also recorded that King Bela III of Hungary sent an embassy to Henry II requesting the hand in marriage of *matildem filiam ducis saxoniæ*, but nothing came of this, her grandfather in his customary way neither assenting nor refusing.

In mid-Lent, or early spring of 1185 Queen Eleanor was summoned to Henry II's court in Rouen, where she learned that Henry's anger with Richard's insubordination had determined him to restore Aquitaine and Poitou to her, in order to bring Richard to heel. Her conditions of life had improved greatly since she was permitted to live with Duchess Matilda's family, who accompanied the ageing queen of England to Normandy, where they learned the reason for her to be allowed to return to France. King Philippe Auguste was rightly arguing for the return of the dowry of his widowed half-sister Marguerite since Henry the Young King had died of dysentery in June 1183 while on a murderous rampage that included desecrating the allegedly miracle-working shrine of St Amadour in Rocamadour. Whether Philippe Auguste was being kind to Marguerite or simply wanted back her dowry of the three castles in the strategically important Vexin, lying between the Plantagenet duchy of Normandy and his territory of the Ile de France, who knows? To this, Henry II declared blandly that it was impossible to return the castles to French control because Marguerite's dowry had passed to Eleanor in 1179, in compensation for her birthright of Aquitaine being given to Richard. As 'proof' of this preposterous argument, Eleanor spent six months living in Gisors castle with Duchess Matilda as her companion.

This was not exactly freedom, but conditions were radically better for her than she had known since first being locked up in Old Sarum. The dispute was settled after a fashion when a treaty was agreed between Philippe Auguste and Henry II, by which Henry kept the Vexin but returned Marguerite and undertook to pay her a handsome compensation for illegally keeping her dowry. Philippe Auguste was not the pliable adversary that his father had been and also raised the awkward status of his other half-sister Alais, who had been locked away in Winchester castle for years, since Richard had no intention of marrying her, or anyone else. Appearing to concede the point, Henry confused Philippe by saying that he intended marrying Alais to Prince John without delay. He then further muddied the waters by swearing fealty to Philippe for the continental possessions, which he had previously refused to do. On 24 August 1186 Marguerite returned to the court on the Ile de la Cité as a ward of Philippe Auguste and was married off by him to Bela III, the disputatious king of Hungary and Croatia later that same year. Widowed a second time ten years later while on pilgrimage to the Holy Land, she there died a week after her arrival in her thirty-ninth year and was buried in the cathedral of Tyre.

It seems that Henry II lobbied the pope to persuade Emperor Barbarossa to allow Matilda's Saxon family to return to Germany, the price being the reduction of Heinrich's titles to just Duke of Brunswick. In October the ducal couple travelled home with their eldest son Heinrich of Hanover, leaving behind William/Wilhelm, Otto and Matilda/Richenza. It was perhaps a disappointment to that young lady after her mooted royal suitors when, aged 17 in 1189 or 1190, she was married to Count Geoffroy III of Le Perche in northeast France, and bore him two sons. After his death in 1202, she married in 1204 Enguerrand III de Coucy, a noble who boasted he was not a king, a prince, a duke or a count, but the lord of Coucy and built the largest castle in France to prove it, but died in that common accident of the time, a fall from his horse, in which he landed on his own sword.

During 1187, while in Paris bathing in the flattery Philippe Auguste always lavished on a disaffected son of Henry II, Richard was informed by his host that Henry's talk of marrying Alais to John after keeping her a prisoner for twenty-two years was a smoke-screen. His real intention, Philippe said, was to get a divorce, marry Alais and put her 2-year-old bastard son on the throne after disinheriting his two remaining sons by Eleanor. It was probably just Philippe's way of winding up Richard. In any case, Alais' little boy died soon after.

Participating in a *mêlée* that Philippe Auguste had arranged to entertain him outside Paris in August 1186, Prince Geoffrey was unhorsed and trampled to death beneath the pounding hooves of the heavy destriers, against which his armour afforded little protection. His widow, Constance of Britanny gave birth on 29 March 1187 to her ill-starred son Arthur. Since he inherited his father's title at birth, Philippe Auguste demanded as suzerain of the deceased Count Geoffrey that Constance, her daughter and son be brought to live in Paris at his court. Henry trumped this move by insisting on his right to re-marry widowed vassals and forcing Constance to marry Ranulf de Blundeville, Count of Chester.

Early in 1189, when 67-year-old Emperor Barbarossa was pressuring his vassals to accompany him on the Third Crusade, he gave Duke Heinrich the option of taking the cross or going into a second exile, to ensure he did not cause problems in Germany during Barbarossa's absence. Himself aged 60 by then, Heinrich judged it prudent to choose the soft option and returned to England, but this time Duchess Matilda remained at Brunswick in the Dankwarderode Castle to defend the interests of her husband and children. However, she died three months later at the age of 33, six months before her father. After her death and the death of Barbarossa, who died after falling into a Turkish river on the journey to the Holy Land, Duke Heinrich returned to Germany and made his peace with Barbarossa's son Emperor Heinrich VI.

Chapter 7

Princess Eleanor becomes la Reína Leonor

In the twelfth century, because the boundaries of counties, duchies and even kingdoms were not yet fixed, there was near-perpetual fighting between counts, dukes, kings and their vassals, who had every incentive to grab neighbouring territory, if they could get away with it, before the neighbours grabbed theirs. Nowhere was this more true than south of the Pyrenees, where four-fifths of the Iberian peninsula was Muslim, known as the emirate of Córdova, and only the northern fifth was nominally Christian. There are no contemporary accounts of the Muslim invasion of the Visigothic kingdom covering the Iberian peninsula that took place between 711 and 788. The absence of records due to the spoliation of monasteries, virtually the only places where they could have been written and kept, reflects the total chaos of the rapid conquest of what the invaders called al-Andalus, a name that lingers on in modern Spanish with Andalucia being the southernmost province of Spain. The speed and ruthlessness of the conquest – literally by fire and sword – is illustrated by the 800-mile northward advance of the Muslim forces reaching Poitiers, after very many battles along the way, in just two decades, which placed them only a week's march from Paris. Its violence is testified to between the Pyrenees and Poitiers, along the route of their northward march, where the place-name 'Sarassins' still means a house that has been burned down, although not necessarily by the marauding Moors in the eighth century.

The Ummayad Moors were driven back south of the Pyrenees following the decisive victory of the Frankish forces under Charles Martel at the battle of Tours or Poitiers, which took place between the two cities at an unknown site and uncertain date in 732. However, by 788 they occupied most of what is now Spain and Portugal. Among the remaining precarious Christian territories in the north and northwest lay the kingdom of Asturias. Some time between 818 and 842 Bishop

Teodomiro of Iria in Asturias put it about that two of his monks had been led one night by a star – echoes of the Star of Bethlehem – to a field in which they found a rock-cut tomb. The worthy bishop identified the skeletal remains in it as those of the apostle St James, who, so legend said, had come to Spain to convert the pagans in the first century CE. The name James is rendered in Spanish as Iago, actually closer to the original Hebrew Ya'akov, and the name Compostela for the tomb site was said to derive from Latin *campus* and *stella*, meaning 'field' and 'star'.

There was nothing miraculous about the tomb and a skeleton being there because the area had been a fourth-century Roman graveyard, but since the kingdom of Asturias had suffered depredations at the hands of the Moors and also Viking raids in 968, when the reigning bishop was killed in combat,[1] the current bishop reasoned that creating a pilgrimage site at the alleged grave of one of the apostles would not only attract pilgrims from all over Europe, but surely justify a moderate crusade to keep at bay the Moslems pressing in on the southern frontier of Asturias. In 997 Santiago de Compostela was attacked and partially destroyed by a mixed Muslim and Christian force; if the Muslims wanted more territory, the Christian element was after loot. A few decades later Bishop Cresconio had walls built around the whole town that had grown up at the pilgrimage site. In 924 the kingdom of Asturias was absorbed into the kingdom of León. Two centuries later the Plantagenets entered the picture.

The ninth child borne by Eleanor of Aquitaine was the sixth of her marriage to Henry II. After the birth on 13 October 1162 at the castle of Domfront in Normandy,[2] the baby girl was baptised Eleanor, after her mother, by Cardinal Henry of Pisa.[3] Having as her godfather the abbot of Mont St Michel Robert de Torigni[4] – a counsellor of Henry II better known as the chronicler who revised the *Gestae normannorum ducum* – the infant had as auspicious a start in life as any other princess. Shortly before her birth, a group of disgruntled barons from Aquitaine had presented to papal legates a genealogical table proving the consanguinity of Henry and Eleanor. A few years later, after her menopause, Henry might have jumped at this chance of ridding himself of the queen who refused to obey his every whim, but at that time he had no immediate intention of doing so, because it would have meant giving up control of her vast territorial possessions. Papal legates being the cleverest lawyers of the time, this conclave turned a blind eye to the family tree, in return for which Eleanor and Henry upped their contribution towards the construction of the new cathedral in Poitiers. Still a very impressive building in Romanesque style, it took more than a century to complete.

In early 1165 at Rouen and at Westminster Archbishop Rainald of Cologne checked out the young Plantagenet princesses and arranged the betrothal of 3-year-old Eleanor to Prince Friedrich, infant son of the German Emperor Friedrich Barbarossa, but the boy died before a wedding could be arranged. For several years, Princess Eleanor remained 'available' for another match. In October 1170 Henry II, who had been so ill for two months, probably with malaria, that he dictated a new last will and testament, went on pilgrimage to the shrine of Rocamadour – still the second most visited tourist town in France – to give thanks for his recovery. In better humour that usual after surviving that crisis, he discussed with Queen Eleanor the idea of betrothing Princess Eleanor, now 8 years old, to the 14-year-old King Alfonso VIII of Castile, the central one of the three main Christian kingdoms in northern Spain, lying between León to the west and Navarre/Pamplona to the east. Although they were all nominally of the same faith, that did not prevent repeated internecine wars, halted by truces that did not last. To the south, in Moorish Spain the same process occurred, usually between Shiites and Sunnis or Arabs and Berbers or simply mutually jealous warlords, as among the Christians. On occasion, a mixed Christian-Muslim force was even formed to attack a Christian or a Muslim area, usually with loot in mind. Treaties to make truces, whether between Muslims and Christians or between same-religion warlords, were constantly being broken or renegotiated.

The Reconquista – as the long process of driving the Muslims out of Spain is known – commenced in 722 at the battle of Covadonga[5] when the Asturian hero Don Pelayo defeated a larger Muslim force. The sporadic, long-drawn-out process lasted over seven centuries, ending with the defeat of the Moors at the battle of Granada in 1492. Henry II considered that the kingdom of Castile would play an important part in the Reconquista, with Alfonso able to considerably expand his territory – as proved to be the case. Henry also thought that the alliance with Castile would protect the Angevin Empire at its southern flank on the Gascony-Castile border in the Pyrenees.

The mooted match was acceptable in Burgos, the capital of Castile, but at this time Henry II was excommunicated and widely blamed for the murder of Archbishop Thomas Becket inside Canterbury Cathedral in the last days of 1170. So, it was not until 1174 that the marriage was celebrated in Burgos, the 12-year-old bride modifying her name to the Spanish form Leonor. King Alfonso VIII was not simply an accomplished warrior, holding his own in the ongoing skirmishes with Navarra, Aragon and León, he also welcomed learned men and troubadors to his court and was later to found the *studium generale* or nub of a university at Palencia.

Having been given personal control of much property in Castile by her husband, including fourteen fortified towns spread throughout the kingdom, Queen Leonor had her own income to support a court of noble ladies and others, including troubadours and minstrels. If this was King Alfonso's generosity, it is said that he puzzled for years over the *quid pro quo*. What exactly was the dowry Henry II had promised in the marriage negotiations? Alfonso had understood that it was the province of Gascony, running from Bordeaux south to the Pyrenees, which did make geographical sense, given the common border. Typically, Henry had not actually given what he said he would give, which led on one occasion in 1205 to Castilian troops invading Gascony to claim what Alfonso VIII thought was his by right. It failed to achieve his ends. Abandoning his claim to the province in 1208, Alfonso contented himself with the arrival in Castile of many Gascon knights and nobles who volunteered to fight with his forces against the Muslims in the more or less continual skirmishing on the borders, Christians pushing them southward resisted by Muslims pushing the Europeans northward again.

In addition to enjoying the pleasures of twelfth-century cultural life at the court in Burgos and elsewhere, Queen Leonor was devout and took particular pleasure in supporting religious institutions. In atonement for her father's responsibility in the death of his rebellious archbishop – he always denied that he had given any explicit order for it – she financed a shrine to St Thomas Becket in Toledo Cathedral in 1179. She also founded in June of 1187 the Cistercian nunnery of Santa Maria la Real de las Huelgas across the river from the city of Burgos, the foundation charter beginning, *Yo, Alfonso, por la gracia de Dios, rey de Castilla y Toledo, y mi mugier, la reína doña Leonor...* I, Alfonso, by the grace of God king of Castile and Toledo, and my wife the lady queen Leonor ... The nuns setting up the new community were brought from a Navarese[6] convent at Tulebras, which was the first all-female convent in Spain. The young Queen Leonor never did things by halves, and therefore arranged for the community of Las Huelgas to be given by Pope Clement III a status placing it above even the papal *curia*, so directly below the pope himself.

She also negotiated with the original Cistercian monastery at Cîteaux in France for her new foundation to be recognised as equal to all the monasteries of the order in Spain, which was effected by Cîteaux declaring the royal convent to be *mater ecclesia*, or mother church of Castile and León. The abbess, being female, could not conduct a Mass, hear confessions or preach, but she alone could license priests to perform these functions in her 'parish' and also had the power to nominate abbesses for several other convents. With the charter of the convent giving it the right to enact laws binding on the inhabitants of the properties with which Queen Leonor had endowed it, and to hold a civil and criminal court, the abbess thus enjoyed as near total independence as anyone could without necessarily being royal. In the city of Cuenca, reconquered from the Almohades in 1177, Leonor had the mosque demolished and the construction of the cathedral of Santa Maria y San Julián commenced in 1183 on the same site, to erase the most obvious sign of the previous Muslim domination. Designed like a French cathedral to please her, it was the first such building in Castile.

Both cathedral and convent still stand, the latter being a national monument. Although deservedly a tourist site, it continues to house a small community of nuns with ten cells kept for women who wish to make a retreat there. Although *huelga* usually implies an industrial strike in modern usage, it was the original meaning of leisure time which gave the monastery its title, the ground on which it stands having previously been a parkland and a pleasure ground for the Castilian royalty with a small palace of hunting tower dimensions, which was demolished for the construction of the convent. To provide the necessary funds to launch the community, Queen Leonor endowed it with forty-nine royal properties,[7] including mills – always a reliable source of income in those days – and the *hospital del rey* or royal hospital adjacent, but construction of the convent still took a hundred years to complete. The convent and its community were also tax- and toll-exempt, privileges that continued until abolished by Pope Pius IX in the nineteenth century. The importance of Las Huelgas to the kingdom of Castile is shown by its use as setting for important ceremonies like the dubbing of new knights and the proclamation of the kings of Castile. In 1199 the convent also became the pantheon of the Castilian royal family on the model of Fontevraud in Poitou for the French line of the Plantagenets.

Certainly Queen Leonor performed all her other queenly duties, her children numbering twelve in all. The first, born in June of 1179 when she was seventeen, was a daughter christened Berenguela. Her next child was born in April 1181, with Robert de Torigni recording the birth as being *circa Pascha* – about Easter – but this prince, christened Sancho, lived only three months, his name mentioned in his father's charter of 13 July 1181 granting a donation to the shrine of Rocamadour in France *cum uxore mea et cum filio meo rege sancio* – with my wife and my son King Sancho. Two weeks afterwards, the little prince was dead.

It seems that another daughter was born the following year and christened Sancha in memory of her dead brother, but she also did not live long. Mentioned in a charter of January 1183, by which Alfonso VIII exchanged some property with the military orders in return for their support against the Moors, her physical existence was proven during restoration of the convent church in the twentieth century. Remarkably well preserved, as though mummified, the small corpse was found tenderly wrapped in a shroud of dressed sheepskin laid in a limestone coffin that bore traces of having been painted in many colours. In a charter dated July 1182 mention is made of another son named Enrique in the list of donors: *regnante el Rey Don Alfonso ... con su mugier Doña Lionor, con su fijo Don Anric.* By the reigning king Alfonso with his wife the lady Leonor and his son Enrique. It seems that this Enrique may have been a twin of Princess Sancha and, like her, died in infancy before his second birthday.

Leonor's next son, named Fernando, also died young. Mentioned in a charter dated January 1184: *regnante rege Alfonso cum uxore sua regina Leonor et filio suo Fernando ...* By the reigning king Alfonso with his wife the Queen Leonor and his son Fernando. It seems that this little prince did not live out the year.

After a perhaps reasoned break from childbearing of three years – or were there other births not recorded, for whatever reason? – in 1186 or 1187 Leonor produced another girl, named Urraca, who did survive infancy. On 4 March 1188 in Palencia the most famous of Leonor's daughters saw the light of day and was christened Blanca. Another son was born in September 1189. Christened Fernando in honour of his father and his dead brother, like Blanca he seemed certain of a great destiny until dying aged 22 in Madrid from a sudden illness in October 1211 while returning from an unsuccessful attempt that summer to relieve the siege of the strategic castle of Salvatierra. Held by the first Spanish order of knighthood, the Order of Calatrava, the castle lay deep in Moorish territory, south of Toledo, and had served as an advanced Christian base in enemy territory. Alfonso VIII was preparing for his greatest battle against the Moors at Las Navas de Tolosa when he was brought the news of his son's death by some of the knights who had been with the prince at Salvatierra. The bereaved father wept, distraught with grief. An anonymous chronicler wrote *quia in ipsum tanquam in vite speculum contemplabatur* – it was as though he saw in Fernando the mirror of his own life.[8]

The corpse was escorted back to Las Huelgas in a cortège of important prelates and barons led by Fernando's sister Berenguela. Presumably, as was customary, the intestines and other internal organs had been removed to delay putrefaction because, on arrival at Las Huelgas some days after the death, Queen Leonor threw herself on the corpse, kissed it on the lips and had to be forcibly removed by attendants. As the chronicler wrote, *vel eum vivificare vel cum eo mori* – it was as though she wished to bring him back to life or to die with him. A troubadour at the court of Castile named Giraut de Calanso wrote a *planh* or verse lament praising the young prince's beauty, courage and accomplishments, rather as the Aquitain troubadour Betran de Born had won round Henry II by writing a *planh* lamenting the death of Henry the Young King in 1183.[9]

Leonor's next child was another daughter, born in 1191 at Plasencia and christened Mafalda. Her life epitomises the web of relationships among medieval nobility and royalty. In 1204 she was betrothed to the *infante* Fernando de León, eldest son of King Alfonso IX by his first marriage and therefore the stepson of Mafalda's eldest sister. However, the marriage was never celebrated, Mafalda dying in the same year at Salamanca.

Queen Leonor's next child was born in 1200 and also christened Leonor. At the relatively mature age of 20 this princess married King Chaime I de Aragon in February 1221. Known in Aragonese Catalan as Chaime lo Conqueridor because he enlarged his kingdom with the reconquest from the Almohade Moors of Mallorca, Menorca, Ibiza, Formentera and Valencia, he also inherited several important counties north of the Pyrenees through his mother, but it was not a happy marriage for poor Princess Leonor. Chaime was known as *o home de fembres* or 'the lady's man' and reputedly had many mistresses, rather like the French King Henri IV, who had twenty-two 'official' mistresses and uncountable one-night stands. After eight years of marriage, including the birth of one legitimate son christened Alfonso in 1222, Chaime sent Leonor away in April 1229, using the grounds of consanguinity to free himself to marry the Hungarian princess Jolán Árpád-Házi, by whom he had several more children. Being the first-born, Leonor's son would have succeeded to the crown of Aragon, but died before his father and the kingdom was divided *post mortem regis* between his other sons. Unusually, Chaime also found time to dictate to some cleric a record of his life titled in Catalan *Llibre dels Fets* – like the Latin *res gestae*. Records of deeds of other medieval kings were mostly composed by chroniclers; in this case the subject himself was the author. The book shows him to be more than just a warrior king; it is also a treatise on the function of monarchy, and on military tactics, a definition of feudal loyalty and treachery and a fascinating examination of the gradual growth in his lifetime of national identity based on geography, language and culture.

There is some doubt about the date of birth of Queen Leonor's last daughter. She was christened Constanza and followed the advice of her sister Berenguela to become a nun at Las Huelgas in 1217. Eventually its abbess, she died there in 1243. The very last child of Alfonso VIII and Leonor was a boy christened Enrique, born in April 1204 at Valladolid. His father's respect for Queen Leonor is illustrated by his written will made shortly after that birth, decreeing that she was to rule as regent with Enrique in the event of Alfonso VIII's death, thus bequeathing her more power than any of his barons or bishops, one of whom could have been named regent.

We can never know the feelings of people in the distant past. With little understanding of the causes of disease, hardly any effective medicines and such frequent deaths of infants and children, as well as deaths of adult offspring in battle or from illness, did they grieve as modern parents do? Queen Leonor's reaction to the death of her 22-year-old son seems to indicate that some of them did. Alfonso VIII's will could, of course, simply be pragmatic reasoning: in every particular, his queen was a loyal consort possessed of an impeccable political acumen. Yet, there is a hint that their emotions were not so different from ours in Queen Leonor's last weeks. After her husband's death in October 1214, just two years after his resounding victory over the Moors at La Navas de Tolosa in 1212, she was reportedly so prostrate with grief that she was unable to preside over his burial, her eldest daughter Berenguela standing in for her at the ceremonies. Although appointed regent by the terms of Alfonso's will, his widow then fell ill and did not recover, dying exactly twenty-four days after her husband. And there is surely a message through time from those who knew them both, and who placed the two bodies side by side in a very unusual double sarcophagus balanced on two stone lions in the church of Las Huelgas. Fortunately, it survived the sacking of the convent by French forces during the War of Spanish Independence (1808–14) because it contained the remains of a French princess. This highly carved and decorated tomb is a testimony to the fact that some arranged marriages did lead to enduring affection and respect between the spouses.

Princess Berenguela, at the age of 8, was betrothed in Seligenstadt to Duke Konrad II of Swabia, but the marriage was never solemnised. Her role as a pawn of realpolitik saw her promised instead to King Alfonso IX of León as his second wife under the treaty of Tordehumos, which ended a state of hostilities between Castile and León, caused by her father breaking a previous treaty of alliance with León. Peace with León meant that Alfonso VIII could afford to defy a truce with the Moors which had held good since 1190 and launch a campaign of incursions into their territory that reached as far as Seville. The marriage with

Berenguela was celebrated in December 1197 but was dissolved on grounds of consanguinity by Pope Innocent III[10] in 1204, her father and Alfonso IX of León being cousins. The marriage nevertheless produced five children: a daughter christened Leonor, who died in infancy; two daughters who survived, Constanza and Berenguela, and two sons, Alfonso and Fernando.

After the dissolution of her marriage to Alfonso IX of León, his wife Berenguela of Castile returned to Castile aged 24, to act as regent for her under-age brother crowned as King Enrique I. This long-lived woman became queen regnant of Castile when Enrique died accidentally in 1217, but she abdicated shortly afterwards in favour of her son Fernando III of León, for whom she foresaw a magnificent future. Having been born during her marriage with Alfonso IX in Zamora – a city liberated from the Moors by the legendary Spanish hero El Cid and where the kingdom of Portugal first came into existence by the treaty of 1143 signed by King Alfonso VII of Castile and King Affonso I of Portugal – he was entitled to succeed to the thrones of both Castile through his mother and León through his father. Becoming king of Castile on the death of his young uncle Enrique in 1217 and of León when his father Alfonso IX died in 1230, he re-united the twin kingdoms[11] and continued liberating more territory from the Moorish occupation, reaching as far south as the line of *la frontera* – a medieval Spanish word meaning the border between Christian and Moorish territory that still graces the names of the southernmost Christian towns on that line, like Jérez de la Frontera, the world capital of sherry. Although Fernando's right to the dual succession was legitimate enough, dissident barons in both kingdoms might have undone Berenguela's plan, had she not used what the chroniclers called her considerable diplomatic talents to block or buy off all resistance to him.[12] Fernando married Elizabeth of Hohenstaufen, known as Beatriz in Spain, who gave him twelve children, his second wife providing five more.

History would indeed have been different, had Fernando of León and Castile succeeded in driving the Moors from Andalucia, which he failed several times to achieve, but nevertheless did place the last remaining Moorish emirates in hegemony to Seville. He had also intended to drive all the Jews out of Spain with the Moors; as it was, they were given a two-century respite before being expelled by *los reyes católicos* in 1492. In each of the areas he did conquer, his policy was to allot the land to his vassals and knights, who introduced Christian peasants – mostly from north of the Pyrenees – to work the land. The measure of his success is that, when he came to the throne, the kingdom of Castile covered about 150,000 square kilometres; when he inherited León in 1230 he added another 100,000 square kilometres and his conquests added a further 120,000 square kilometres. His ambitious plan was to complete the Reconquista of Spain and, after driving out every last Moor from the Iberian peninsula, to carry the war across the strait of Gibraltar and into the Maghreb – Muslim North Africa. But it was not to be: he died in May 1252 at Seville, allegedly telling his son and successor on his deathbed, 'You will have more lands and loyal vassals than any other king in Christendom.' His remains still repose in a gold and crystal coffin in the cathedral of Seville, inscribed in Castilian, Latin, Hebrew and Arabic.

Despite his significant contribution to the Reconquista, Fernando was not canonised until Pope Clement X recognised his achievements in 1671, belatedly making Queen Leonor's mother, Eleanor of Aquitaine, the only great-grandmother of two saints.

Chapter 8

Joanna, the Pregnant Nun

One of King Fernando's sisters had a bizarre life, even by the standards of medieval princesses. In 1223 53-year-old Jehan de Brienne, who held the title of King Jehan I of Jerusalem, travelled to Santiago de Compostela, ostensibly as a pilgrim. Having been twice widowed, he was actually looking for a new wife in the Christian courts of northern Spain, much as Louis VII had done after his divorce from Eleanor of Aquitaine. Alfonso IX of León offered Jehan de Brienne his daughter Sancha, but his divorced wife Berenguela of Castile proposed her 19-year-old daughter from the Leonese marriage, also called Berenguela. King Jehan I accepted her offer and married daughter Berenguela at Toledo in 1224, introducing his bride into a tangled web of relationships. In 1225 she had a daughter, who was christened Marie. In 1229 the 12-year-old Baudouin II de Courtenay was chosen to be the next emperor of Constantinople in order to prevent the succession going to candidates from Nicea and Bulgaria, both states being enemies of Byzantium. Because of his youth, Baudouin's barons imposed on him an experienced older co-emperor until he attained his majority, an appointment that Jehan de Brienne accepted, having ironically participated in the Fourth Crusade that sacked Constantinople in 1204.

To form a family link with his co-emperor, while at Rome he betrothed his 4-year-old daughter Marie to Baudouin in April 1229. Prudently waiting until this had been accepted in Constantinople, he and Berenguela travelled there in 1231, when he was crowned as co-emperor and she as co-empress consort. The marriage of Marie and Baudouin did not take place until 1234, when she was about 9 years old and Baudouin 16.[1] This made Marie de Brienne the junior co-empress consort, with her mother the senior one. The troubles of the once-great city being far from ended, in 1235–6 Constantinople was besieged by Bulgarian and Nicean troops, whose leaders fortunately fell out over their shares of the loot when the city surrendered. Jehan de Brienne assumed command of the inadequate forces within the walls, after despatching Baudouin II to Europe in search of money and reinforcements.[2] When Jehan de Brienne died on 27 March 1237, probably aged 61[3] and his much younger wife died two weeks later, aged 33, the only member of the imperial family left in Constantinople was Marie, still only 12 years old. The remains of the late co-empress Berenguela were transported all the way to the Cathedral of Santiago de Compostela and placed in a marble coffin there. However, it is not just modern readers who get confused with all the similarly named personalities in this period; some earlier writers have claimed that the body in that sarcophagus is that of Berenguela of Castile, her mother, or of Berenguela or Berengaria, the sister of King Alfonso X of Castile.

The one certain thing is that, if the date of her mother's reported death is correct, a 12-year-old girl was left in nominal command of Constantinople as a result. This was hardly a sinecure for the young empress, even though her magnates governed the city and her generals commanded the inadequate forces at their disposal. After much toil and trouble, Baudouin returned in July 1239 with some funds, with which to pay mercenaries and, following him, a small force of volunteer crusaders, whose numbers are disputed. Among the various deals he had negotiated in Europe was a gift from Queen Blanche of France, who was Marie's great-aunt, of 20,000 pounds on conditions that included sending her great niece Marie back to Europe, ostensibly on a visit.

Given four armed vessels to transport her and her escort across the Mediterranean, Marie arrived in Cyprus to find the French King Louis IX, son of Queen Blanche, leading the army of the Seventh Crusade. All might have been well for Marie, given their close blood relationship, but Louis had no intention of coming to help with the defence of Constantinople, nor of helping the Templars, who pleaded that they were close to losing Syria to the Saracens. His mind stayed fixed on conquering Egypt as a base for the reconquest of the Holy Land. Then a westerly gale caused Marie's ship to drag its anchor with her aboard and blew it across to the coast of what is now Lebanon. Narrowly avoiding destruction when the gale blew itself out, the skipper managed to hug the coast southwards and reach the crusader port of Acre, modern Akko. All Marie's belongings on the other three ships were apparently lost, but at least she was in friendly hands. Given a fresh ship, she recommenced her journey to France, where she was eventually welcomed by Queen Blanche, ruling the kingdom as regent for Louis IX during his absence on crusade. Marie stayed with the court in Paris until her great aunt's death in 1252, after which she took up residence in Baudouin's estates at Namur – which, fortunately, he had been dissuaded by Queen Blanche from selling off when he was raising funds for the defence of Constantinople. History was not yet finished with Marie. Sometime in 1260 she returned to the court of Castile to obtain a loan enabling her to ransom her son Pierre, held hostage by Venetian bankers to whom he owed money.[4]

Queen Blanche was far from the only woman to rule her husband's, brother's or son's domain while he was on crusade. It is interesting that even the misogynist celibate chroniclers could find little wrong they had done; in many cases they improved the patrimony entrusted to them by respecting the Peace of God that protected the property of absent crusaders and punished any infringement of that provision with excommunication. Accordingly, they did not waste money and lives in attacks on their neighbours' lands. In a number of cases, their good stewardship was in vain, as their crusading menfolk returned to inform them that, while in foreign parts, they had mortgaged or sold all their property to raise funds for their crusading activity, much as Duke William IX of Aquitaine had mortgaged the county of Toulouse in 1095 so he could depart with a suitably large contingent of vassals and men-at-arms on the First Crusade. It was that action by Eleanor of Aquitaine's grandfather that was to cause much grief to her unfortunate third daughter, Joanna.

Born in October of 1165, Joanna was barely 4 years old when she was betrothed to King William II of the *regnu di sicilia* – the Norman kingdom of Sicily. Henry II having done penance for his part in the killing of Becket, Pope Alexander III lent his weight to the betrothal of Princess Joanna to the young king of Sicily. The pope's motive was thus to block a possible alliance by marriage between Sicily and the German Empire, which would outflank the papal territories in central Italy. This was not Henry II's first plan for Joanna on the geopolitical chessboard, and William II had recently been snubbed by a Byzantine princess he intended to marry. As to how the Mediterranean island came to be a Norman possession, during the eleventh century the Lombards of northern Italy and the Byzantine emperors were both hiring Viking mercenaries to curb Muslim influence in the Mediterranean. Since the duchy of Normandy was gifted to the Viking warlord Rollo[5] in 911 by the French king aptly nicknamed Charles the Simple in return for Rollo's promise to halt other Norsemen's incursions in France, later Vikings looked further afield for territory to conquer. A force of 700 Norman knights under Count Roger of Hauteville beat back the Muslim occupying forces of Sicily in a slow process ending in 1091, when he declared himself ruler of the county of Sicily. Unlike the Christian kings in Spain, Roger did not drive out Muslim inhabitants because he needed every citizen to put the island back on its feet after three decades of war, and thus welcomed Muslims, Christians, Jews and Byzantine Greeks as his subjects, respecting their different customs and religions. In 1130 Count Roger II declared that the strategic island of Sicily, the Maltese islands and Apulia henceforth constituted a kingdom of which he was monarch, installed as Roger II by Antipope Anacletus II on Christmas Day of that year.

Did that go down well with the current legitimate pope, Innocent II? To list all the miseries it unleashed would sound like a game of musical allies, with everyone changing sides each time the plainsong stopped. In the final episode, Roger II's son, also called Roger, captured Innocent II. To regain his liberty the Pope changed his mind and gave his blessing to the Norman *kingdom* of Sicily. Complete peace was not, however, restored until the reign of William II, known as 'William the Good' for the two decades of peace he ushered in. As to his morals: although boasting that he was a Christian monarch, he spoke and wrote Arabic and kept a harem of beautiful Christian and Muslim girls in the palace. In 1176 he sent ambassadors to England requesting Henry II's permission to marry Joanna, then 11 years old. There was no shortage of channels of communication, one of them being Peter of Blois, who had been William II's tutor during his minority after inheriting the throne at the age of 13 and was now archdeacon of Bath after serving as secretary to both Queen Eleanor and Henry II.

Towards the end of August 1176, Queen Eleanor bade farewell to a daughter for the second time. With gifts of fine horses, gems and bullion for her husband-to-be and escorted by Bishop John of Norwich, Joanna crossed the Channel and landed at Barfleur in Normandy, whence she was escorted southward to Poitiers[6] by her brother Henry the Young King with a retinue sufficiently strong to discourage any attempt to kidnap or rob her. There her 20-year-old brother Richard took charge and escorted her across a landscape ruined by war to Toulouse and thence to St Gilles in the delta of the river Rhône, where William's emissary Richard Palmer, bishop of Syracuse, took charge of her while Prince Richard headed west to to 'pacify' southern Gascony, his *casus belli* the argument that its barons had been robbing pilgrims en route to Compostela.[7] On 9 November Joanna embarked on a Sicilian galley, but the weather was against them and the 11-year-old English princess was so violently seasick that Palmer was worried enough to cancel the voyage and continue the journey on land. They reached Palermo at last on 2 February 1177.

> When she had arrived in Palermo, in Sicily, together with Bishop Gilles of Evreux and the other envoys [of Henry II] the whole city welcomed them and lamps were lit, so many and so large that the whole city almost seemed to be on fire, and the rays of the stars could in no way bear comparison with the brilliance of such a light, for it was by night that she entered Palermo. The said daughter of the king of England was then escorted, mounted on one of the king's horses, and resplendent with regal garments, to a certain palace, that there she might await in becoming state the day of her marriage and coronation.[8]

When that day came on 13 February 1177, wearing a bejewelled dress that had cost the staggering sum of £114 4s 5d, Princess Joanna was married to William II at the cathedral of Monreale outside Palermo, whose bishop was an English cleric named Roger of the Mill, with possibly Richard Palmer also officiating. At the age of 12, Joanna thus became queen consort of Sicily, duchess of Puglia and princess of Capua, not that she was often to share William II's bed, at first because she was still a child, who had grown up largely in the abbey of Fontevraud, and later because he preferred the compliant concubines in his harem. According to Robert de Torigni, she did, however produce one son for William, in 1181. Of this prince,

Boamundus, declared Duke of Apulia, little is known, although he cannot have lived long because when William II died in 1189, he left no legitimate heir. This placed Joanna in a parlous state as a series of underhand moves saw Roger II's illegitimate grandson Count Tancred of Lecce elected to succeed him, as a way of preventing the German Emperor Heinrich VI from claiming the throne on the strength of his marriage to William's aunt Constanza of Hautefort. Tancred, of small stature and unprepossessing appearance, had two nicknames in Sicily: *il re scimmia* meant 'the ape king' and *Tancredulus* translates as 'little Tancred' and is also a play on *incredulus*, which means the same in Latin or English.

Instead of freeing Joan to return to Angevin France or England, as would have been customary, Tancred placed her under house arrest in the Muslim west of Sicily in order to keep his hands on her considerable dowry. Fortunately for her – or maybe not – Joanna's brother Richard the Lionheart arrived a few months later on Christian eastern Sicily to overwinter there on his way to the Holy Land in the Third Crusade. Occupying the port-city of Messina by force of arms,[9] Richard demanded that Tancred release his sister and hand her dowry over to him, together with the substantial funds that William II had promised for the crusade. Whether he had his sister's interests at heart or was, as ever, greedy for funds from any source, is anyone's guess. Tancred hesitated until Richard threatened to do to Palermo what he had done to Messina and won the day. Tancred had Joanna escorted to Richard at Messina with most of her dower possessions and 40,000 ounces of gold, as promised by her late husband. Although her own bed had been among the goods delivered to Messina, Richard also dunned Tancred for the rest of her furniture including a gilded table eight feet long and a gold and silver dinner service of twenty-four settings, some of which Tancred eventually handed over with great reluctance.[10]

Also present on Sicily was the French army under King Philippe Auguste. When he set eyes on Joanna, a spirited 25-year-old woman raised for a greater destiny than she had known with William II, he wanted to marry her, his previous consort having recently died. In one of a number of acts hostile to Philippe, Richard seized the priory of Bagnara on the Calabrian mainland to serve as Joanna's residence so that there could be no contact between them. This was hardly the freedom that Joanna had been hoping for. The Sicilians exploiting the rivalry of Philippe and Richard, Richard betrothed his nephew Arthur of Brittany to Tancred's elder daughter[11] and Tancred coughed up the remaining 40,000 *bezants* – named for Byzantium – of Joanna's dowry promising in addition nineteen Sicilian galleys for the crusade, the timbers of the crusaders' original ships being badly affected by teredo wood-boring molluscs. At the other end of the island, the disputes between the two crusading kings growing worse, Philippe Auguste demanded that Richard marry after the crusade his half-sister Alais, who had been betrothed to him as a child by Philippe's father and handed over to grow up in Henry II's household until reaching marriageable age. Henry II having later used this French princess for sex, as a result of which she bore him one or more children, Richard retorted that it was unnatural for a man to marry his father's mistress.[12] Where this spat might have led, we cannot know but Count Philippe of Flanders came up with this: that Alais would be handed back to the Capetians after the crusade with her dowry, enhanced by 10,000 marks so that Philippe could marry her off to whom he pleased.

As the stay on Sicily drew to an end, Richard received unwelcome news from his mother. Queen Eleanor had been deeply worried by the departure on the crusade of Richard, a king of England who had no heir, which would become crucially important, should he die in the Holy Land, as did three out of four crusaders from drinking bad water, food poisoning, sand tick fever or some contagious disease – never mind combat. Uninterested in women, Richard had managed to avoid all possible previous matches. Instead of entrusting the hunt for a suitable wife for him to a couple of her bishops, which would have been normal, towards the end of 1190 Eleanor herself travelled across the Pyrenees to the court of King Sancho the Wise of Navarre. His 25-year-old unmarried daughter Berengaria was no sexy nymphet to tempt a sex-starved crusader into bed, but was described as gentle and virtuous – in other words, of such a submissive character that she would not demand anything of a husband, and be content to do her duty by him. Sancho was delighted at the idea of getting this long unmarried daughter off his hands and becoming the father-in-law of the king of England, which would be a very useful trump card to play against neighbouring monarchs, with whom hostilities were always breaking out in northern Spain.

Eleanor, shrewd as ever, refused to hand over to Berengaria the English queen's marriage portion, which she intended keeping for herself. Instead she promised Berengaria the county of Gascony – shades of Henry II and Alfonso of Castile! – and several towns on both sides of the Channel. One wonders what advice she gave, setting off with Berengaria back to her court at Poitiers. Sixty-eight years old, she did not rest there for long, but continued escorting Berengaria through southern France and the Alpine passes and down the long Italian peninsula, buying safe conducts from local lords on the way. Why the long and exhausting journey? To ensure that Richard did not invoke his oath of celibacy as a crusader as excuse not to marry Berengaria when she arrived on Sicily or hide behind the pope's ban on women accompanying the crusader armies. Richard had currently some 200 seaworthy ships, apart from those still being repaired, and could easily have sent one of them to collect his mother and Berengaria and speed up the final stage of their journey, but he did not.

Trapped on Sicily by the winter gales, Philippe and Richard were no longer on speaking terms. Aware of the ill feeling over Alais and her dowry, Eleanor waited until the French fleet had set sail, and crossed the strait of Messina with Berengaria on 30 March 1191. Her timing was impeccable. In the absence of Philippe Auguste, Eleanor may have hoped that the wedding of her favourite son could be celebrated on Sicily to avoid the further insult to Philippe of nuptials in the Holy Land while his half-sister was still locked up in the castle of Rouen. This was not to be: Richard invoked the Church's ban on marriages in Lent. We do not know what arguments Eleanor employed but, after four days with Richard and a visit to Joanna in Bagnara, she set off back to England, where Prince John's flagrant disloyalty to his brother the king and his accretion of power needed Eleanor's presence and political sense to stave off a civil war between his supporters and the barons loyal to Richard. Eleanor departed with letters bearing the king's seal appointing the Cornish-born Archbishop Walter of Rouen to replace Richard's universally unpopular chancellor William Longchamp. As to Berengaria, Richard despatched her to Bagnara, there to be exiled with his sister Joanna, who at least had a companion at last. The chronicle of Pierre de Langtoft described their frustrating existence there by recording that they were as happy as two doves in a cage.[13]

To circumvent by a technicality the papal ban on women travelling with the crusaders, Richard despatched Joanna and Berengaria three days before the departure of his fleet on board a *dromon* – a fast armed merchantman with a lateen sail and fifty oars on each side, plus two escorting vessels to protect it against the pirates infesting the Mediterranean. Blown ashore by a gale near Limassol on Cyprus, two of the ships were pillaged by wreckers in the service of the Byzantine self-styled Emperor of Cyprus Isaac Comnenus, who attempted unsuccessfully to entice Joanna and Berengaria to come ashore and 'accept his hospitality' – in other words, let themselves be taken hostage. On arrival there, Richard demanded compensation; when Comnenus refused, the crusading army was unleashed in a violent 3-week conquest of the island by land and sea. In one dawn attack, Comnenus fled in his night clothes from one end of his camp while the crusaders fought their way in at the other end. Finally trapped at the northern tip of the Karpaz peninsula, with no possibility of escape, Comnenus pleaded not to be put in irons, so Richard had him fettered hand and foot with silver chains in a dungeon and his daughter placed in the custody of Joanna as the first of her many keepers.

With Lent at an end and no shortage of bishops on the island, Richard agreed at last to marry Princess Berengaria. Before he could do that, it was necessary to confess himself as guilty of much spilling of blood and the sin of sodomy. His act of expiation was to be flogged in public, clad only in his underpants. In the next day's ceremony, poor Berengaria was married to Queen Eleanor's very reluctant 33-year-old son in the citadel chapel of St George in Limassol. Crowned queen of England by the bishop of Evreux, she became the only queen of England who never set foot in the country. Whether the 8-year-long marriage was ever consummated, we do not know: it is possible that Berengaria was England's first Virgin Queen. At the convent of L'Epau near Le Mans, which she founded, the feet of her effigy rest, not on a cushion but on a carved lion in the act of mounting a sheep.

Queen Eleanor had meanwhile broken her return journey with Archbishop Walter of Rouen in Rome, visiting Pope Celestine III, whom she had known in Paris during her marriage to Louis VII as Cardinal Giacinto, or Hyacinth. Speaking to him as queen-regent of England, she requested that he immediately consecrate Henry II's illegitimate son

Geoffrey the Bastard as Archbishop of York, which disqualified him from seeking secular office in the turbulent island kingdom during Richard's absence, where Prince John was already causing more than enough dissension. He was also planning to divorce his wife, Isabel of Gloucester, before leading an invasion of Normandy by a mercenary force and 'rescue' Princess Alais from house arrest to marry her and declare himself Duke of Normandy. He would then pay homage to Philippe Auguste, who had returned to France prematurely after surviving serious illness in the Holy Land. To speed things up, Eleanor persuaded the Pope to give her the *pallium* – a bishop's symbolic scarf of lambswool, which normally required a new prelate to travel to Rome to receive it from the pope's own hand. A second request granted was the dismissal of Richard's close friend and chancellor William Longchamp from his post as bishop of Ely. Travel being so slow in those days, she had taken the precaution on Sicily of securing letters bearing Richard's seal which covered every possible move that Longchamp or Prince John could make. That done, she continued the journey, reaching Rouen on 24 June.

What were conditions like for Joanna, Berengaria and Comnenus' daughter in the Holy Land? Although not required to live in the stinking, hot, disease-ridden siege camp outside Acre with Richard, they were not left in peace. Indeed, the reason for Richard insisting the three women come to the Holy Land was to serve as possible pawns in some political game. The campaign against the Muslim forces under their brilliant general Salāh-ad-Dïn Yūsuf[14] having reached stalemate after long months of combat with no likelihood of ever recapturing Jerusalem – which was the avowed purpose of the crusade – Richard made overtures to Saladin in the hope of pulling off some coup that would disguise the failure of the crusade. He offered to marry his sister Joanna to Saladin's brother al-Adil or Saphadin and give the throne of Jerusalem to the happy couple, to reign there as king and queen. It was a far from original idea, having been proposed many times as a way of converting the Saracens. Convincing himself, if no one else, Richard dubbed al-Adil a knight, called him 'my brother' and ordered some compliant bishop to arrange al-Adil's baptism. Saladin wisely kept clear of the whole mad scheme, which foundered when Joanna – in an outburst of passionate indignation rare among medieval women – refused outright to marry a Muslim. Saphadin in turn refused to change his faith. Undeterred, Richard offered him his niece Eleanor of Brittany as a bride, but that did not succeed either.

Having alienated virtually all his allies, Richard had to beg a single ship from the Templars in return for the Saladin tithe that Henry II had paid to them. It was a sorry contrast with his arrival in command of a fleet and an army. Berengaria and 31-year-old Joanna, virtually penniless because Richard had spent on his crusade all her dowry recovered from Tancred, had been sent on ahead ten days previously, to await his arrival in Rome. When all the other surviving crusaders had returned to Europe and Richard was known to be a prisoner in Austria and Germany, the two princesses journeyed on to France, where Joanna's troubles were not over. She had, like her grandmother Empress Matilda, kept her title as queen of Sicily, which enabled Eleanor of Aquitaine to incite the young Count Raymond of Toulouse to divorce his second wife Bourguine de Lusignan and become the husband of a titular queen, thus reuniting his breakaway county with the duchy of Aquitaine and defying his duty of vassalage to his cousin Philippe Auguste. There were complications: Raymond had been excommunicated for sending away his first wife and would dig himself deeper into the spiritual mire by repudiating a second wife while Joanna was understandably not keen to become the property of another unfaithful husband.

Insisting that she had no more right to object than when she had been despatched as a child to Sicily, Eleanor inserted into the marriage contract a clause providing that Joanna's children in the marriage would inherit the county lost to her family two generations earlier, and arranged her wedding to Count Raymond VI in Rouen cathedral during October 1196 in the presence of Berengaria who otherwise kept out of the limelight in her own dower possessions. The reluctant countess-consort of Toulouse was to be survived by two children by Count Raymond: a son born in 1197 also called Raymond, who would succeed his father; and a daughter, born in the following year. In addition to this traditional female role, in March 1199, when Count Raymond VI was putting down rebellion in the east of his county and the lord of San Feliu took advantage of this to rebel against him, Joanna courageously led some of Raymond's knights to besiege the rebel count at a place known as Les Cassés – a corruption of the Occitan word *cassos* meaning oak trees.

After some of the knights betrayed her by allowing food and weaponry into the besieged fortress, Joanna abandoned the siege but, before she could leave the camp, was badly burned when some of the turncoats set fire to her tent. Already pregnant again, she fled from Toulouse to seek the protection of her brother Richard in Aquitaine, only to learn that he had died at the siege of Châlus and that John was now the king of England after Queen Eleanor had belatedly announced that he was to succeed Richard on the throne of England, as duke of Normandy and Aquitaine and count of Touraine, Anjou and Poitou – the empire that stretched from the Scottish border in the north to the peaks of the Pyrenees in the south.

Travelling northwest, Joanna caught up with Queen Eleanor at Niort but, either because of her advanced pregnancy or injuries she had suffered in the fire, was too weak to keep up with her mother's customary pace of travel. Sent back to Fontevraud abbey, to be cared for by the nuns, Joanna recovered some strength and headed north again in June, meeting John and Eleanor in Rouen and begging their help as she had no funds, Count Raymond having kept all her possessions. Refusing her daughter any financial help, although the richest woman in the world, Eleanor did persuade John to allot his impoverished sister an annual pension of 100 marks and a lump sum of 3,000 marks to tide her over.

At the end of August 1199 the 33-year-old sick and pregnant ex-queen of Sicily was again in Rouen, nearing death and pleading to be buried in Fontevraud. Advanced pregnancy normally disqualifying a woman from joining an order of nuns, Eleanor ordered Hubert Walter, Archbishop of Canterbury, to solve the problem. Often mocked by Richard for his inadequate knowledge of Latin, the archbishop came up with an ingenious compromise: only the abbess of Fontevraud had the authority to fulfil Joanna's wish. Rapidly, he assembled a council of clerics including some nuns from Fontevraud, who decided that Joanna's request was so extraordinary, it must be divinely inspired.[15] She was admitted to the Order shortly before dying in childbirth on 4 September 1199. Her baby was delivered by Caesarean section, which was permitted by the Church in those circumstances, and baptised with the name Richard after his dead uncle. Shortly afterwards, he too died and the bodies of mother and child were transported to Fontevraud for burial. Fifty years later, Joanna's son Count Raymond VII of Toulouse was interred by her side.

Chapter 9

Princess Blanca Becomes Queen Blanche

After the death of Joanna, Queen Eleanor had outlived all her ten children by Louis VII and Henry II except Queen Leonor of Castile and John, now the king of England. This extraordinary woman in her seventy-eighth year overcame her grief at the death of Richard and turned her mind to the pieces she still held on the chessboard of history. After John was crowned in Westminster Abbey on 27 May 1199 – a ceremony in which the prelate's blessing was rendered inaudible by John's constant joking to cronies present and him dropping the ceremonial sword of office – he returned to France, to try and impose his rule in the continental possessions, with which he was still struggling, six months later.

At the Christmas court at Bures in Normandy, a meeting was arranged on the border of Plantagenet Normandy and Philippe Auguste's territory in the Seine valley not far from Richard's reputedly impregnable castle of Château Gaillard. Among the matters being negotiated[1] was the confirmation by John in his capacity as duke of Normandy of Richard's promised cession to the French crown of the long-disputed Vexin, that strategically important territory lying between the northern border of Philippe's Ile-de-France and Normandy. The financial settlement was enshrined in the Treaty of Le Goulet, signed on the neutral island of Gueuleton in mid-Seine near Vernon – incidentally severing the *îles normandes* from the duchy of Normandy to become the English Channel Islands. The treaty required John to pay 20,000 pounds or marks[2] for the right to become overlord of Brittany, a device by which Philippe Auguste dispossessed John's nephew Arthur of Brittany.

To raise this large amount, John imposed an additional *carucage* tax[3] on ploughland in England, earning from his resentful Anglo-Norman barons a second unfortunate sobriquet – *mollegladium*, which translates as 'softsword'. In addition to this and other political matters that needed to be resolved between the two kings, Philippe raised the question of a Plantagenet wife for his son Louis, whose progeny might thus inherit the continental possessions of the Plantagenets. In mid-June, Queen Eleanor travelled to Tours and swore fealty to Philippe for her lands in France after refusing to give John her birthright of Aquitaine and Poitou. During the Capetian-Plantagenet truce after the death of Henry II there had been negotiations with a view to marrying Philippe Auguste's son Prince Louis to Geoffrey Plantagenet's daughter Eleanor of Brittany, as a way of uniting the two royal families, but that came to nothing when renewed hostilities broke out. At the meeting in Tours Queen Eleanor therefore proposed marrying another of her granddaughters Princess Urraca of León to Prince Louis, thus re-uniting the house of Capet and the Plantagenet line two generations after her divorce from Philippe's father King Louis VII in 1152.[4]

While John was travelling through an England that was financially exhausted by Richard's fiscal voracity followed by him dunning his vassals and vavasours for payment of the *carucage* tax, Eleanor set off from Poitiers on the long journey to Castile with a retinue that included Hélie de Malemort, Archbishop of Bordeaux, and several representatives of Philippe Auguste. Having lived more than twice the average age of women at the time, it is unlikely that she still rode a horse and more probable that she was conveyed in a horse litter. Like a one- or two-seater sedan chair with the passenger or passengers protected from the elements, it was carried on two long poles harnessed on both sides to one horse in front and another behind, with a postillion riding on each. The litter horses, like soldiers marching across a bridge, were trained to walk out of step, which stopped the litter from swaying from side to side. The advantage of this form of travel over wheeled transport was that the roads not repaired since Roman times were full of potholes, which slowed carts and carriages down for fear of breaking a wheel and also made life very bumpy and uncomfortable for the passengers.

The journey of nearly 500 miles had hardly begun when her cortège was ambushed on the very first day by the Lusignan family. Although vassals of Eleanor as Countess of Poitou, they had many grievances against Henry II, Richard, John and Eleanor herself, and now demanded in satisfaction the return of their former part of the county of La Marche, lying between Aquitaine and the French territory of Berry to the east. Her mind set on winning a more important political chess game, Eleanor gave them the pawn they desired and was allowed to continue on her way, initially along the old pilgrim trail to Santiago de Compostela, later branching southwest after skirting the Pyrenees along the coastal route through the Basque country and passing through Miranda del Ebro and Burgos to reach Palencia, where Alfonso VIII was currently holding his court.

The reason why she had come all that way in person became apparent when she met her granddaughters Urraca and Blanca, the two available Castilian princesses of marriageable age whose elder sister Berenguela was already betrothed to the heir of the neighbouring kingdom of León. People said that among their ancestors was a Muslim noble named Moussa, whose daughter Garcie had married King Sancho III of Navarre, whose second son became king of Castile when part of Navarre was annexed by Castile in 1033. If true, that made her a descendant of the prophet Mohammed,[5] but this was not something either Queen Eleanor or the chosen princess was likely to boast about in the rigidly Christian Capetian court.

Meeting the doyenne of European royalty in the presence of Philippe Auguste's ambassadors who had travelled with her, the two young princesses may have heard that a marriage with the French crown prince had been discussed in Tours, but, never having met their grandmother before, had no reason to think that they were both being assessed. Reputed for her *admirabilis astucia*, or shrewd judgement of people, Queen Eleanor sized the girls up. It had been assumed by Philippe's envoys that the more beautiful older girl, 13-year-old Urraca, was to marry Prince Louis, but Eleanor ignored them, declaring that her name would sound alien to Frankish ears whereas Blanca translated easily as Blanche. This granddaughter was then a girl of eleven or just twelve, whose long brown hair, cool, classical beauty, broad features and fearless gaze bore an uncanny physical resemblance to the young duchess of Aquitaine who had married Crown Prince Louis all those years ago in the summer of 1137. When he became King Louis VII two weeks later, after his father Louis the Fat died, she became the teenage queen of France. More to the point, Eleanor judged that this granddaughter of hers was like her also in intellect and would make a wonderful match for Philippe Auguste's son, becoming queen consort of France when Philippe died. She sensed in her something of that quality which, according to historian Gérard Sivéry, earned Blanche not the love of her subjects, but their respect.[6]

Princess Urraca was therefore betrothed instead to Prince Affonso of Portugal, marrying him in 1206. Although he succeeded to the throne as Affonso II aged 26 in March 1212, being king of Portugal was no sinecure. He had serious disputes with his three sisters, who all claimed territorial rights conferred by their father and which Affonso disputed. Portugal being a young kingdom, he also found it difficult to control his restless barons, all of whom were greedy for greater power. Worst of all, his grandfather Affonso I had been captured by Castile after a fall from his horse and forced to cede the province of Galicia, which he never recovered. In order to get the support of the Pope for Portuguese independence in 1143, he had also granted too much power to the Church in Portugal, where it had become a state within the state. Affonso II was determined to change the situation so that he was undisputed ruler. As a result he was excommunicated by Pope Honorius III and the kingdom placed under interdict. And for Urraca, he must have been a difficult and unattractive spouse for he was grossly overweight, perhaps from some glandular problem, and known to his people as 'Affonso o gordo' – Alfonso the Fat. In his last years, he acquired an even less flattering sobriquet, his hostile people hurling at him, *'Fora, gaffo!'* Begone, leper! Whether he died of the leprosy that afflicted him or from gross overweight, is unknown, but he left three sons by Urraca, two of whom became successive kings of Portugal, and a daughter christened Lianor, who was sent to Denmark to marry the prince who became King Valdemar III.

Blanca, however, was destined for greater things. She was born in Palencia in 1188 and, after leaving her richly rewarded wet-nurse, but still described as *puerula infantissa domina blanca* or 'infant princess the Lady Blanca', was sent by her parents to be brought up in the household of Pedro Rodríguez de Castro in the province of Palencia.[7] From that quiet but noble retreat, she was about to be precipitated into the high life of the Capetian royal family.

For a woman of Eleanor's age the long journey south must have been exhausting. Fortunately, there was no reason for her to hurry back to

France since, for practical reasons, a wedding could not be celebrated before the end of Lent yet had to be concluded before 1 July under the terms of the marriage contract. At least she could relax for a while and regain her strength in the elegant surroundings of the Castilian court of Alfonso VIII and Eleanor's daughter Queen Leonor, where both learned debate and the compositions of troubadours from north of the Pyrenees were valued and the game of courtly love played as a distraction for the ladies.

Eleanor had intended to chaperone her chosen granddaughter all the way to Paris, and doubtless enjoy her new status as grandmother of the future queen of France expunging the disgrace of the long-ago divorce from Philippe's father. The first stage was to cross the Pyrenees by the pass of Roncevaux, where the Augustinian abbey offered rude accommodation for the night and was accomplished against the springtime stream of pilgrims heading towards Santiago de Compostela.

However, even she was feeling her years and had to end her journey at Easter in Bordeaux. It says something of the untrustworthiness of her Gascon vassals that she had made her loyal mercenary commander Mercadier the constable of Aquitaine during her absence in Spain and wanted him to escort her and Blanca – now called Blanche – north to the Ile de France. Just before Easter, Mercadier was killed in a street brawl with a rival band of mercenaries. Some said they were in the pay of John, but whether he was guilty or not, this was a blow to Eleanor, who did not trust any of her vassals. She summoned up the strength to accompany Blanche to the abbey of Fontevraud, where she rested to recover her strength.[8] There, she entrusted Blanche to the care of Archbishop Hélie de Malemort and the bishops of Poitiers and Saintes, who escorted her to Richard's castle of Château Gaillard in Normandy, which within four years would be captured after a long siege by Philippe Auguste.

In 1200 Château Gaillard was still John's property and there Blanche was accommodated while being prepared for her marriage to 14-year-old Prince Louis. Instead of being celebrated with due pomp in Reims cathedral, it took place on 22 or 23 May 1200 at the small church of Port-Mort in Norman territory near Château Gaillard because Philippe's royal domain lay under an interdict imposed by Pope Innocent III to punish him for bigamously marrying his mistress Agnès de Méranie after putting away in a convent his second wife Ingeborg of Denmark. In the royal domain no Mass could therefore be said, church bells had all been lowered to the ground and the dead could not be buried in consecrated ground. A complication was that for the Capetian wedding party to be safe in Plantagenet territory, King John had to constitute himself a hostage on French territory for as long as the Capetians were in 'his' Normandy.

Also present at Port-Mort was John's unfortunate nephew Arthur of Brittany, posthumous son of John's brother Geoffrey, whose widow, Countess Constance of Brittany, could not attend because she was afflicted by leprosy and thus debarred from all contact except with other lepers. Otherwise, the chronicler Mathew Paris described a gay enough scene attended by the nobility and monks, priests, counts, barons, as well as ordinary local folk who would never have dreamed of seeing such splendour under normal conditions.[9] As the wedding party split up to go their separate ways in truce, Philippe Auguste consented to Arthur paying homage to John for Brittany. For a moment it looked as though some peace might be due for the Bretons, but John was a man who nurtured hatred and never forgave Arthur for having been a possible contender for the throne after Richard's death. With no celebration meal delaying the departures, all concerned returned to the safe sides of the Capetian/Plantagenet territorial divide and Blanche departed with the royal household to Paris, following part of the way in the footsteps of her grandmother when arriving in the royal palace on the Ile de la Cité with Louis VII in 1137. Due to the interdict, no public acclaim greeted her and no church bells rang out to salute the arrival of the girl who was to be among France's most important queens, governing the country for several years when her husband departed on crusade.

The royal household in which she found herself after marrying Prince Louis included several children and young people – Louis' cousins and half-brothers born to Agnès de Méranie and several noble children who had been taken hostage by the king to ensure the loyalty of their parents. From the beginning, Prince Louis was solicitous towards her, sensing her bewilderment in Paris, the most populous city in Europe that was still expanding, noisy day and night with traders and artisans at their business and not infrequently disturbed by street fights between students from many countries, whose only common language was Latin – hence the name 'Latin quarter' even today for the area where they then lived. In all this Babel, lacking almost totally was her own mother tongue *castellano*, any unconscious use of which enabled her enemies in the gossipy court to label her *la fille étrangère* – the foreign girl – a slur that stuck to her for life. On the Ile de la Cité itself, Philippe Auguste's court, from which troubadours and other entertainers had been banned by Louis VII after the divorce from Blanche's grandmother, was a grim affair compared with her mother's elegant and spirited life in Burgos or Palencia.

Notwithstanding the strength of character she developed, and which made her a great and powerful queen, in the early months after the wedding, Blanche was given to fits of depression and hysterical weeping. With no queen resident on the Ile de la Cité, Prince Louis thought that perhaps his young bride was simply missing a sympathetic female ear. His concern for her prompted him to consult Bishop Hugh of Lincoln, known in his native France as Hugues, who travelled a great deal and was at that time visiting the bishop of Paris. Bishop Hugh agreed to come to the royal palace, where he both talked with Blanche and listened to her tale of woes, letting her pour out all her sadness and worries, after which he reminded her of her obligations. Brought up in northern Spain, where her father and his vassals were constantly either fighting off the Muslims or squabbling lethally with the neighbouring Christian states, she took heart, accepted her destiny and learned to smile again.[10]

Chapter 10

Two Isabels at King John's Court

When bidding farewell at Fontevraud to Archbishop Hélie, Queen Eleanor had charged him with another task. That was to accelerate the dissolution of King John's marriage to Countess Isabel of Gloucester,[1] who seemed unlikely to provide a male heir to inherit the English throne. Although not born a princess, Isabel was the youngest daughter, and co-heiress of William, 2nd Earl of Gloucester after the death of her brother Robert. Once again, no chronicler noted the exact date of her birth, but she was aged about 3 when King Henry II betrothed her to 9-year-old John Lackland in 1176.

Herodotus coined the word *'istoria* meaning the pursuit of knowledge by enquiry. Unfortunately, researching even the most prominent women in medieval Europe is complicated by the misogynist chroniclers often not bothering to note the birth date of girls. That influential abbot and inveterate letter-writer Bernard of Clairvaux could not bear even to look at his own sister in her nun's habit and attributed the perpetuation of mankind's original sin to each child being 'conceived in sin and born in filth'. The mother of Yeshua bar Josef, better known by his Hellenised name Iessous Khristos which became Jesus Christ, was considered the only exception to this rule.

Although hostile to Jews, the all-powerful Christian Church in Europe had adopted the Torah-ordained view that women were unclean when they had performed the very purpose for which these royal and noble girls, sent away young to marry a stranger, later risked their lives in childbirth. They remained unclean, shut away like lepers for forty days or, in some countries, eighty days if the child was a girl, until the Church ceremonially pronounced their bodies usable again for sex by their spouses. It seems strange that the ceremony of the 'churching of women' after giving birth continued into modern times – certainly well into the twentieth century – although latterly dressed up as a blessing on the new mother. Some priests of the Anglican Church continue to perform the ritual of *benedictio mulieris post partum* – or blessing of a woman after giving birth. It was discontinued in the Catholic Church after the Second Vatican Council in 1965, although some Catholic priests of the Roman Rite continue to perform churchings. The Christian rite was inherited from Jewish tradition based on Leviticus 12:1–8, which considered a woman unclean after giving birth or even menstruating. Even today, every Orthodox synagogue has a *mikveh* for the ritual monthly 'purification' by total immersion of the female members of the congregation, usually supervised by the rabbi's wife, who keeps a record to ensure no other wife cheats.

At an early age, these girls betrothed so young in the Middle Ages became aware that that their only justification for living in a palace and wearing silks and velvet was their own *untried* fecundity. If they did not produce children, they would be sent away in disgrace, no matter that the fault might lie with the husband. Even that formidable daughter of Henry I, Matilda, who married the 28-year-old German Emperor Heinrich V when she was not yet 12 years old, was 'returned to sender' on his death eleven years later, having failed to get pregnant.

Her equally powerful daughter-in-law Eleanor, who inherited in her own right at age fifteen the vast duchy of Aquitaine, married Louis VII of France a few weeks later produced two living daughters by him. Her failure to produce a male heir was her ticket to freedom after fifteen years as Louis' wife, when she immediately married her much younger neighbour, Count Henry of Anjou. Her possessions allied to his, including the duchies of Normandy and Aquitaine, enabled him to gain the English throne. Producing five sons and three daughters for Henry, she more than fulfilled her wifely duty. When he sought to be rid of her at the menopause, she raised her surviving sons in a rebellion that failed. Betrayed to Henry, she spent fifteen years as his prisoner under house arrest or worse. Emerging from that punishment at the age of 67, she immediately declared herself the only queen in England and held the country by sheer force of character for her son Richard Lionheart until he arrived from France for his coronation. During his long absence on the Third Crusade and afterwards, she acted as regent and found the time and energy to travel into Spain to find a suitably submissive wife, by whom he *might* father a son who could succeed him, if he died in the Holy Land. She then escorted Berengaria all the way to Sicily, to ensure Richard went through with the wedding.

Although it was always 'the wife's fault', a failure to conceive could be because the husband was too old, or diseased, or rendered sterile by daily damage to his sexual organs from the hard, unyielding saddle of a warhorse, with its high pommel and cantle. Be he old, gross or diseased, she had to suffer his advances all the same. And, if these girls did produce children, but only daughters – like Eleanor of Aquitaine with her first husband, Louis VII of France – what then? In Eleanor's case, that shortcoming enabled her to escape the marriage with monkish Louis and marry by her own *political* choice the virile young Henri d'Anjou, in whose bed she had no trouble producing children of both sexes. But she was extraordinary.

In September 1176 King Henry II had arranged the betrothal of the richly endowed 3-year-old Isabel of Gloucester to his youngest son 9-year-old Prince John as compensation for his lack of titles and expectations, already shared out among his older brothers. Thirteen years later, on 29 August 1189 Isabel was married to John in Marlborough castle, although the union was opposed by Archbishop Baldwin of Canterbury on the grounds of consanguinity, each spouse being a great-grandchild of Henry I. To increase the wealth for John, Isabel's two sisters Mabel and Amicia were bought out with annuities of £100 each, in which they had no say. When John succeeded to the throne on the death of Richard ten years later, Isabel had produced no children for her husband, while he continued busily sowing his seed elsewhere. It seems she was a barren woman, who never did get pregnant in her two subsequent marriages either. Her penalty was to find Archbishop Hélie had obeyed Eleanor of Aquitaine's instructions and pressured the Norman bishops of Lisieux, Bayeux and Avranches and three bishops in Aquitaine into annulling the marriage on the grounds of the consanguinity that had been known all the time. For fourteen years, Isabel remained a ward of court, her considerable inherited wealth accruing to the husband who had rejected her. In January 1214 King John was desperately raising funds for a war in France to recover the lost Plantagenet possessions there, and sold Isabel of Gloucester's wardship to Sir Geoffrey Mandeville, Earl of Essex, for

20,000 marks, which included the right to marry her and claim the title of earl of Gloucester *jure uxoris* – by the entitlement of his wife.

Mandeville was obliged to make the huge payment within a year. When he defaulted on the debt, John confiscated Isabel's estates once again. In 1215 de Mandeville sided with the rebel barons, which meant that, when he died of wounds received in a tournament one year later, all his lands and titles were forfeit to the Crown. Not until a year after John's death were Isabel's lands returned to her, at which point she became a desirable wife, married by Earl Hubert de Burgh of Kent, who was a chief justiciar of England and would be a regent during the minority of Henry III. Whatever Isabel's expectations at that point, she died within a few months.

To return to historical chronology, when visiting Eleanor at Fontevraud after the wedding of Louis and Blanche in Port-Mort, John found that his mother had selected for him a suitable Portuguese princess to wed. She had already despatched ambassadors to the court of King Sancho I, known as *o povoador* – the settler – on account of his policy of settling Christian immigrants on lands formerly held by the Muslims he had driven out. Nothing came of this because John had other ideas. His Aquitain vassals the Lusignan family, who had caused so much strife for Henry II, for Eleanor and for Richard, were so pleased with their deal forced on Eleanor on her way to Castile that they offered to bring the disaffected counts of Limoges and Angoulême back into the Plantagenet fold.

John was apparently never able to separate affairs of state from his personal desires. Staying with Hugues IX de Lusignan, known as 'le Brun', his lust was aroused by Hugues' beautiful blonde, blue-eyed 14-year-old betrothed, Isabella of Angoulême.[2] Although advised by her father, Count Aymar Taillefer – who liked the idea of becoming father-in-law to the king of England and seeing his daughter crowned in Westminster Abbey – that stealing Isabella from the powerful Lusignans would cause a dangerous rift in relations with them and probably open warfare with serious strategic consequences, John came up with a devious plan. He despatched Hugues and his brother to visit their estates in Normandy and England, then took advantage of their absence to follow a confusing itinerary to Angoulême via Bordeaux, so that he could collect Archbishop Hélie de Malemort en route.

Isabella was called home by her complicit father and on 24 August – the day before she was to have been married to Hugues – she was informed by Archbishop Hélie that the man she was to marry on the morrow was not he, but the king of England. Far from the submissive daughter required by custom, the often tempestuous Isabella preferred the idea of being queen of England with John to being a countess with Hugues. And so it was, with Hélie officiating in Angoulême cathedral. Isabella was afterwards blamed for the trouble her desirable body and good looks had caused and also slandered as an immoral creature by the chroniclers, Matthew Paris labelling her, 'an animal'. Eleanor, residing in Fontevraud, gave her the cities of Niort and Saintes as a wedding gift, which was not generous, but she was not in the best of tempers after having to inform the frustrated envoys of Sancho I, who came from Portugal with her returning ambassadors, that John's wedding to a daughter of the Portuguese king was not going to happen. An alternative interpretation of John's stealing the girl betrothed to Hugues IX is that it was an astute move, preventing the Lusignans from uniting the county of Angoulême with their territory, which would have created a power bloc that could have destabilised Aquitaine.

Before departing blithely on a leisurely journey north, obsessed with his new wife, John sent one of his wards, who was a cousin of Isabella, to Hugues de Lusignan as a replacement bride. Hugues le Brun played it cool and accepted the cousin, but bided his time for revenge. Eleanor sent her Poitevin vassal Amaury de Thouars to John, suggesting that he sort out the problems he had caused with the Lusignans, but John did the reverse, ordering the constable of Normandy to seize the Lusignan castle at Driencourt and all their other possessions in the duchy. North of the Channel, on 8 October, John was re-crowned and Isabella crowned queen in Westminster abbey. In the following fifteen years she bore him five children, all of whom survived childhood.

Staying in poor health at Fontevraud in the care of the nuns, Eleanor should have been able to relax in the knowledge that she had just achieved her greatest betrothal coup in matching Blanche and Prince Louis, but this was marred as visitors coming to pay their respects brought her news of all the mistakes she had foreseen John making – and others. In 1201 the truce between the Capetian king on the Ile de la Cité and his vassal John as duke of Normandy was fêted in the royal domain with a luxurious reception for John and his beautiful young wife, whose custom it reportedly was to dance into the small hours and rise at midday, having detained her husband in bed well after the time a king was expected to be up and about his duties.[3] Blanche was presumably scandalised and continued her pious observances, while Philippe Auguste indulged John and Isabella, smothering them with presents. It seems that John had expected his niece Blanche to use her influence on his behalf out of family loyalty. On occasions elsewhere this had been known to happen – and was indeed part of the reason for sending royal daughters away to foreign husbands – but she regarded herself now as a Capetian, and caught her uncle off-guard when relaying to him Philippe Auguste's demand that the remainder of the Norman Vexin be handed over. The visit over, John was summoned as duke of Normandy to appear before his suzerain Philippe on 28 April 1202. When John refused to attend, Philippe dispossessed him of all his possessions on French soil, knighted Arthur of Brittany and endowed him with the counties of Anjou, Maine and Touraine, Arthur kneeling in homage and swearing fealty to him.

Philippe Auguste bided his time as John committed error after error in the continental possessions, alienating other important vassals like Count Aymar of Limoges and his neighbour Count Raymond of Toulouse. Philippe's mistress Agnès de Méranie having died in childbirth, he was no longer living in sin, so from Rome Pope Innocent III – *il papa innocentius tertius*, as he was known – revoked the excommunication of the French king and legitimised his bastards, which caused sighs of relief in the royal domain. Although Philippe's rejected consort Ingeborg of Denmark was allowed to return to court, Philippe Auguste did not live with her and she was never accorded the respect due to her title. The pope's revocation of the interdict was good fortune for Arthur of Brittany, who was betrothed to Princess Marie, but his new titles and rank rather turned the head of her betrothed, who lacked the shrewd brain of his father Geoffrey Plantagenet. Rashly invading Normandy at the head of only 200 knights and some foot-soldiers, he was chased off and arrived in Tours with his knights and men-at-arms, where he was informed by the Lusignans, seeking their revenge, that Eleanor had left Fontevraud, where she was protected by the Peace of God, and was heading for the temporal safety of her palace inside the walls of Poitiers.

Currently in the border town of Mirebeau, she was under the personal protection of King John, but Arthur ignored saner counsel from his Norman knights and allowed the Lusignans to persuade him that together, they could capture Eleanor and force her to confer the county of Poitou and the duchy of Aquitaine on him, after which he could hand her over to the Lusignans as a very valuable hostage. When Arthur's force broke into Mirebeau, Eleanor retreated to the citadel with a small number of loyal knights and men-at-arms after despatching messengers to find John, who was known to be near Le Mans, eighty miles to the north. Coming to the gate of the citadel to speak with her, Arthur seemed to find nothing wrong with besieging his own grandmother, who did not lose her head, but dragged out the negotiations so that help could arrive. John, for once, did not hesitate, but rode day and night with a band of knights and mercenaries under Guillaume des Roches, the seneschal of Anjou, arriving at Mirebeau before the early dawn of 1 August.

They found that Arthur's men had forced the citizens to wall up all the town gates except one, through which supplies and reinforcements could be brought in. Thinking themselves far from any enemy, Arthur's men had left that gate open and unguarded, allowing John's men to steal quietly into the town. Half-asleep, Arthur's Breton and Norman knights and men-at-arms were cut down in the streets. Reacting fast, Guy de Lusignan, who had been eating breakfast with Arthur, managed to mount his warhorse and head for the gate. The horse was killed under him by Guillaume de Braose, who took him prisoner and went on to capture Arthur too.[4] De Braose had been a favourite of John for some time, and may have thought that taking so valuable a prisoner was the next step in his rise to fame and fortune. It was instead the first step on his path to disgrace, dispossession, bereavement and the grave.

Defying feudal custom that ransomable hostages were the property of the men who had captured them, John demanded that all the male captives taken at Mirebeau – including many who were blood relatives of knights who had helped him take the town – be handed over to him. To overcome the reluctance of the captors, he gave promises that the men handed over would be well treated and that he would share out the ransom money, when received. Driven in chains to various of his castles in Normandy, many suffering castration and/or blinding, Arthur's knights were shuttled hither and yon to confuse any possible rescue attempt.[5] With John's vindictiveness alienating his vassals who had fought with him at Mirebeau, Eleanor must have despaired anew at the inappropriate behaviour of her sole surviving son, who had himself been pardoned by King Richard for conspiring with Philippe Auguste to keep Richard a prisoner in Germany indefinitely. She left Mirebeau and returned to Fontevraud, where she took the veil and put the Peace of God between her and 'the evil that men do'.

In England the barons who resented being taxed for John's putative invasion to recapture Normandy gathered with 2,000 of their knights and men-at-arms on 13 April 1215 at Stamford, led by two of the nobles whose wives had been abused by John, Robert Fizwalter and Eustace de Vescy. Their king, as was his wont, delayed attending by all means in his power, cancelling rendezvous and attempting to subvert or bribe individuals in one-to-one meetings. On 5 May the barons' patience was exhausted and they formally declared *diffidatio* – the feudal equivalent of a vote of no confidence – revoking their oaths of loyalty to the king. It was a declaration of war against John and those barons who remained loyal to him. On 15 June a temporary truce permitting the meeting at Runnymede saw the dissident barons force John to agree the terms of the Magna Carta, or great charter, that created a council of twenty-five nobles who assumed many functions of the monarch. On 24 August John's technical overlord Pope Innocent III declared it invalid and excommunicated thirty of the principal barons responsible.[5] Sending his family to the security of Corfe castle, John sailed to Dover in expectation of the arrival of a considerable reinforcement of Poitevins, Gascons and Flemings, but their vessels were scattered in a gale on 26 September. Many sank, drowning passengers and sending treasure to the bottom of the Channel.

Starting out overland for London, John was at Canterbury when he heard that the barons were advancing down the pilgrim route from London and were already a short day's ride away. He hastily returned to Dover castle. The barons in turn did an about-face at the pilgrims' hospital in Ospringe and retreated to Rochester castle. Besieging the castle, John had to provision his forces, which he did by sending out foraging parties in all directions, to plunder or steal by force what they needed from the local population. It was to forestall this that well-planned warfare included a scorched earth prelude, to deny the enemy sustenance. His multiple setbacks brought out the worst in John. After receiving some particular piece of bad news, he shouted at Isabella, 'You see what you have cost me?' Never a woman to take a reprimand lying down, she spat back, 'You cost me the greatest knight in Christendom.'[6]

In England, John's winter campaign against the barons laid waste their lands as far north as Nottingham by Christmas and then continued to the Scottish border at Berwick, returning to confront the anticipated French invasion after reducing twenty of more rebel strongholds. As during King Stephen's war against Empress Matilda, his Flemish mercenaries robbed and raped as they went, while in the south and east, another loyalist army blockaded the city of London, held by the rebels, and attacked the barons' fiefs with fire and sword, cutting down orchards and burning crops and homes. That was the medieval equivalent of total war, its progress watched with interest by the observers on the Ile de la Cité.

Chapter 11

The Tragic Pearl of Brittany

H enry II had governed *per vim et voluntatem* – by force and willpower. He had also legitimised the Angevin concept of *ira et malevolentia*, or ruler's right to indulge his anger and ill will against a subject of whatever rank. This accorded perfectly with John's personality. His upbringing in the closed world of Fontevraud, with little family contact and no great future to look forward to, had produced a embittered, deceitful and jealous man. Arthur having been named successor to Richard in the treaty of Messina in March 1191, his children would have a prior right over John's offspring, since Arthur's father was senior to John. To remove the risk of 15-year-old Arthur ever having children, John ordered him to be castrated and blinded. The grim twin *donjons* of William the Conqueror's castle[1] at Falaise in Normandy still glower down at the town below. Simply being locked up there must have caused Arthur to fear the worst; there was no chance of rescue and King John's defiance of custom in grabbing and ill-treating all the ransomable captives at Mirebeau hinted that worse was to come. It did.

In the dungeons of this forbidding fortress three men-at-arms were ordered to inflict the grim punishment decreed by the king. Two of them refused to carry it out after recognising the victim. The third man involved botched his first cuts – perhaps because Arthur was not held down with enough force by the others – before stopping his grisly work on the order of Hubert de Burgh, castellan of Falaise. Partly mutilated, Arthur was again shackled hand and foot and fed only scant rations of bread and water in that castle, as ordered by his uncle John. The news of his resulting emaciation and increasingly poor health caused Guillaume de Braose to resign from John's service after swearing in front of three witnesses that Arthur had been in good health when he delivered him to the king.[2] The evidence of Arthur's last days is confused because John had his nephew secretly transferred in shackles to Rouen castle, where there was no castellan of similar probity to Hubert de Burgh or any other person of similar stature to protect him from his uncle's wrath. The ups and downs of de Burgh's career epitomise the dilemma of Norman lords with property on both sides of the Channel, but he managed to reinstate himself in the king's good books, to the extent of marrying Isabel of Gloucester, John's discarded first wife, in 1217.

The castellan of Rouen was one Robert de Vieux Pont, known in England as Vipont, who was to be richly rewarded by John for his collaboration. On a Thursday in April 1203 the enfeebled count of Brittany, whose sixteenth birthday was less than a week past, was taken out of his cell through the postern gate at dead of night, forced into a small boat and stabbed to death in mid-river by John or possibly the castellan himself, for John could not afford to have any witnesses who might talk. Arthur's emaciated body was weighted down, tipped into the Seine and sank out of sight. A few days after the death of Arthur, Queen Eleanor received a confidential letter from Guillaume de Braose telling her that a monk named Brother Jean de Valerant was bringing from Rouen an oral message for her, which was far too important or dangerous to be put in writing.[3] In those times before royalty routinely used codes for confidential communications, a trusted messenger was the best way to convey them.

For the part he had played in the carefully orchestrated murder without other witnesses, Robert de Vieux Pont was rewarded with the castles of Appleby and Brough in far-distant Westmorland, plus the lordship of that county and the office of sheriff there and in Devon, Cumberland and Wiltshire. John also made him high sheriff of Nottinghamshire, Derbyshire and the royal forests and gave him responsibility for the sees of York and Durham. Arthur's sister Eleanor of Brittany was placed in his custody. This was a rich reward, matching the harsh punishment of Guillaume de Braose after his wife inadvertently admitted her knowledge of the part John had played in Arthur's murder. Fined the colossal sum of 40,000 marks or more than 25,000 pounds, which he had no way of paying, De Braose fled with his family to his estates in Ireland,[4] where John had his wife and son hunted down and later starved to death in a dungeon below Windsor castle.[5] It was said that the doorway to their shared cell was bricked up, so that their cries could not be heard, and that, when it was unbricked, she was found to have attempted to gnaw parts of her dead son's body, to still the pangs of her own hunger.[6] Dispossessed of all his lands and wealth, De Braose died in exile in 1211, and his grandsons remained in prison until 1218, two years after John's death.[7]

The many ways in which John had defied all normal feudal practice between monarch and barons caused widespread anger among the nobility, already made restive by his fiscal demands. If the king could behave like this with De Braose, they thought and said, which of us will be safe from his anger? It was not just the barons themselves who might be his next victims. It was normal for kings to keep mistresses, to sate their lust without producing too many legitimate children, but John also had a habit of forcing his attentions on noble wives. He took advantage of his half-brother William of Salisbury being a prisoner in France after Otto of Brunswick's defeat at the battle of Bouvines in 1214 to seduce William's wife; Eustace de Vescy claimed that the king tried to rape his wife; Robert Fitzwalter accused John of forcing himself on Fitzwalter's daughter. The wife of Hugh de Neville was reduced bizarrely to paying 200 chickens to the king so that she might sleep with her husband for one night.[8] According to French sources, even before succeeding to the throne John had fathered at least nine sons and three daughters out of wedlock. The chronicler known as 'Anonymous of Béthune' wrote that the English king 'lusted after beautiful women and because of this he shamed the great men of the land, for which reason he was greatly hated.'[9] Other kings also having made free with their vassals' wives and daughters, the complaints about John's sexual predations are considered as symptomatic of the widespread and growing dissatisfaction among his barons with John's rule, although in May 1215 only thirty-nine had openly declared their hostility to him. Interestingly, only the same number declared for him, the remainder waiting to see which way the political and military winds blew.[10]

While it is difficult to assess the comparative reliability of the contemporary sources, the indisputable fact is that Arthur was never seen again after his disappearance from Rouen castle. Under Angevin custom, his death brought his sister Eleanor, known as *la Brette* or the Pearl of Brittany,[11] into line for succession to the English throne. Exactly when she fell into John's clutches is not recorded, but it seems to have been *before* Arthur was captured at the Battle of Mirebeau on 1 August 1202.

Being the daughter of Geoffrey, who was the fourth son of Henry II and Eleanor of Aquitaine, on the death of King John, their fifth son, and with her brother Arthur dead, Eleanor of Brittany would have a claim prior to those of John's descendants – as would any children of hers. She was in any case heiress to an impressive tally of lands in Brittany, Aquitaine, Anjou and England, where she inherited the county of Richmond in Yorkshire from her father. Her inheritance was also her death sentence: she died after nearly forty years as the prisoner of five successive kings, denied the right to marry and produce any child.

Four months after the death of Arthur, on 6 December 1202 John left Normandy in a hurry, but spared the time to collect Eleanor of Brittany and bring her to England as his prisoner. Escorted by four knights, who were actually her keepers, she was detained in several castles, where the local nobility was instructed by the king to visit her and bear witness that the conditions of her confinement were not too harsh. Was this his way of countering the rumours of what he had done to Arthur? Early in 1204 Philippe Auguste, whose vassal she was, demanded Eleanor's release, so that she could marry one of his sons, but John refused. Later, she was known to have been taken to Brough castle in Cumbria and placed under the control of Robert de Vieux Pont,[12] the very man deeply implicated in the murder of her brother. If she knew that, or had heard rumours about Arthur's death, every day and night there must have been sheer terror for her, wondering whether her uncle had sent her there, knowing that he could count on her jailer to do whatever was required of him, if John wanted her dead, too. But she still had some cards to play and, whether the king changed his mind or for another reason, she was shuttled from there to Bowes castle, also in the custody of Vieux Pont, to meet the king, who visited it about this time.[13]

Possibly because she protested about her custodian, her uncle John then moved her all the way back south to Corfe castle in Dorset, one of his favourite residences because of the nearby hunting in the forest of Purbeck. Construction of the castle started under William the Conqueror, with the grim and forbidding five-storey stone keep built by Henry I. King John added the outer bailey and a range of buildings adjacent to the keep, which were known as the *gloriette* – a French word for a pavilion in a garden – including his luxurious royal apartments. Henry III and

Edward I later added the outer and southwest gatehouses, which were like small fortresses barring access to the inner buildings. The extensive outer gatehouses and walls, now in ruins, suffered greatly after Dame Mary Banks held the castle for the King during the civil war for three years, resisting attacks and sieges by parliamentary forces using artillery. To punish her tenacity, the castle was 'slighted' by Parliament in 1645–6, with the result that many of the outer walls lean over at alarming angles.

Castles were both to keep enemies out and prisoners inside, confined in often damp and dark dungeons. John imprisoned twenty-five of the French knights he had taken at Mirebeau in Corfe castle. When they forced their way out in a bid for freedom, twenty-two of them were recaptured and starved to death in dungeons beneath the Boutavent Tower on the king's orders. His treatment of his niece Eleanor was, in contrast, a state of luxurious confinement, receiving from the king delicacies like figs and almonds – and once a saddle and bridle among other presents, which implies that she could go out riding under guard. Obliged to entrust her birthright of Brittany and the county of Richmond to John, Eleanor was referred to by him as his 'dearest niece' in letters to Brittany,[14] which included correspondence about liberating her. The only surviving document written by Eleanor is a description of her life in captivity, implying that an embassy of nobles and churchmen coming to England might be able to negotiate her release. In 1208 the bishops of Nantes, Vannes and Breton Cornouaille attempted and failed to achieve this. In any event her chief Breton vassals had elected Eleanor's younger half-sister Alix in 1203 to be their countess because they had no wish to come under the English crown, should Eleanor be sent back to Brittany by King John, forcibly married to an Anglo–Norman noble loyal to him. She was literally without a friend in the world.

Always guarded closely – *in custodia diuturni carceris reservata* – Eleanor was permitted to exercise in the fresh air by daily walks along the walls of Corfe castle. The ruins today, maintained by the National Trust, do not give a good impression of what the castle was like then because they are the result of the later extensions. In Eleanor's time, the triangular inner curtain wall enclosed only the square keep, the gloriette and the Boutavent tower. She took her meals in lonely state in the Long Hall, composed from a long list of food enjoyed by the nobility, including different meats, eggs, eels, sea and freshwater fish, fruit and vegetables, honey and pepper – the last an expensive luxury at the time. It was a diet far removed from the meagre rations of bread and water on which her brother had been kept barely alive in his last months. A small household was employed for her, comprising three maids; other allowances from the king provided material for clothing and bed linen for them and their mistress.

King John's generosity may be seen either as a bribe or an expression of guilt for her long confinement, knowing all the time that she would never be released or know a husband even after her menopause, When John died on 19 August 1214, she was thirty-two and still being shuttled from castle to castle, although there was little chance of being rescued by subjects of Philippe Auguste and even the Anglo-Norman barons who had hated John and rebelled against him showed no desire to be ruled by a woman, should her claim to the throne of England ever succeed. John's 9-year-old son by Isabella of Angoulême, who was knighted and crowned in Gloucester abbey as Henry III on 12 October 1216, was perhaps unaware at the time that only his father's long incarceration of this cousin enabled him to inherit the kingdom that should have been hers, her claim as daughter of the fourth son of Henry II taking precedence over his own as a child of the fifth son. On one occasion at least, Henry III later visited Eleanor. One wonders what they discussed. Was it a proposal that she should renounce all her rights and enter a nunnery?[15] How would he sweeten that bitter pill? And how did she find the strength of will to refuse all the pressure during her entire adult life?

What thoughts can have gone through her head during the long confinement? Brought up as a disposable ward of King Richard, having more contact with her grandmother, Eleanor of Aquitaine, than with her own mother the leprous Countess Constance of Brittany, and with her brother Arthur the heir presumptive to England on John's death, she must have been anticipated a royal betrothal like the other Plantagenet princesses. Instead, when Richard's sister Joanna refused to marry a Muslim during the Third Crusade, Richard offered Eleanor of Brittany as second-choice bride to Saladin's brother al-Adil in his mad scheme to invest the couple as king and queen of a Christian Jerusalem – the plan that collapsed when al-Adil showed what he thought of it by refusing to convert to Christianity. In 1193 her betrothal to Friedrich, son of Duke Leopold V of Austria, Richard's original captor on the return journey from the Holy Land, was part of the ransom package put together by Queen Eleanor for his release, since Duke Leopold liked the idea of his son marrying Richard's niece.

This project collapsed when she was already being escorted to Austria in 1194 because Leopold's foot was badly crushed when his mount fell on top of him during a tournament. Advised to have the foot amputated, but finding no surgeon prepared to risk the operation, Leopold ordered his servants to chop it off with an axe. Although this was clumsily and agonisingly done, it was of no avail, for the gangrene was already higher up the leg. Thus the Austrian duke[16] died the same agonising death that was later to claim his erstwhile prisoner. Being excommunicate for the sin of taking captive a fellow crusader, he was facing eternal hellfire until Archbishop Adalbert of Salzburg persuaded him on his deathbed to make substantial gifts to the Church as the price of revoking Leopold's excommunication and permitting the duke's burial in consecrated ground. Hearing the news, Queen Eleanor had this bartered virgin bride escorted back to England.

The following year, in summer 1195, marriage between Eleanor of Brittany and Philippe Auguste' son Louis was mooted, as a way to create an alliance between Philippe and King Richard but came to nothing. With the two kings falling out yet again, a possible betrothal to Duke Odo of Burgundy in 1198 was also aborted by Philippe Auguste forbidding Duke Odo to marry any Plantagenet princess without his permission, which was not forthcoming.[17]

After all this, to spend her life as a prisoner, albeit in a gilded cage, must have been cruel indeed for the princess who in her youth had been known as 'the Pearl of Brittany'. After thirty-nine years' detention at the whim of five English kings, she died in Bristol Castle on 10 August 1241, aged about 59.

Chapter 12

Siwan, Lady of Wales

An independent Wales was a constant challenge to the Norman and Plantagenet kings of England. Like Afghanistan, the country was easy for them to invade, but impossible to occupy – for the same reasons, a combination of difficult topography and the mutual hostility of the native peoples inhabiting the various valleys and plains, who were constantly changing alliances. Henry I, Henry II and Richard had attempted and failed to subdue this troublesome neighbour to the west of England, although using Welsh mercenaries in their wars, especially in France. These Welshmen fought together as a cohort because their language of command was their mother tongue. In 1174, Henry II used 1,000 Welshmen when marching to the relief of Rouen. In the last months of John's fight to hold Normandy, 740 Welsh infantry and twenty mounted men-at-arms were transported across the Channel, their advantage being that they would not go home after the mandatory forty days' service required of feudal levies.[1]

Yet, throughout the Angevin rule there was almost incessant skirmishing between the Welsh and *ffrancwr*, or the French, as they called the various armies sent against them by the English Crown and not *saeson* or Saxon-English, because all were commanded by French-speaking Anglo-Normans, whether the ruling monarch or his Marcher lords, universally hated by the people of the valleys. Ironically, the Anglo-Normans called the Welsh by a Latin name *walscii*, or foreigners. At the same time, some Welsh princes – the title 'count' would be more appropriate really – were exiled to England for their own safety in the internecine bloodshed more typical of the Dark Ages than the imposed civilisation of England a century and more after the Conquest. One of these exiles, who spent his childhood in England with his father, and may have been born there in or about 1173, was Llywelyn ap Iorwerth from the northern principality of Gwynedd, ruled at the time by a usurping half-brother of his father named Dafydd ap Owain. When still barely adolescent, Llywelyn returned to Gwynedd and, with the support of Dafydd's full brother Rhodri, lord of Mona and Snowdon, who was Llywelyn's uncle, drove Dafydd into exile.[2] It was a tangled web.

Although only fourteen when Richard came to the English throne in 1189, Llywelyn learned fast and later proved an able commander in the irregular skirmishing and ambushes that characterised Welsh-English hostilities, earning himself the honorific Llywelyn Fawr, or Llywelyn the Great. One of his earliest successes was against his own cousin Mareddud ap Cynan,[3] driving him out of the rainy Lleyn peninsula. In a reign of forty years Llywelyn was the most prominent of the Welsh princes, dominating most of Wales while defying repeated incursions from Marcher territory. One of King John's better ideas was to try and convert this intransigent enemy into an ally by the well-tried expedient of marrying off a daughter to him. Any legitimate daughters would be worthy of a more prestigious match, so he followed the example of his grandfather Henry I, who had married off a natural daughter among his twenty-five illegitimate offspring named Sybilla to the Scottish king Alexander I. Similarly John turned to a *filia notha* or illegitimate daughter named Jeanne living in Normandy, whom he is thought to have fathered in 1191.

Royal or noble males spreading their seed far and wide was generally regarded as an enrichment of the race, with the rape of solitary shepherd girls by itinerant knights so common as to cause little notice. Horses were the most important animals in the Middle Ages, when a knight was often judged by his mount, and it was proven in horse-breeding that the bloodline of a good mare could be greatly improved by putting her to a superior stallion. So, John had certainly 'enriched' the Norman race by fathering many bastards, both before and after obtaining the succession – although not so many as his father and grandfather. When he was dying at Chinon in 1189 Henry II was cursing his legitimate sons and found solace in Geoffrey the Bastard, later Archbishop of York – the ecclesiastical appointment arranged by Eleanor of Aquitaine being designed to prevent him contesting the throne while Richard was on crusade and later a prisoner in Germany. After Geoffrey read out the list of Henry's sons and vassals to be pardoned for siding with Philippe Auguste during the great rebellion – the list was headed by the name of

Prince John – Henry is reputed to have said that it was his legitimate sons who were the bastards, with future Archbishop Geoffrey alone staying true to his father.[4] John continued siring bastards after becoming king, with so many mistresses that it can be difficult to know with certainty who was the mother of which child. One lady-in-waiting to his queen was euphemistically described as *domicella, amica domini regis* or 'friend' of the lord king.

The early years of King John's illegitimate daughter Jeanne are a mystery, but were spent in Normandy in the household of her mother Clemence. In December 1203 John summoned her at his expense to England, where she was known as Joan, for the purpose of marrying her to Llywelyn ap Iorwerth. Aged 14 or 15, Joan was married in May 1205 to the groom some eighteen years older than her in St Werburgh's Abbey at Chester, now Chester cathedral.[5] Llywelyn had already been married several times, although whether always with the blessing of the Church is unclear. He also appears to have kept a long-time concubine named Tangwystl Goch or 'Red Tangwystl' in reference to her hair colour. At the time of Joan's birth in 1191, he had asked King Raghnall IV of the Isle of Man for the hand of his 8-year-old daughter, but, for whatever reason, she was married off to Llywelyn's uncle Rhodri ab Owain and Llywelyn married instead a sister of the earl of Chester, who died a few years later.

In 1199 Llywelyn was a widower and Rhodri was dead, so Llywelyn attempted again to marry the Manx princess, but Pope Innocent III ruled that it was against canon law for a man to marry a woman who had been his uncle's wife although this relationship was not included in the Table of Kindred and Affinity established by the Church of England in 1560, which was displayed in every church porch in England until recently, forbiddingly headed *A man may not marry*, and which was modified by the several English Marriage Acts of the twentieth century. In 1204 Llywelyn totally lost interest in that prospective bride when King John offered him his illegitimate daughter from Normandy. Royal letters close indicate that Jeanne and he were betrothed before 12 October 1204, and were married at Ascensiontide, or mid-May, of the following year, with the manor of Ellesmere granted to Llywelyn as her dowry.

On arrival at her husband's 'palace' known as Garth Celyn in Abergwyngegyn, Jeanne/Joan – now referred to by the Welsh name of Siwan – must have been disappointed to find it unlike the imposing castles she knew in Normandy and totally unlike the elaborate palace/castles that King Edward I was later to build in and around Wales. Garth Celyn was better described as a keep without bailey or curtain walls. Also, although Llywelyn would presumably have learned to speak the Anglo-Norman dialect of French during his childhood exile, most of his dependents and servants spoke only *cymraeg canol* or Middle Welsh, a language of which his bride had no knowledge apart from a few borrowed words like *eglwys* for church and *pont* for bridge. Isolated both physically when Llwewelyn was travelling and fighting, and linguistically too, except for a couple of maidservants she had brought with her, Siwan's hunger to hear her mother tongue, or something like it, was later very nearly to lead to her undoing.

When Llywelyn used the excommunication of John in 1209 to pose as the champion of Rome, Innocent III absolved him and his allies of their oath of loyalty to the English king, which they had sworn to gain a truce. He also relieved their territories from the 5-year interdict on England and blessed their campaigns against John's invasions and those of his vassals. One of the important roles of a married-off princess was her ability to serve as a diplomatic channel between her birth family and her married one. Siwan's usefulness to Llywelyn was demonstrated in that same year, when King John prepared a great expedition to punish the lord of Gwynedd for attempting to drive John's protégé – and Llywelyn's sometime ally – Prince Gwenwynwyn out of the neighbouring county of Powys. In the autumn of 1209, the earl of Chester and justiciar Geoffrey FitzPeter followed up with an invasion of Gwynedd, rebuilding the English castle at Deganwy that Llywelyn had destroyed and building a new castle at Holywell on Anglesey. Long taken to mean 'island of the English', Anglesey was very Welsh and referred to by the natives as Ynys Môn

In August 1211, after King John's successful campaign in which several Anglo-Norman armies and Welsh enemies of Llywelyn made a temporary alliance to drive his loyal forces back into the fastness of Snowdonia, the Welsh chronicle *Brut y Tywysogion*, meaning 'Deeds of the Princes', records that Llywelyn was forced by his supporters to sue for a truce.[6] He sent Siwan to her father 'to make peace on whatever terms she could'. She was at the time probably just twenty-one.

The terms were punitive: Llywelyn had to acknowledge John as his overlord, surrender four *cantrefs*,[7] pay a fine in cattle, and hand over a number of high-born hostages including his own first-born son, by the concubine Tangwystl, Gruffudd ap Llywelyn.[8] That son was effectively deprived of any inheritance rights by a clause specifying that the county of Gwynedd would escheat to the English Crown in the event that his father died without fathering any legitimate heir by Siwan. How she softened the blow to Llywelyn, we do not know, but that idea almost certainly came from Siwan in the first place. The following Easter the couple attended John's court in Cambridge as a display of reconciliation.

In the summer of 1212, when Llywelyn's Welsh allies formed a confederacy with him against the Anglo-Norman incursions, he broke the truce. Forfeited territory was recaptured, among the Anglo-Normans driven off Welsh soil being Ralph Vipont. At Nottingham John planned a new invasion but called it off when Siwan managed to send a warning to him that some of his barons planned to assassinate him during the campaign, or betray him to the enemy, to be taken hostage. The chroniclers Mathew Paris and Roger of Wendover recorded that John received a similar warning from William the Lion, King of Scotland. Being at the time excommunicate, if killed in that spiritual state, John would spend eternity in hellfire according to the Church. Although he had little respect for Christian beliefs he nevertheless thought it more prudent to abandon his planned invasion, rather than place himself at risk of betrayal on Welsh soil resulting in capture or death at the hands of the enemy or one of his own tenants-in-chief. Instead, he contented himself with hanging twenty-eight of his Welsh hostages at Nottingham castle.[9] In response to Siwan's pleading, he did release four of his Welsh hostages in 1214 and a fifth in 1215. John's death in 1216 and the succession of his eldest son as Henry III did not end the Norman-Welsh skirmishing, but the following years were less violent.

Siwan bore at least three children to Llywelyn. Elen ferch Llywelyn, who inherited Joan's manors of Bidford and Stuckley, was born in 1207, marrying firstly John the Scot, Earl of Chester and, in second marriage,

Robert II de Quincy. Dafydd ap Llywelyn was born in 1212, and married
Isabella de Braose, dying near Siwan's palace in 1246 – a scant six years
after his father. Where Susannah, who was sent into England purportedly
as a hostage at Henry III's orders in 1228, came in the sibling order, is
unknown. Three other children were fathered by Llywelyn during the
marriage. Gwladys Dhu, or Gwladys of the dark eyes, who was born in
1206, married the Marcher lord Reginald de Braose around 1215 and
Ralph de Mortimer after her first husband's demise in 1227 or 1228.
Of Angharad ferch Llywelyn, little is known except that she bore four
children by Maelgwn Fychan. Marared ferch Llywelyn married Sir John
de Braose around 1219, when she was thirteen and then Sir Walter de
Clifford after her first husband's death in or about 1232. Whether Siwan
was mother to any of these daughters of Llywelyn, is not known with
certainty. Although one of the most famous medieval chroniclers, Gerallt
de Barri, the archdeacon of Brecon better known by his Latin name
Giraldus Cambrensis, was Welsh, strict records – even of noble families
– were not generally kept in Wales at the time. But the time-honoured
expedient of marrying off a daughter to convert an enemy into an ally did
not always work. The contact with the de Braose family to arrange the
marriage of Gwladys Dhu at the age of 9 to the elder de Braose, who died
in 1227 or 1228 was probably – although no one knew at the time – the
first step in what was very nearly Siwan's undoing.

Whether her husband's attitude to her was one of genuine affection
or because her relationship to the English king made her a very useful
diplomatic envoy, by the rude standards of those days Siwan was well
treated by Llywelyn. Known initially as *domina norwalliae* – Lady of
North Wales – on her early diplomatic initiatives, she profited from the
custom of using *dominus* and *domina* to describe rulers who had not been
crowned. To save her a 2-mile walk through the mountains to the nearest
church in Llanrhychyn, Llywelyn had a chapel built for her at nearby
Trefriw. Why she did not either ride to Llanrhychyn or walk there, we
do not know. The absence of a church or chapel already near the palace
suggests a more lax approach to the formalities of religion than in
England at the time.

Siwan's political activities seem to have been suspended for four
relatively peaceful years after her half-brother Henry came to the throne,

but in 1220 she persuaded him to endorse the nomination of her son Gryffudd ap Llywelyn as the heir to the lordship of Gwynedd. This was further strengthened by Llywelyn's request granted by Pope Honorius III in 1222 to abolish the Welsh custom of recognising illegitimate children as equal heirs – an idea that surely began in Siwan's mind.

In April of that year, Siwan requested, and was granted by Honorius III, legitimation as the daughter of King John, making her truly royal. The papal secretary who wrote the document expressed the reason succinctly in Latin as *Johannes rex anglie solutus te genuerit de soluta*[10]– the unmarried king of England fathered you by an unmarried woman. The reasoning was that, because neither parent was married at the time, there was no adultery involved, but the papal legitimation gave no entitlement of succession to her father's title or estates. Adultery was, however, seriously to tarnish Siwan's image.

The 1222 betrothal contract between Llywelyn and Ranulf III, earl of Chester, giving Siwan's daughter Elen to Ranulf's nephew John of Scotland, mentions Siwan's manors at Bidford in Warwickshire and Suckley in Worcestershire as Elen's dowry, the contract stating that Siwan would issue her own charters to confirm these as gifts in free marriage. Importantly, this is the only surviving document in which Siwan and Llywelyn act as a jointly ruling couple.

Siwan was particularly active following the unsuccessful English invasion of Wales in 1223, when she travelled to meet her half-brother King Henry III on 19 September at Worcester, but could do nothing to prevent Archbishop of Canterbury Stephen Langton excommunicating her husband, or Pope Honorius III placing all Llywelyn's lands under interdict. In September 1224, when as 'Lady of North Wales' not only was Siwan granted safe passage to meet Henry III at Worcester and prepare the groundwork for a peace conference, but Henry also ordered the Exchequer to reimburse the sheriff of Shrewsbury the sum of £8.7s.4d. advanced by him towards Joan's travel expenses. Her political efforts were rewarded by Henry granting her the manor of Rothley in Leicestershire in 1225. In that year, William Marshal II was given the king's sister Eleanor in marriage as a reward for his constant sparring with Llywelyn, capturing and destroying his castles. In August 1226, Siwan accompanied Llywelyn and Dafydd to meet, and negotiate with, her half-brother once more at Shrewsbury, when she was rewarded by him with the grant of another manor at Condover in Shropshire. Further, she was exempted from payment of the tallage tax[11] on her manors, Henry III even recommending that her tenants should pay her a reasonable aid.

Yet, two years later, in early 1228 he deprived her of the manors of Rothley and Condover, although permitting her to harvest and keep the crops planted on her orders there, and to remove livestock. Diplomacy was Siwan's forte: on 13 October she travelled to Westminster to witness the homage of her son Dafydd to his uncle Henry. Shortly afterwards, after receiving a safe conduct from the king, she travelled to his court at Shrewsbury without Llywelyn to successfully negotiate a truce and, it seems, to persuade Henry to release her daughter Susannah – although not to go back to Wales. Henry III also showed his appreciation of Siwan's diplomacy by restoring the confiscated manors to her on 8 November.

The mystery of Siwan's parentage was cleared up for the historical record in 1228. Her Norman mother Clemence – Clementia in Latin documents – was referred to by an overly respectful anonymous monk in the annals of the Benedictine monastery of St Mary the Virgin at Tewkesbury12 as *regina clementia*, although Clemence was not of royal blood. Yet, from the *Patent Rolls of the Reign of Henry III* comes this entry from 1228, being a copy of a letter from King Henry III when sending Siwan's daughter Susannah to Normandy:

Rex dilecto et fideli suo Nicholao de Verdun et Clementie uxori sue, salutem. Sciatis quod nos vobis benigne concedimus quod fidelis noster et dilectus frater L. princeps Norwallie et Johanna uxor sua et dilecta soror nostra Susannam filiam suam, neptem nostram ... vobis committere duxerit nutriendam, eam salvo et secure et sine omni dampno et occasione suscipiatis et penes vos retineatis. In cujus rei testimonium etc. vobis mittimus. Teste me, apud Westmonasterium, xxiiij die Novembris anno MCCXXVIII.

The king to his favoured and faithful Nicholas de Verdun and his wife Clemence, greetings. Know that we are sending to you Susannah, the daughter of our favoured and faithful brother [Llywelyn] prince of North Wales and his wife Joan/Jeanne, to bring her up safe and sound. In which matter we send you this testimonial. As witness, at Westminster 24 November of the year 1228.

It was a gesture of clemency, certainly, but the only conceivable reason why King John's son and successor Henry III would send his cousin Susanna, the daughter of Llywelyn and Siwan, into the care of Nicholas de Verdun and his wife is that Clemence de Verdun was the Clemence known to be Siwan's mother, who could be trusted to care for and bring up her own granddaughter.

Although Siwan's legitimation was based on the grounds that there was technically no adultery in the relationship between the then uncrowned John and Clemence de Verdun, by which this princess was conceived, the most scandalous episode in Siwan's life occurred around Easter of 1230. Two years previously, in that hectic year of 1228, the Norman Marcher lord William de Braose – a son of Reginald who titled himself 'baron of Abergavenny' – was taken prisoner by Llywelyn's forces and held for ransom. As an honoured hostage, he would have spent some time with Llywellyn's itinerant court, where he would have met Siwan. Was there a sexual spark between Llywelyn's wife and this important hostage, or was it just an overwhelming relief on her part at having a noble companion with whom to talk at last in her mother tongue – until then only possible when on her diplomatic missions in England? Something happened, as events were to show. As part of the ransom settlement, which included payment of a fine of £2,000 and a sworn undertaking not to invade Llywelyn's territory again, de Braose betrothed his daughter Isabella to Siwan's son Dafydd, the lordship and castle of Builth being her dowry. De Braose was released early in 1229. Although obviously intended as a diplomatic gesture, the union of these children angered many of Llywelyn's people as the Norman Marcher lords like Gwylim Ddu, or Black William as William de Braose was called west of the border, were hated throughout Wales.

For whatever reason – it was possibly in connection with the betrothal of his daughter – William de Braose paid another visit to Garth Celyn around Easter 1230, and was discovered in bed with Siwan, by whom is unclear. Given the cramped conditions in Llywelyn's claustrophobic castle/palace and the number of servants present, de Braose must have been persistent to the point of foolhardiness to place himself in that position. Fleeing back to the presumed safety of his own territory, de Braose was ambushed by some of Llywelyn's men and taken back by them to Gwynedd. Whatever Llywelyn's feelings were in the matter, his household and court gave him little choice but to agree that de Braose must die. Honour was satisfied when Siwan's lover was hanged from the branch of a tree adjacent to the palace on or about 20 May 1230 in the presence of many witnesses, possibly including her. To William de Braose's widow and four daughters Llywelyn let it be understood that he had no choice in the matter. They presumably accepted his explanation, for the following year Isabella and Dafydd were married, as agreed.

To punish his wife for her part in the affair after twenty-five years of marriage, Llywelyn imprisoned Siwan in the palace and kept her there for twelve months before allowing her to resume her status as his consort and her title changed to *domina walliae* – Lady of Wales. It is unclear whether a daughter she seems to have given birth to early in 1231 was the result of her night or nights of lovemaking with William de Braose. Whether her reinstatement was because Llywelyn truly forgave her or because the insult to his pride was overridden by the need for her diplomatic skills again in disputes with the justiciar Hubert de Burgh, is not clear. In February 1232 and on two other occasions that year, she led embassies to negotiate with Henry III, being accompanied in May by her son Dafydd and Llywelyn's *distain* or seneschal Ednyfed Fychan, reaching an agreement for territory recently captured by Gwynedd to be restored to English sovereignty.

Evidence exists of safe conducts issued by Henry III for Siwan and Dafydd to travel to meetings in August and December although in all her diplomatic career only one document is directly attributable to Siwan herself. Written most probably between March and May 1232, it is a masterpiece of pleading, in which *johanna domina walliae* assures the king that she is 'grieved beyond measure' that he has been influenced by ill-wishers to sow discord between the Crown and Llywelyn, and begs Henry 'on bended knee and shedding tears' to accept the word of her clerk-emissary, referred to as 'Instructus', in negotiations. Instructus seems to have been a confidential go-between, used for setting up meetings of the principals. The Lady of Wales also crops up in a letter patent, or open letter, dated 8 November 1235 mentioning the request of the Lady of Wales that Henry pardon 'Robert, son of Reginald' for the death of 'William, son of Ralph of Credenshull'.

In early 1237 Siwan died at the age of 46 or 47 in the palace at Abergwyngregyn, her succinct obituary in the Tewkesbury Annals reading: *Obiit domina johanna domina walliae, uxor lewelini filia regis johannis et regine clemencie, iii. kal. aprilis.* Joanna, Lady of Wales died. She was the wife of Llywelyn and daughter of King John and Queen Clemence. Although the mention is dated in early April, she died on 2 February.

In a display of grief, Llywelyn founded a Barefoot Franciscan friary at Llanfaes on Anglesey in her honour, whither her remains were conveyed across the Menai strait after the friary was consecrated in 1240, shortly before Llywelyn also died. The friary was destroyed during Henry VIII's dissolution of the monasteries, when it seems that someone salvaged her sarcophagus. Many graves and tombs of past royalty were smashed to pieces during the dissolution, as in the French Revolution. Yet, Siwan's sarcophagus – if it is hers – may have been carted off by some local farmer who needed a horse or cattle trough and simply threw away her remains before carting it off. It stands now in the church of St Mary and St Nicholas in Beaumaris. Above it is a slate panel inscribed:

> *This plain sarcophagus, (once dignified as having contained the remains of Joan, daughter of King John, and consort of Llywelyn ap Iowerth, Prince of North Wales, who died in the year 1237), having been conveyed from the Friary of Llanfaes, and alas, used for many years as a horsewatering trough, was rescued from such an indignity and placed here for preservation as well as to excite serious meditation on the transitory nature of all sublunary* [i.e. earthly] *distinctions.*
>
> *By Thomas James Warren Bulkeley, Viscount Bulkeley, Oct 1808.*

The coffin lid beside the sarcophagus may have come from a totally different source, some experts ruling that the woman depicted in low relief on it is dressed in a style much later than Siwan's lifetime, although wearing a coronet, which suggests a member of a royal family.

After her death, the strife between the Welsh princes and the English Crown and individual Marcher lords continued, Llywelyn's power and prestige growing all the time until he was virtually lord of all Wales, but the one enemy he could not confront was his age. A partial paralysis caused by a stroke led to him increasingly devolving power upon his son by Siwan named Dafydd. In October of 1238 Llywelyn called all the Welsh nobility to the Cistercian abbey of Strata Florida in Ceredigion and made them all swear fealty to Dafydd, who made sure of his position by imprisoning his eponymous half-brother by Llywelyn's concubine Tangwystl the Red. After a lifetime of bloodshed and battle, Llywelyn Fawr donned the habit of a Cistercian monk and devoted himself to charitable works for the good of his immortal soul, his previous martial prowess being celebrated by the accolade of 'the second Achilles' by Welsh bards in poetry and song.

Rather poetically, Siwan was given a new lease of life in 1956, when Seymour Lewis' masterly play *Siwan a cherddi eraill*, or *Siwan and other tales*, was first produced and became a staple of the Welsh Language 'A' level syllabus. So a thirteenth-century princess has become a romantic heroine for two generations of Welsh-speaking teenagers.

Chapter 13

Blanche, the Warrior Wife of Prince Louis

There is no record of what Blanche of Castile made of the fate of her cousins Eleanor and Arthur of Brittany when these were related to her by the court gossips on the Ile de la Cité. At the age of 17, she bore Prince Louis a daughter, which was either still-born or lived so few days that the chroniclers did not even mention the birth. Not until 9 September 1209 did Blanche produce another child – a son christened Philippe. Recording his birth, an anonymous royal clerk expressed the hope that he would reign not only over the French, but also England, on the strength of his mother's descent from Queen Eleanor and Henry II. Although officially the crown prince, the boy never reigned anywhere because he died before his father, at the age of 9. On 26 January 1213 Blanche produced twins, who died shortly afterwards.

However, in the following year on 25 April in the royal castle at Poissy, Blanche bore the son who was to become famous as Saint Louis, but news of the birth was overshadowed by all the courts of Europe agog at the deal King John had pulled off with Pope Innocent III, enshrined in a papal bull dated four days before the birth. It was a clever move by John which, he thought, made it impossible for the French ever to invade Britain. England had been under interdict since 1208 and John excommunicate since 1209, but in May 1213 he had placed his territory north of the Channel under the temporal lordship of Rome, which gave it back to him as its vassal for an annual tribute of 1,000 marks, or £666 plus 200 marks for Ireland. Once the interdict and his excommunication were lifted by Stephen Langton, the archbishop whom John had refused entry into England on his appointment in 1207, the English king could flatter himself that his country was safe from invasion, while he was still free to invade France to recover his parents' lands there. Innocent's declaration that the Magna Carta was illegal and unjust reinforced John's natural tendency to metaphorically tear it up, after which the barons also refused to abide by its provisions. The result was the first baron's war.

In 1216 Blanche gave birth to the prince who became Count Robert of Artois. In 1218, when Prince Philippe died prematurely, Blanche's son Louis became crown prince. In the following year another son named Jean was born, followed by a fifth son born in 1220, who was christened in honour of his Castilian grandfather Alfonso VIII, becoming Count Alphonse of Poitiers and Toulouse. Thus, Blanche fully performed her duty to produce male heirs, although a sixth son named Philippe Dagobert, born in 1222, also died in childhood at the age of 10.

Throughout this time, she managed to lead a delicate balancing act between the pious devotion required of a Capetian queen, ensuring her son was educated by the most eminent theologians, and the cultured life she had known in Castile, which involved a generous royal patronage for poets and writers of *la littérature courtoise*, much on the model of the court of Marie, the daughter of Louis VII and Eleanor of Aquitaine who became Countess of Champagne. Although this scandalised some Frankish courtiers on the Ile de la Cité, they could hardly point the finger at Blanche, who, throughout lived a life of irreproachable devotion to her husband that was obviously reciprocated.[1] If they could not publicly find fault with their 'foreign queen', they did take revenge for the young royal couple's tolerance of Amaury de Bène, a master of the schools accused of pantheism because he preached that God was in all things and men, and not accessible exclusively through the Church.

Although this original thinking did not prevent him, following an oral retraction, being buried in sacred ground after his death in 1207, his followers were subsequently accused of constituting a heretical sect. Hauled before the *curia regis* or king's court, which also served as a law court under Philippe Auguste, they were accused of conducting licentious orgies with adultery and other sexual debauchery. The women were pardoned, but four men were sent to prison for life and nine were burned alive as heretics in 1210. Amaury was posthumously excommunicated and his remains dug up and scattered.[2] Harsh punishments were imposed on free-thinkers prosecuted by the Church in early medieval Paris but perhaps the extreme venom with which Amaury and his followers were prosecuted was due to his effrontery in attaching himself to the royal household and not confining his philosophy to the more tolerant students of the schools.

Was resentment of this liberalism on the part of Blanche and himself also the reason why Prince Louis was not dubbed a knight immediately after attaining his majority, nor given a traditional Capetian coronation as a minor? This would have meant that, on the death of Philippe Auguste, the criers could indeed announce throughout the kingdom that the monarchy continued uninterrupted? '*Le roi est mort. Vive le roi!*' As to the dubbing, Prince Louis had to wait until he was in his twenty-second year, which Blanche must have feared he would never reach, his childhood health having been frail. His dubbing at Compiègne during Pentecost 1209 in the presence of the great vassals of the kingdom was preceded by a number of oaths he had to swear. One was not to take part in tournaments, which killed so many young knights. If that was reasonable for the heir to the throne, he was also denied household knights, unless each one swore obedience to the king first. Prince Louis had also to swear not to seek loans from the independent cities ruled by guilds under various titles, unless they had been previously approved by his father. Instead, he was given several territories to provide income for his own household, but no right to demand fealty from his vassals living there! As Blanche's father-in-law aged, there was an air of paranoia in the restrictions with which he fenced around his son and heir, gradually according him more duties but no more rights, while more power accrued both to the Church and to a coterie of the king's counsellors and vassals who constituted his *curia*, each seeking to raise himself above the others.

When Louis was 27 years old and constantly denied much of what would have been normal for his position, he or Blanche saw the unrest across the Channel and Philippe Auguste's unwillingness to intervene as an opportunity for Louis to make a name for himself after all the years of frustration, kept in check by his father. In England, the Anglo-Norman barons rebelling against King John's refusal to abide by the spirit of Magna Carta wanted a figurehead for their campaign against him. Blanche being a granddaughter of Henry II made Prince Louis a grandson-in-law. If John could be ousted and Louis put on the throne with Blanche as consort, that would have sufficient air of legitimacy.

Additionally, either Philippe Auguste or Louis was the overlord of many of John's barons who held fiefs in France.

Louis' first move was to send a token force of between 120 and 140 knights from the Artois district centred on Arras, who landed with a contingent of foot-soldiers at the mouth of the river Orwell in Suffolk to support the rebellion in early December 1215. Technically they were breaking their sworn fealty to Philippe Auguste, but that sort of problem could always be sorted out. While he had no wish to confront the pope, his considered judgement was that Rome could not blame him for what Prince Louis was up to on his own account. Louis' plan, shared with Blanche, was for a full-scale invasion of England, led by himself, which would inevitably result in his excommunication, since it was now papal territory and John had sworn to take the Cross, which made him personally protected by the Church as a crusader – although he had no intention of actually going on crusade.

Prudently, Philippe Auguste arranged for the Anglo-Norman barons to send twenty-four noble hostages to France, to be held there until the safe return of Prince Louis, who was busily preparing logistics and funds for his cross-Channel invasion. Before that took place, a delegation from King John, led by William Marshal and the bishop of Winchester, came to Paris, requesting that Philippe forbid Louis to cross the Channel. At a meeting in Melun on 24 April between Philippe, Louis and papal legate Guala Bicchieri, argument and counter-argument attacked and defended John's title, Philippe Auguste contending that his treachery to King Richard and murder of Philippe's vassal Arthur of Brittany, for which he had been tried in absentio by the *curia* in Paris, disqualified him from the throne. Bicchieri nevertheless threatened the French king with excommunication, after which Philippe was careful to keep in the background, leaving Prince Louis and Blanche to assemble a fleet of 800 ships of all sizes, an army of 1,200 knights and several thousand men-at-arms.

Not until the night of 18–17 May 1216 did Louis set sail in a storm that made any interception by English ships unlikely, to land at Stonar on the Isle of Thanet with just seven ships, the others having turned back or been blown off-course. Crossing the Wantsum channel, which then separated the island from the mainland, on the following day he entered

Aged 22, Eleanor of Aquitaine (left) defied the pope to accompany her first husband Louis VII on the Second Crusade. The couple is shown below in the royal portal of Chartres cathedral.

Rejected by her second husband Henry II of England, she raised their adult sons in rebellion. Betrayed, she became Henry's prisoner, and is shown being led away with her daughter Joanna in a contemporary fresco at Chinon (above). Her first prison was in the left-hand tower of Chinon castle (below).

There are few images, even of royalty, from the twelfth century, but when Eleanor paid for the nuns' kitchen at Fontevraud abbey (below) the mason carved her likeness at age 78 on a corbel below the eaves (left).

The carved image in Brunswick cathedral (above) of Eleanor's first daughter Matilda shows a powerful duchess, but she was only 11 when married to 48-year-old Henry the Lion, who had to kneel, to bring his head level with hers at the wedding (below).

Eleanor's eponymous second daughter became Queen Leonor at the age of 12 when wed to King Alfonso VIII of Castile. She built a French cathedral (below) at Cuenca. This marriage of mutual respect is epitomised by their unique double sarcophagus in Burgos (above).

This was life for most of the traded princesses. The husband rides off to perform deeds of derring-do (below at Angoulême cathedral) while his wife is left behind. Glorified in the golden Virgin and Child at Beaulieu (right), her job was to produce sons for the succession and daughters to be traded in their turn.

Even that powerful stateswoman Eleanor of Aquitaine gave Louis VII two daughters and produced eight more children with Henry II (contemporary diagram above). A wife employing contraception, known as 'womanly arts' risked eternal torture by demons in hell, like the ones in the tympanum above the door of Souillac church (below).

The two functions of medieval
kingship. The great seal of
Edward I (right), showing him
as the hammer of the Scots and
terror of Wales. Below, he holds
the symbolic sword of state
when wisely dispensing justice.

His wife Eleanor of Castile travelled everywhere with him (below at Lincoln cathedral). When she died after bearing him fifteen children, he mourned her for ten years. The nineteenth-century sketch (left) is of her effigy in Westminster cathedral.

King John loved hunting, and also seducing his vassals' wives and daughters, which was one reason why the barons forced him to sign Magna Carta.

This tiny miniature from a genealogy chart (left) is the only vestige of Eleanor of Britanny, daughter of Eleanor's son Prince Geoffrey. She had no children because her uncle King John locked her away in Corfe castle (below). For thirty-nine years she was held captive by five successive kings because she had a claim to the throne of England.

The body language in the sketch of Isabelle of France and Edward II says it all (right). She managed to get him to father four children, but his two lovers were executed, one tied to a ladder (below) for a crowd to watch the final agony.

With her lover Roger Mortimer, Isabelle led an army across England (right) to force Edward II to abdicate in favour of her son Prince Edward. The king's arrest is depicted rather fancifully below, with her and Mortimer watching on the right.

Princess Blanca of Castile (right), was only 11 or 12 when taken by her grandmother Eleanor of Aquitaine to France to marry Crown Prince Louis and become one of France's most famous queens. She was also a very dominant mother for her son, even after he became King Louis IX, known as Saint Louis (below).

Departing on the Seventh Crusade (above), Louis IX took his queen, Marguerite of Provence with him to Egypt. During the crusade, she bore him two more children, while he oscillated between devout pilgrim and Christian warlord. So many men were blinded at the battle of Damietta (below) that Louis founded a hospital for them in Paris.

Medical ignorance and untrained midwives caused many princesses and queens to die in childbirth.
Yet, in Salerno (above) and Montpellier there were schools for properly trained midwives.

the port of Sandwich as the rest of the French fleet arrived – some 600 vessels transporting reinforcements and eighty cogs carrying supplies.[3] When news of this significant landing reached King John, he rode towards Sandwich but fatally hesitated to attack before the army was all ashore and supplies unloaded, instead fleeing through Guildford to the ancient capital of Winchester. Finding no significant resistance in Kent, although harassed by irregular bowmen hiding in the Kentish forests under a royalist partisan leader nicknamed Willikin of the Weald, Louis marched his men westward through Canterbury to Rochester, where they were welcomed by some of the disaffected barons, who swore fealty to him. On 2 June Louis rode triumphantly into London, its mayor and citizens proclaiming him the uncrowned king of England – although not in Westminster abbey, which refused him entrance as an excommunicate. The commandant of the Tower also did not permit him entrance until 6 November.[4] Louis swore an oath that he would restore the ancient rights to all men and behaved as though already crowned, splitting his forces into two: half to subdue the eastern counties and half to ride out of the city with him on 6 June to confront John at Winchester. That he could not speak English was irrelevant, since the language of everybody of importance in England was still a version of Norman French that was gradually becoming a separate dialect.

Capturing Winchester was a push-over because John's garrison was demoralised by the king having fled again. Soon Louis was acclaimed by his supporters as ruler of half the kingdom. Actually, it was only one-third his, with John's loyalists holding out in the west and north. Fate had a few surprises in store for Louis, despite Innocent III dying in Perugia on 16 July. Exactly how Philippe Auguste was kept up to date with developments in England, is unknown, but his criticism of the failure to attack the strategic castle at Dover resulted in a belated siege of it by Louis' forces beginning on 19 July. Blanche meanwhile showed her customary perseverance in haranguing Louis' feudal vassals in the Artois and the new communes in the towns there into supporting the cross-Channel initiative, both in manpower and money.

Philippe Auguste received the thanks of Pope Honorius III for remaining 'neutral' in the conflict. He did indeed refuse to give money to Louis in support of the invasion, because he did not wish to be seen as attacking John's kingdom while it was a fief of Rome. He was accused by Blanche of failing in his paternal duty to his own heir apparent, who was likely to die in England and never succeed to the throne, if not supported. This was exaggeration: no vassal of John's had proposed harming Prince Louis personally, although he could have died in battle or from disease. Furiously, Blanche walked out of the audience. Philippe Auguste called her back and promised to provide funds to her, with which she could do as she willed.[5]

So she did, raising on her own initiative a new force of 300 knights and mounted men-at-arms and 800 infantry – sufficient to replace Louis' men taken prisoner at the battle of Lincoln, who were trickling back to him as their ransoms were paid. In early August she had at Calais a fleet of eighty vessels including ten large ships of war, many laden with the supplies and treasure that Louis' force lacked in England. Leading the fleet that set sail on the night of 23–24 August was the famous pirate Eustace the Monk. This led to the battle of Sandwich, when an English fleet, raised by William the Marshal largely from the Cinque Ports, attacked the French ships. At the time, sea battles were fought as on land, with archers and crossbowmen firing into the opposing vessels. Riding higher in the water, since they were not loaded with supplies, the English force had the advantage of of firing arrows and crossbow bolts down on the French sailors and passengers and catapulted at them large terracotta pots of quicklime, which broke on landing and released clouds of stinging lime that blinded the French. The English ships also had a secret weapon in the form of iron beaks on their prows, which pierced holes in the French vessels below the water-line.

Eustace was beheaded, despite offering his captors a large ransom, the more valuable knights on board were taken prisoner and the mercenary men-at-arms had their throats slit and bodies dumped overboard. By dawn on 24 August, Blanche's fleet was scattered, the other large ships driven off and the smaller craft captured or driven into the shallows and wrecked. Better news for Louis was the arrival of an ally in the shape of King Alexander II of Scotland, who had led his army all the way to Kent in a forced march of over 400 miles. To show his appreciation, Louis rode west to welcome him at Canterbury, where Alexander swore fealty to him as 'the king of the English' for his fiefs south of the border.

Hubert de Burgh, John's castellan at Dover, did not lose his nerve. Having made adequate provisions, he held out against siege engines and a major sap beneath the walls until 14 October, when Louis agreed a truce and headed back to London, permitting de Burgh's men to sally out and plunder the surrounding area for supplies. King John was in East Anglia at King's Lynn on 11 October, when he fell ill, probably with dysentery. Panicking at the strong local support for Louis – and perhaps his judgement was affected by illness – he left a garrison in the town and took a short cut across the Wash, during which the tide changed, quicksands claimed many victims in the baggage train and were said to have swallowed up John's treasury. That misfortune and news of the truce at Dover, added to his increasing illness, saw him arrive in agony at Newark castle, where he died in the night of 18–19 October.

What should have been good news for Louis, turned out to be the reverse. Since their enemy had been John himself, many barons willingly accepted his unimplicated 9-year-old son Prince Henry as their new liege lord under the regency of William Marshal, considering that the boy, currently in the West country at Devizes, would be a more pliable ruler than Louis, son of Philippe Auguste, who had fought Henry II and Richard and driven John out of Normandy. No one seems to have spared much thought for that unfortunate other contender for the English throne Eleanor of Brittany, who was still languishing in prison.

Prince Henry could not be crowned in London because Louis and the dissident barons refused to leave the city, so he was taken to Gloucester to be crowned in its abbey church as King Henry III on 28 October 1216 after being knighted by William Marshal. Not until three and a half years later was he formally crowned in Westminster Abbey. At Gloucester, the crown and royal jewels being inaccessible in London, a gold necklace refashioned as a coronet for his small head was loaned by his mother Isabella d'Angoulême and used instead. It was a time of chaos with no organised government, no Exchequer, no royal seal even – and half the shires of England were occupied by enemy forces.[6] A revised version of Magna Carta naming William the Marshal *rector* of the realm was rushed out on 12 November, with Hubert de Burgh – who was still at Dover castle – named as regent. By the time the approval of the new pope Honorius III arrived in England, most of the barons had already changed sides. On 6 December Louis took Hertford castle, generously allowing the defenders to march out with arms and mounts, as he did at Berkhamsted later that month. Casualties and wastage had taken their toll, however, so early in the New Year Louis turned tail and fought his way back to the south coast through territory that had been for him and was now against. After an ambush at Lewes, the rump of his invasion force took refuge at Winchelsea, where the arrival of Blanche's rescue fleet with supplies and reinforcements saved them from having to choose between starvation and surrender.

Hubert de Burgh having repeatedly blocked Louis' communications with Blanche across the Channel in Boulogne, Louis decided, too late in the day, to follow his father's advice and re-start the siege of Dover castle, despite news that his remaining Anglo-Norman allies were steadily being reduced by the advice of William the Marshal that they should seek pardon for their rebellion and swear allegiance to Henry III. After the civil war had dragged on for several more months, Prince Louis decided it was time to go home, so he did, leaving England at the end of February 1217. During his 8-week absence, his remaining forces attempted to hold the ground they occupied. Louis' return to England did not turn the tide: defeats at Lincoln in May 1217 and at Dover and Sandwich in August forced Louis to negotiate an end to his campaign.

The treaty that ended the first barons' war may have been signed at Staines or Chertsey, or somewhere else, but no copies exist, although it is sometimes referred to as the Treaty of Lambeth and said to have been agreed by Louis and Henry III's representatives on 11 or 20 September at Lambeth Palace. Under its terms, the rebel barons were given amnesty and Louis was paid 10,000 silver marks for abandoning his wife's claim to the English throne and swearing never again to attack England. The allied Scottish troops under Alexander II also withdrew. The reasonableness of the terms sound as though the far-sighted William the Marshal had devised them, for the kingdom was so impoverished by Richard's and John's swingeing taxation that he, as rector, had to borrow heavily from two prosperous merchants in the Norman town of St-Omer, who had still not been fully repaid three years later.

Louis went home to Blanche in France, to put his first major failure behind him. Having done so much to support his English adventure by sending funds and reinforcements and assembling the second fleet at Boulogne and Calais,[7] Blanche's considerable debts for ships and other property lost in the several phases of the invasion were also outstanding as much as a decade later,[8] which accounts for her unpopularity in the Artois, which she no longer visited, confining her absences from Paris to trips to royal palaces in the Ile de France. Prince Louis did go there several times, but took no part in its government, safely in the hands of a nominee of Bishop Guérin of Senlis. For some reason – perhaps his agreeable temperament – Louis nevertheless still had a following among the *petite noblesse* of France. The Welsh chronicler Geraldus Cambrensis knew him personally in Paris and was said to find the Capetian prince-in-waiting a literate, cultivated art-lover and patron of the arts – but patently not a violent man of war like Blanche's uncle Richard.

Because of John's device making himself a vassal of the papacy, Pope Honorius III had, through his legate Guala, blessed John's and Henry III's forces, who wore crusaders' crosses in their conflict with the barons. By the time Guala left England in November 1218, peace had been made at Worcester with Welsh warlord Llywelyn ap Iorwerth, a truce agreed with Alexander II of Scotland, the Exchequer was reopened, a great seal had been made for Henry III and the business of government was returning to normal.[9]

King John's death had left Isabelle d'Angoulême in the awkward position of a royal widow and mother of the new under-age, king. Many royal widows exercised considerable power as the guides and instructors of their sons. Blanche would prove to be one of them. But 70-year-old William the Marshal kept Henry away from his mother. This may have been because she was considered to share the guilt for John's misdeeds or because she was, like Louis, from France and therefore, although the mother of five children by John, still a 'foreign queen'. Or maybe the slurs against her as a sexually active woman were recycled. Perhaps it was a complex of all these considerations. Nine months after John's death, Isabelle left Britain for good, returning to southwest France, where she was since 1202 *suo jure* Countess of Angoulême. Importantly the behaviour and innocent character of the young king – so different from his father – gained him increasing popularity and the loyalty so necessary for ruling a land in peace. Yet, curiously, during Henry III's long reign none of the four major taxes raised contributed toward the government of the realm, much being siphoned away for the long struggle in Gascony.[10] Reflecting this and his own use of the great seal, the charter rolls began again until after he declared himself of age in January 1227.[11]

Knowing that she would never be accepted in England and with her blonde-haired, blue-eyed looks still turning heads wherever she went, in the spring of 1220 Isabella d'Angoulême married Hugues X de Lusignan, Count of La Marche and son of Hugues IX, to whom she had been betrothed before John spirited her away in 1200. Her daughter Joan was already present in his household, being brought up as his betrothed under a contract with King John that named her dowry as the city of Saintes and the Ile d'Oléron, but Hugues X nevertheless preferred the mother to the daughter – and married her! To re-marry anyone, Isabella, as the widowed ex-queen of England, should have asked the consent of the English *curia regis*. Because she did not wish to ask a question to which the answer would have been negative, in the name of her son Henry her dower lands were confiscated and her pension stopped. Isabella and her new husband retaliated by threatening to keep Joan, who had meantime been promised by the regency council in marriage to the king of Scotland. The council first responded by sending furious letters to Pope Honorius III, signed in the name of young King Henry, and urging the pope to excommunicate Isabella and Hugues X Lusignan. Prudence dictated they later come to terms with Isabella, in order to have Princess Joan available for marriage to King Alexander II of Scotland. As reward for her cooperation, and in compensation for her confiscated dower lands, Isabella was granted the revenues for four years from the valuable stannary towns in Devon and the city of Aylesbury, and was paid the £3,000 arrears withheld from her pension. It was a very good deal for her.

She bore nine further children to Hugues X, but never accepted that she was now 'only a countess' and refused to behave as appropriate to her reduced station. Matters came to a head in 1241, when summoned to Paris with her husband to pay homage to King Louis IX's brother Alphonse in his capacity as count of Poitou. There, Queen Blanche treated her as a mere countess who called herself a queen and Isabella blamed Blanche for responsibility in Louis' invasion of England, which, she was convinced, had caused or hastened King John's death. Conversely, in 1244 it was even alleged that Isabella had paid two of the cooks at Louis' palace to poison him. Although even the Romans had realised that torture produces many false confessions just to end the agony, the cooks were arrested and tortured into admitting that they had been in her pay. Isabella moved fast. Fleeing to the sanctuary of the abbey of Fontevraud, where she died on 4 June 1246, she was buried outside the abbey at her own request, as a sort of posthumous penance. Visiting the abbey later, Henry III was horrified that an ex-queen of England should be treated like a commoner and had the remains of his mother re-buried inside the abbey church close to the tombs of Henry II and Eleanor of Aquitaine. Several of her children accompanied their half-brother Henry III back to England after his visit, and prospered there, Aymer of Lusignan becoming Bishop of Winchester. Alais de Lusignan married Jean de Warenne, 6th earl of Surrey. Guy de Lusignan was killed at the Battle of Lewes in 1264 during the Second Barons' Rebellion. Guillaume de Lusignan survived that battle and became first earl of Pembroke.

Chapter 14

Blanche, Queen of France

Warfare then was nothing like even the worst of what cinema re-enactments show us. The stabbing towards an enemy's eyes, the thrusting of a lance into his internal organs, the hacking of a *heavy* sword into another man's shoulder or, if in the hands of a foot-soldier, into the thigh of a mounted adversary, all required immense strength. So did driving a lance into a knight's mount, so that it would collapse and throw the rider to the ground, stunned and probably injured. For a moment until he gathered his senses, he was helpless and could be despatched by any common man-at-arms. Even when plate armour was worn later, the lethal thrust of a narrow stiletto-like dagger between the joints of his armour might come next, unless he was valuable enough to be taken hostage for ransom.

Every action on the battlefield was exhausting, bloody and brutal. Men lost hands and feet, whole arms and legs, and very frequently lost ears and noses from the swipe of a cutting edge. At a gathering of warriors who had never met before, they could often recognise each other by the mutilations their faces bore, missing fingers or hands or damaged legs causing them to limp. It was for this reason that the *cervellière* or simple pudding-basin helmet evolved side-flaps covering the ears and the nasal – a strip of metal running from the brow down along the ridge of the nose, affording protection from a frontal cut, but not for a slash from the side. This in turn was modified in the great helm, an iron enclosure for the whole head from the crown to the neck, which had the disadvantage that it weighed 15–20 lbs and was very stuffy, the only ventilation in some cases being through the horizontal eye-slits. Even those bishops who considered drawing blood inappropriate for their holy office went into the field at the head of their vassals when summoned by their overlords, and chose to wield, instead of a sword, a mace with heavy metal-spiked or flanged head, which alone weighed 4lbs – 6lbs. One blow of this could fatally crush an opponent's helmet and skull. That long-distance weapon with a long history, the longbow was five feet long and required a pull of up to 150lbs to fire the 28-inch-long steel-tipped arrows which could pierce chain mail.

Descriptions and depictions of Prince Louis did not suggest the sheer strength required for that kind of fighting, but he could not escape being drawn several times into border disputes in the long-drawn-out war with Henry III over the Plantagenet possessions in France. In addition to his enemy across the Channel and in western France, there was also a perceived internal enemy in the south of France. From 1209 to 1229 the Capetian monarchy was conducting an intermittent genocide against the inhabitants of southern France, who came from a pre-Roman Celtic race with different patterns of blood groups, darker skin and shorter stature than the northern Franks, who originated in Franconia in the Rhine valley. These southerners did not even speak the northern tongue *la langue d'oïl* but dialects of Occitan or *la linga d'oc*, a different Latin-derived language closer to Spanish than the tongue of the Franks. In addition, the French king had subjects in the northeast speaking low-German Flemish and in the northwest, Celtic Breton, which was why the administration of the kingdom was in the hands of monks and bishops. They could all communicate with each other in Latin, until King François I – who reigned 1515–1547 – broke the power of the Church by decreeing that henceforth the sole official language of France was the one he spoke – *la langue d'oïl*.

The justification for the Frankish genocide of the Occitan-speakers, which was approved by successive popes, was that many of these southerners supported the heresy of Catharism.[1] The genuine Cathars – or Albigensians, as they were often called because many lived in and around the city of Albi – were also known as 'perfects'. The name was not their proud boast, but a translation of the Latin accusation *hereticus perfectus* meaning 'a thoroughgoing heretic', for whom there was no salvation, according to the Church. The Cathars believed that God was in everyone, but that there was in the world also a force for evil, tempting each person into sin. They eschewed the slaughter of animals for meat and adopted an ascetic vegetarian regime. Other proto-Protestant sects, like the *pauperes de lugduno* or Poor of Lyons and the Poor of Lombardy were equally harassed by inquisitors and suffered terribly for their independence, being known as *vaudes* or sorcerers, which was one of the articles in the condemnation of Joan of Arc in 1431.

The Italian monk Giovanni Gratiano, who was a counsellor to Pope Innocent II, compiled in the 1140s a compendium of 3,800 canonical laws in order to resolve conflicts between them. The *Decretum*, as it was known, was regarded as the authority on human activities ranging from praying to sex. According to it, sex was necessary for procreation, but not to be indulged in for pleasure, even by married couples: in Gratian's words, 'whorish embraces' were not allowed between spouses.[2] These and other Cathar precepts might have been tolerated by the Church, but the Cathars preached openly that, since God was everywhere, no one needed priests and monks or even the Pope himself to make contact with Him through a sort of heavenly telephone exchange based in Rome. By extension, since He had created everything, there was no reason to pay taxes and tithes to the Church, as to a temporal overlord. This, to Rome, always greedy for political power and money, was anathema. So, as early as 1207 Pope Innocent III declared that the war against these heretics was a crusade, with all the indulgences and the remission of sins granted to crusaders going to the Holy Land automatically extended to all who went to kill these in-country heretics and their uninvolved neighbours. His successors endorsed this ruling.

The excesses to which this led included the siege of Beziers during Philippe Auguste's reign in 1209, where a crusading army of around 20,000 armed men invested the city and took it on 22 July. Bishop Renaud of Beziers had a list of 220 allegedly dangerous heretics living there, but the mercenary foot-soldiers were ordered to slaughter every one of the 14,000 men, women and children living within the walls. They complained that killing so many with sword, knife, axe and hammer – or simply the strength of a man's arm to hold a baby by the foot and dash its head against a stone wall – was extremely hard work under the summer sun, and asked if they could kill just those on the bishop's list, since the rest were not proven guilty of any sin. The papal legate Arnaud Amaury is said to have ordered them to continue the slaughter still called in Occitan *lo gran masèl*, or great massacre, until no one was left alive because God in Heaven would know which were the innocent: *'Dieu saura connaître les siens,'* he reportedly said.

The Inquisition – later so infamous in Spain – was first instituted to judge and persecute all heretics in Germany, France and Italy with interrogation under torture by iron, fire and water. Surviving Cathars fled from all over the south of France into the foothills of the Pyrenees, where they constructed castles so difficult of access that they thought themselves safe there. Even young and healthy tourists visiting the ruins today find this exhausting and sometimes dangerous. The final siege of Montségur by a force of more than 10,000 knights and foot-soldiers had a bishop commanding the artillery of trebuchets hammering away at the walls of the castle,[3] perched at the height of 3,000 feet above sea level atop a limestone outcrop between Mirepoix and Ax-les-Thermes in the modern Ariège *département*. It continued for ten months in the hope that the defenders would run out of water and food, and surrender. On 2 March 1244 the survivors finally did so. Those who recanted, or said they had never been perfects, were allowed to depart over the following two weeks, when only 207 unrepentant Cathars of both sexes and all ages were still there. Eventually marched down to a field below the castle still called locally *lo prat dels cremats* – the field of the burned people – where a huge common pyre awaited them, they climbed onto it, praying and singing hymns, parents holding their children close. Then it was fired, burning them all alive – the fate decreed for all heretics. A stele on the spot bears the Occitan inscription *Als catars, als martirs del pur amor crestian 16 marc 1244.*

What part did Philippe Auguste's son and grandson – and their wives – play in this long drawn-out war? Although Queen Blanche has been blamed for taking an active part by historians reasoning that she wanted a French army to conquer Pyrenean territory which would enable her to threaten her native Castile and claim the succession to that kingdom, documentation is sparse, and no proof exists that she saw in the harrying of the Cathars a way to reclaim her family's possessions. Whatever Blanche thought about the slaughter of thousands of people – eventually the genocide was calculated to have killed a half-million peaceful men, women and children – there was no need for her to intervene because the French Archives Nationales contain letters from Rodrigo Diaz de los Cameros and other important Castilian nobles reporting the dying wish of King Alfonso VIII that, should his son Enrique die without issue, the succession should automatically pass to a son of Blanche and Prince Louis.[4]

Although there is no record of Blanche travelling anywhere near Cathar territory, her husband Prince Louis is known to have been involved. Early in 1219 Alix de Montmorency, the widow of Simon de Montfort, led a small contingent of reinforcements from the north to back up her son Amaury VI de Montfort, who was continuing his father's harrying of the Cathars. This in turn was joined by Prince Louis, sent by Philippe Auguste with twenty bishops, thirty counts and reputedly a force of 10,000 bowmen, all of whom arrived on 2 June 1219 at Marmande on the river Garonne. The commandant of the town, Count d'Astarac halted its defence and agreed to surrender to Prince Philippe's forces on 10 June, on condition that he and his men should be allowed to leave alive. The papal legate and the bishops decided to revoke the agreement, despite the knights with them protesting that this was contrary to the rules of warfare. In the renegotiations, soldiers from Louis' force broke into the town, sacking it, raping indiscriminately, setting fire to the houses and killing the 5,000 inhabitants.

The Frankish army then marched eastwards to resume the siege of Toulouse, its numbers shrinking daily as feudal vassals completed their obligatory *quarantaine* or forty days of service and went home with their followers. This problem was at the root of the tax known as *scutage*, whereby a vassal could pay to be released from the obligation of knight service, enabling his overlord to hire mercenaries, who would continue fighting until their pay ceased. On 1 August 1219 Prince Louis followed the example of many vassals, abandoned the *chevauchée* to Toulouse and rode north, destination Paris.

Having learned the lesson that it was not advisable to go against the will of Philippe Auguste or Chancellor Guérin, Blanche and Louis generally led a frustratingly circumspect life, eschewing invitations to join political initiatives that might have been entrapment by their enemies. It is an illustration of the precariousness of medieval times, even for the most favoured in time of peace, that Philippe Auguste was the first French king to live long enough to know a grandchild. His rule also saw the title of the

Capetian king changed from *rex francorum* – king of the Franks – to *rex franciae* – king of the geographical entity of France. It was an important difference. When Philippe died and was interred in the cathedral at St Denis, Blanche's husband finally succeeded to the throne of France on 14 July 1223 as Louis VIII, following which both spouses were crowned in the opulent setting of Reims' new cathedral on 6 August 1223. Officiating was Archbishop Guillaume de Joinville, with the chrism brought from the nearby abbey by Abbot St Rémi.

A minor hitch came when the chrism – sanctified oil that was said to have served also at the baptism of Clovis six centuries earlier – was found to have solidified in the abbot's phial during the intervening centuries, obliging the archbishop to extract a few small pieces and mix them with holy water for the anointing, ordinary holy water also being used for the anointing of Blanche. With a sceptre placed in her right hand and a crown upon her head, she was every inch the queen of France. Clouds of incense and the chanting of a choir of monks made a ceremony to more than compensate for the hurried nuptials at Port-Mort in Plantagenet Normandy twenty-three years earlier and the couple's precipitate retreat to Frankish territory afterwards. This time, the royal couple processed in a dignified cortège of noble vassals to preside over a great banquet costing the enormous sum of 4,000 pounds, paid for by the archbishop and the citizens of Reims as the price of their town's prestige.

The royal couple's return to Paris was by a roundabout route through Soissons and Compiègne. After a brief rest, their travels continued to Melun and Sens, Bourges, Tours, Fontainebleau, Orleans, Chauny, Peronne, Arras and Douai, to show the new monarch and his spouse to as many subjects as possible. Further such trips lasted into the New Year. Back in Paris, Blanche lived in great pomp, but little comfort, in the Capetian palace on the Ile de la Cité, her household or *familia* embracing not just herself and Louis and their growing children, but also Philippe and Marie, the belatedly legitimised children of Philippe Auguste and Agnès de Méranie.[5] Her political life is more mysterious, with few documents in the royal archives bearing her seal, or even naming her. Mathew Paris, however, considered that, like many powerful wives, she preferred to act by prudently influencing her husband in private. The Church also recognised her influence over Louis VIII, Pope Honorius III on one occasion requesting her to persuade her husband to lend support to the threatened Latin kingdom of Constantinople.[6]

Blanche gave birth to her first daughter, christened Isabelle, in 1225. The following year, she bore another son named Etienne, who died in infancy. The delicate health of the boy's father eventually catching up with him, Louis VIII died just three years after the coronation. Falling ill in October 1226, he died on 8 November, when Blanche was again pregnant, giving birth to another son shortly after Louis's death. Christened Charles, the new prince became the count of Anjou and Maine, and eventually King of the Two Sicilies. In this way, his mother mingled Eleanor of Aquitaine's DNA with the Capetian bloodline but, as the future was to show, Queen Blanche did much more than this for the French dynasty founded by Hugues Capet in 987. During his final illness in the castle at Montpensier, Louis VIII called some important barons and bishops to his bedside. Dying of 'the bloody flux', as dysentery was known, he refused their advice that he might be cured by sex with a virgin, rejected the girl on offer, and made the assembled religious and temporal lords promise to swear fealty to his eponymous son after his death.[7]

It was a prudent gesture, there being much resentment among the nobility of the royal domain and in France generally at the idea of being ruled by a child controlled by a woman as strong as Blanche had shown herself to be over the years – and who was still regarded by many as a foreigner. She still is, being known seven centuries later as 'Blanche de Castille'. Fortunately, she had, before Louis' death, cultivated close relationships with the most important churchmen of the kingdom, who testified that it had been the expressed intention of Louis VIII on his deathbed that his son be *sous le bail et la tutelle* of Queen Blanche – in other words, that she be the regent[8] and chief counsellor of the young king whom she had so strictly and piously educated.

The news of his father's death in Montpensier, 250 miles south of the capital, reached Paris several days later while the funeral cortège was still en route. Somewhere along the way it met Prince Louis riding south to accompany his father's body on the final stages of the journey. Back in Paris, Blanche was so distraught with grief that she talked of killing herself until calmed by her courtiers into realising that her duty lay with her living children and especially with Prince Louis. Together, he and his mother supervised the burial of Louis VIII in the cathedral of St Denis, near to the grave of Philippe Auguste. In 1793, when Paris was in revolutionary turmoil, with Louis XVI and Marie-Antoinette beheaded on the guillotine before screaming crowds, and young Napoleon Bonaparte was making a name for himself at the siege of Toulon, Louis VIII's coffin was among the royal ones opened at St Denis and elsewhere, the remains despoiled. This skeleton of Blanche's husband, wrapped in layers of oiled cloth and cowhide, was that of a short man. The sceptre, with which he had been buried, had disintegrated; only the bones and a skullcap and satin head-covering were still intact.

Crowned as Louis IX – France's forty-fourth king and ninth in the Capetian line – in Reims cathedral on 29 November 1226, Blanche's tall blond 12-year-old son remained firmly under the guidance *and control* of his mother until he attained his majority eight years later, in 1234. His 'book-learning' she entrusted to Franciscan and Dominican monks while at the same time seizing property of the archbishop of Reims for defying the royal power. That dispute lasted a long time until resolved by Pope Gregory IX ordering Louis IX and Blanche to behave, granting in return to the royal chapel and that of Blanche herself an exemption from the imposition of interdict, except by himself, and thus freeing them from threats by French bishops who used spiritual weapons for temporal aims.[9]

Determined that her son should be no bookish man like his father, Blanche had Louis instructed in the skills of hunting and warfare by tutors authorised by her to beat her son on occasion when he fell short of *her* expectations. In between, young Louis IX was obliged to attend audiences and councils of state, which was normal for the sons of the nobility and royalty – learning to use the reins of government by observing his elders' behaviour. Harsh as her regime sounds to modern ears for a boy not yet in his teens, her guidance and teaching continued to bear fruit later in Louis' reign, when he ended the open conflict between Capetians and Plantagenets in France and gradually extended the royal domain to include undisputed rule over Normandy, Anjou, Touraine, Maine and Poitou, plus Aix-en-Provence, Beaucaire and Carcassone and the counties of Blois, Chartres, Châteaudun and Sancerre. So far as we know, the young king never opposed his mother, but she was unpopular with many of the nobility, especially in Champagne – and once again the

Lusignans were manoeuvring for power. Mostly, these differences were resolved in the traditional manner, by truces and the restoration of fiefs that had been confiscated by Philippe Auguste.

It was, of course, not the youthful king these dissidents wished to replace; their intent was to get rid of Blanche and replace her by a regent more sympathetic to their priorities. One of the ways in which a strong female figure could be brought low was by imputing immorality. This was the root of the scandals that pursued Blanche's grandmother Eleanor of Aquitaine for years when she was known by her political enemies as 'the whore of Aquitaine'.[10] In Blanche's case, the death of Bishop Guérin in April 1227, after rumours of his alleged improprieties with the queen, saw a more elaborate scandal. To explain Count Thibaut of Champagne's change of political sides to become a supporter of Blanche, she was accused of having him poison her husband so that she could take the count as her lover. There were no limits to this unpleasant game, it seemed, when Thibaut was replaced as the alleged paramour of the queen by the papal legate Cardinal Frangipani. This time, it was whispered in the corridors of power that she was pregnant by him. When this scandal reached Blanche's ears, she decided on an original method of ridiculing the rumour-mongers. Arriving at a session of the all-male royal *curia*, she had the ushers announce her presence and strode in, climbing onto a table and dropping her cloak to reveal herself clad only in a thin shift. Turning, so that all the men present in the council chamber could inspect her body, she demanded whether any one of them considered that she was *grosse* – in other words big with child. Hurriedly, she was helped down by the embarrassed barons and escorted back to her quarters, to get dressed.

That object lesson to her detractors did not stop the unruly students of the Paris schools, many of whom were not even French, but all of whom were male – only Bologna university admitted female students at the time – from insulting the queen by singing songs and declaiming poems accusing her of immorality. On occasion, this resulted in rioting, as on Mardi Gras – Shrove Tuesday – of 1229, with damage to property which had to be put down with force by Blanche's guards, involving some cracked skulls and bloodshed. The schools considering that the Crown had no authority to do this, rebellious students and their masters fled to Reims, Orleans and other cities, inciting Henry III, when the news reached London, to invite them to cross the Channel and instal themselves in London.[11] It was a reversal of Henry II's ban in 1167 of English students attending the schools in Paris, which founded the schools in Oxford, likewise subject to intermittent riots between 'town and gown'. Blanche, realising that it was time to show clemency, persuaded Louis to endorse Philippe Auguste's exemption for students of the schools and their masters from the civil power. But she was just as adamant in her dispute with the chapter of Notre Dame cathedral, which insisted on its right to tax the serfs on its manor of Orly, south of the capital. The chapter then confined male and female peasants and their children in its private prison, where some died. Blanche had her men-at-arms break down the prison door and release the survivors. A judgement against her, on the grounds that she had acted *ultra vires*, was not given in favour of the chapter until after her death,[12] which implies that the *curia* was dominated by her right to the end of her days.

After the more or less incessant feudal warfare in the tenth and eleventh centuries, her son's firm application of Philippe Auguste's *quarantaine-le-roi*, did much to make France a law-abiding country. This imposed a 40-day cooling-off period before any noble could revenge himself for an insult or injury under *lex talionis* – the law of revenge – giving time for the Church and the king's appointed law officers to intervene, Even more modern in outlook was his institution of the presumption of innocence and reduction in the number of circumstances where torture or trial by ordeal were admissible; the Mediterranean *vendetta* was banned; and a right of appeal to the monarch was instituted – which obviously not everyone could claim, but at least the concept existed. In all of these measures can be seen the farsightedness of Blanche, as can her religious grounding in Louis IX's generosity to churches, abbeys and hospices for the poor and pilgrims. Avoiding the scandals surrounding his predecessors, the young king of France seemed to his subjects a true Christian monarch, subtly eroding the feudal powers of his vassals and transforming France into a true monarchy.

Chapter 15

Marguerite of Provence

M
any people have wondered how these princesses traded young into foreign lands – for treaties that may, or may not, have worked out – behaved when the passage of years made them dowager queens in their turn. Remembering what their own early experience in the adopted country had been like, were they sympathetic and helpful to the foreign brides chosen for their sons, or on the contrary so toughened by their own experiences of fending off the hostility of their husbands' bishops and barons that they passed on the harshness which had been meted out to them?

A good example is the case of Blanche who, in 1233, decided that it was time for 19-year-old Louis IX to marry. There was a story, which may or may not be true, of a maverick monk who shouted abroad in the streets of Paris, to anyone who would listen, the scandal that Queen Blanche had employed a discreet older woman to teach Prince Louis what was required of a husband in bed. If true, that would still strike many mothers in Mediterranean countries as normal, to make sure that their son's sexual equipment works and that he is not averse to intercourse with a woman. Blanche cast her eyes over the courts of southern France and northern Spain for a suitable bride in what was perhaps an indication of her continuing mistrust of the northern, Frankish nobility, which had never taken to her. The chronicler Jean de Joinville, who knew the court well and later accompanied Louis IX on crusade to the Holy Land, wrote, '[Blanche] had neither relatives nor friends in the realm of France.'[1] This was not quite true, in that supplicants from the Christian courts in Spain did come to Paris from time to time, seeking her support, influence or money. At the time of which Joinville was writing, Blanche's niece Berenguela of Leon and her husband Jehan de Brienne, king of Jerusalem, were lobbying for support in Paris. But none of these people had any influence in the *curia* and they were all careful while in France to avoid attracting notice.

The county of Provence had been reduced by a swirling history of conquest, invasions, insurrections and ravaging by Muslim pirates from the Magreb, all complicated in the thirteenth century by the cities of Marseille, Avignon and Arles constituting themselves self-governing *podestats*. Count Ramón Berenguer IV of Provence and Forcalquier – the two counties were divided by the river Durance – spent much of his time and energy fighting and intriguing to reunite the land whose rump he ruled, and needed 'friends in high places' since his territory was hemmed in by the county of Toulouse to the west, several smaller counties to the north, Italy to the east and Barcelona to the southwest. Most importantly, it lay east of the river Rhône and thus within the German or Holy Roman Empire. Its current ruler, Count Ramón had three daughters; the eldest was 13-year-old Marguerite, followed by 10-year-old Eleanor and 8-year-old Sancha. In the following year, a fourth daughter was born and christened Béatrice after her mother, Béatrice of Savoy. Their father's itinerant court accustomed them when young to spending a few days and nights in one Provençal castle before moving to another. Within the limits of this lifestyle, Countess Béatrice of Savoy kept a very civilised and animated court, where poetry and music were regularly enjoyed and noble troubadours like Guy de Châtillon and Boniface de Castellane sang of her beauty when they were not in the field, shedding blood. Countess Béatrice also ensured that her daughters were well educated and literate because letter-writing was the only way that the four girls, who were unlikely ever to meet after despatch to their foreign husbands, could later keep in touch – as did Marguerite and Eleanor throughout their lives, although married to the kings of France and England, who were often enemies at war with each other.[2]

These four girls illustrate perfectly the medieval confusion of royal and noble bloodlines. In May 1234 Marguerite married Louis IX of France; in 1236 her sister Eleanor, with whom Marguerite remained close all her life, married Henry III of England; in 1243 Sancha married Henry III's brother Richard of Cornwall, who became German emperor in 1257; in 1246, Béatrice married Louis IX's brother Charles d'Anjou, who became King of Sicily and King of Naples. The complication for Ramón

Berenguer and Béatrice of Savoy was that all the required dowries for their daughters' matches far exceeded their ability to pay them.

But all that lay in the future when Queen Blanche was deciding on a wife for her son in 1233. Some sources indicate that Louis IX chose his future wife for himself while travelling through Provence, but Blanche's history of governing every detail of his life during his minority and continuing to do so very intrusively after his marriage, makes it unlikely that she would have accorded Prince Louis complete freedom to decide whom he should marry. Marguerite shared a common great-great-grandfather with Louis, but Blanche succeeded in getting Pope Gregory IX to clear the planned union of accusations of the fifth degree of consanguinity.[3] It was conventional for the chroniclers to describe noble women, especially royal brides, as beautiful, but Marguerite was described as being cultivated, witty, lively and playful, with dark hair and a clear gaze. The marriage contract was signed on 30 April 1234 at Sisteron on the border of Provence and Forcalquier, with the comtal family agreeing to find a dowry of 8,000 silver marks and give as security for its payment the castle of Tarascon, as recorded by Queen Blanche's envoys Archbishop Gautier le Cornu of Sens and royal counsellor Jean de Nesle.

On 17 May Count Ramón added another 2,000 silver marks, guaranteed by Archbishop Audibert of Aix-en-Provence together with income from the town and castle of Aix. It was a considerable dowry, exceeding Count Ramón's resources, but less than half of it was ever paid.[4] On Marguerite's journey to the north, at Lyons two of her maternal uncles still living in Savoy joined the cortège and accompanied the young bride to Sens for the ceremony, arriving there on 26 May 1234. The considerable expenses listed in the royal accounts include fine dresses for several noble ladies to wear, and the bride was the recipient of a very expensive wardrobe of clothes, a gold cup, from which she would drink on special occasions, several golden spoons and a new golden crown, whereas Louis had to make do with a refurbished one. Jewels too are listed in the accounts, although it is not clear for whom they were purchased.

Sens had been chosen by Blanche for the ceremony because its archbishop had been a counsellor of Philippe Auguste and continued to be a member of her own *curia* during her regency. On 27 May Marguerite was married at the cathedral there to Louis before noble and royal witnesses including two of his brothers. Grandstands were erected at royal expense so that those not privileged to enter the cathedral could at least have a good view of the young king and his bride arriving and leaving – also of the ceremony which began outside the cathedral, with the couple's right hands being joined by Marguerite's Savoyard uncle William, bishop of Valence. After the exchange of rings, he blessed them and they were asperged with holy water. Marguerite was also presented with an abridged version of the dower contract listing the property conferred upon her, which included the city of Le Mans and the castles of Mortagne and Mauves-sur-Huisne in the county of Le Perche. Lastly she was given *le treizan* – thirteen *deniers* symbolising her right to funds from the couple's joint wealth, with which to make charitable bequests.[5]

Following a Mass conducted inside the cathedral by Archbishop Gautier le Cornu, he gave the kiss of peace to Louis, who in turn kissed the bride, symbolically transferring the benediction. On the day after the wedding came the coronation in the same cathedral as queen consort of this 13-year-old girl, clad in precious silks that had come either all the way from China along the Silk Road or perhaps from Sicily, where silk worms stolen at risk of death in the Celestial Kingdom were already founding a competition for China's most precious export. The bridal chamber was also blessed, to make the couple fertile, although it was reported that Louis respected the archbishop's public requirement at the wedding mass that he did not touch Marguerite during their first three nights together.[6] The roundabout route taken for the return to Paris, to show the young king and queen to as many citizens as possible on the way, meant that they did not arrive there until 9 June, from when the three nights of abstinence were counted. The festivities at Sens continued with a ceremonial dubbing of young knights, who afterwards showed their martial prowess in a tournament, from which Louis was banned by his oath. The royal accountants also listed a considerable amount of food purchased for a mass banquet, including 20,000 litres of wine! A good time was evidently had by all, with the press of public causing some accidents, of which the victims were compensated from the royal purse. A certain jealousy was evident in Louis' brother Charles d'Anjou, who complained when marrying Marguerite's sister Béatrice in 1246 that his nuptials were not celebrated with equal lavishness.[7]

What was the reaction of 13-year-old Marguerite on seeing the vast expanse of France – then the most populous country in Europe with 13 million inhabitants or more – during the journey north and at Sens and onward to Paris? We do not know. Nor do we know her feelings on first meeting her deeply religious husband and his powerful mother, but all was not well after the return to the royal palace on the Ile de la Cité. Whether because Louis showed too much attention to his barely nubile bride and neglected his duties of state or religious devotions to be near her, or just because of his mother's desire to dominate him without interference from another woman, even one so young, Queen Blanche exercised her power as dowager queen by dismissing Marguerite's uncles and all the household familiars she had brought with her from Provence. This left Louis' young bride isolated among the Frankish courtiers who spoke a different language, the *langue d'oïl*, which to her ears sounded cold and hostile, being very different from the Provençal dialect of Occitan, which Marguerite had grown up speaking.

Having herself had to adapt to the Frankish tongue after speaking Castilian Spanish before her own marriage to Louis VIII, Blanche knew exactly what she was doing. She also accused her daughter-in-law of being insufficiently pious and courtly in her behaviour. This was curious in a court where Louis' brother Robert d'Artois once ordered his servants to pelt Count Thibaud de Champagne with food, filth and old rags – which was taken as a permissible joke by all present! So, was this a classic case of a very powerful and possessive mother considering her daughter-in-law as a chattel necessary for childbearing to prolong the dynasty, but otherwise unworthy of the son she had brought up?

Paris itself was an eye-opener to the young queen, the busiest city in Europe, with more than 100,000 people living there, both inside Philippe Auguste's walls and outside. Day and night there was the noise of people, animals and iron-shod cartwheels on cobbled streets – although most in Paris were still unpaved mud tracks – and the activities of tradesmen from the stinking tanners to butchers, bakers and, literally, candlestick makers. In the palace, the queen's quarters were, strangely, on the ground floor near the audience hall, the chapel and the accounts offices, although Louis' bedroom was upstairs on the first floor. Day and night, servants, lawyers, monks, merchants trying to sell jewels and fine cloths and members of the public passed in and out of the palace. When not staying in the royal castles at Vincennes, St Germain-en-Laye, Fontainebleu and a dozen other places, the palace on the Ile de la Cité was hardly a haven of peace for the young queen, except possibly in the royal gardens and the orchard at the western end of the island, shielded by high walls and the palace itself from some of the noise.

Even there, the stink of human waste thrown into the streets and animal excrement and putrefying offal deposited there was inescapable. Philippe Auguste had had several wells sunk to provide Parisians with clean drinking water, but the aquifers were polluted by seepage from cesspools and people used the wells to dump rubbish in. Sewers had been constructed a thousand years earlier in Roman cities, but there was no sewerage in Paris at the time. The Romans – or some of them – had flushing toilets, but in Paris even the king and queen had to relieve themselves into pottery vessels that were carried away by servants and emptied into the Seine. By one means or another everything, including whole rotten carcases, ended up in the river, floating slowly seaward. Even heavy downpours did little to clear the streets because they caused the river to overflow and flood streets, leaving more filth when the waters receded. It was by barges sailing on the stinking Seine that most food arrived for both palace-dwellers and common folk.

Although the newly-weds shared many tastes, enjoying riding together outside Paris, and reading and listening to music, Blanche did everything possible to keep them apart. Was that the reason why Marguerite did not become pregnant for five years, despite being forced by Queen Blanche to make pilgrimages with her and pray at shrines for divine, or at least saintly, intervention to help her conceive a son and heir for Louis? If medieval advice on getting pregnant was all about finding the right moment in Hippocrates' and Galen's theory of bodily humours, the Church countered this by laying down that no marital copulation should occur on Sundays, Wednesdays or Fridays, on any feast day or during Advent or Lent. It was also prohibited during pregnancy and after childbirth before churching of the woman. In Gratian's *Decretum* it was also recommended that a husband abstain from sex for up to eight days before accepting the eucharist, for fear of passing on his wife's 'contamination' of the Host. We know that Louis was devout, so he would have been aware that only one position was not sinful: what is now called the missionary position. Sex with the woman on top was forbidden because it was believed that gravity was necessary to drain the husband's sperm into the wife's vagina.[8]

In the early years of their marriage, the young couple's favourite residence was the castle twenty miles north-east of Paris at Pontoise built by Louis VI. It has been conjectured that the dowager queen interfered so much in their personal lives when in Paris that Pontoise was chosen to give them some privacy which was simply impossible to find on the Ile de la Cité. At Pontoise, the *valets de chambre* were expressly charged to warn the king and queen every time Blanche chose to pay a visit. As time passed without any pregnancy, rumours abounded that the marriage of Louis and Marguerite would have to be dissolved, because *Causa* 33 of Gratian's *Decretum* laid down that one of the few legitimate reasons for the dissolution of a marriage was the husband's impotence preventing him from paying what was labelled his 'conjugal debt'.[9]

Fortunately, in 1240 Marguerite gave birth to a daughter christened Blanche in honour of the dowager queen, with whom the young mother lived in a state of constant hostilities. In one of the early births, Marguerite suffered a long labour and could well have joined the terribly high number of women who died in childbirth, had not an attendant trained at the enlightened medical school in Montpellier used some early form of forceps to assist the delivery. Even today a difficult birth like Marguerite's forceps delivery can put the mother's life at risk. Princess Marguerite haemorrhaged so badly that Louis was deeply troubled. When he was led away by Queen Blanche, who told him there was no point in staying in the room, Marguerite roused herself sufficiently to scream, 'On the point of death, how can you not let me see my husband!' She then fainted from loss of blood while Louis ignored Blanche's orders, staying with his wife until she was brought round and the bleeding stopped.[10]

Two years after the birth of Princess Blanche another daughter was born and christened Isabelle. By this time, Marguerite no longer gave way to her domineering mother-in-law and was gradually displacing her as the senior queen on the Ile de la Cité, where the whole court must have heaved sighs of relief that Marguerite's next child, born in 1244, was a boy christened Louis, followed by his brother Philippe the following year.

Despite the infertile first five years of the marriage, Marguerite more than fulfilled her obligation to ensure the succession, producing five more sons – one of whom died in infancy – and three more daughters. The births of his children seem to have given Louis the courage, not only to send Blanche away from court, but also to dismiss her traditionalist counsellors inherited from Philippe Auguste in favour of new ones who shared his aims and intentions.

The other way in which the Capetians ensured their future was by building – castles of course, but also abbeys and cathedrals, like the abbey of Maubuisson, founded by Blanche in 1236. Under her influence too, Louis began the construction, in 1241 or 1242, of the Sainte-Chapelle in Paris to house some religious relics looted from Constantinople when the Byzantine capital was sacked by the Fourth Crusade in 1204, including what was alleged to be the Crown of Thorns and a piece of ancient wood supposed to have come from the True Cross, which he bought from the emperor of Constantinople. As the Protestant leader John Calvin remarked four centuries later, if all such fragments were assembled, they would fill a very large ship, although Catholic theologians argued at the time that contact with the blood of Christ had given the wood the quality of being infinitely divisible.

The Sainte-Chapelle is a miracle of slender Gothic columns and enormous windows comprising 1,133 stained glass panels that still awe the modern visitor with the beauty, conception and execution of their apparently unsupported radiance. Construction lasted seven years, an amazingly short time due to the priority allotted to it by Louis IX and by Blanche in his absences, the consecration taking place on 28 April 1248. Although the alleged relics were stolen in the Revolution or destroyed, even that manifestation of godlessness rightly called the Terror refrained from destroying the building or integrating it into the adjacent Palais de Justice.[11]

Chapter 16

A Confusion of Kings

In the summer of 1242, a not unusual marriage tangle centred on Isabella d'Angoulême, King John's widow who had returned to her native southwest France and married Hugues X de Lusignan. When King Louis' brother Alphonse de Poitiers required her to perform homage to him for her birthright county of Angoulême, she refused, considering it below her status as the former queen of England. Louis led the French army into Poitou in support of his brother, confronting Henry III's English-Poitevin army, mobilised in support of his mother and her second husband. With Henry came his brother Richard of Cornwall, whom Henry had named count of Poitou in 1238. On 21 July the husbands of Marguerite and Eleanor of Provence fought a full-scale battle outside the castle of Taillebourg, followed by a second battle the following day at Saintes, after which Henry III fled to the coast and took ship for England.

The tangle of the French and English kings being brothers-in-law came about because Henry III had been searching for a wife for many years. Part of the reason was the hostility of Louis VIII of France to the idea of any daughter of his vassals marrying the king of England. Looking further afield various matches were proposed, including a daughter of Leopold of Austria, a daughter of the king of Bohemia and a daughter of the count of Brittany. It was said that he fell in love during 1231 with a sister of the king of Scots, but this alliance was ruled out by his vassals. In 1235 Henry was actually married by proxy to a daughter of the count of Ponthieu, but when Louis IX refused to countenance this, Henry had to get Pope Gregory IX to release him from his marriage vow on grounds of consanguinity. It is worth noting that the Lateran council of 1215 had reduced the degrees of prohibited consanguinity from seven to four.[1] At last, in January 1236 Henry married Eleanor of Provence, a sister of Louis' wife! This was possible, of course, because Provence was then within the German Empire, so there was little that the French king could do about it.

Louis IX used the rebellion as cause to justify a host of administrative changes he planned. His travelling tax inspectors were themselves made subject to inspection, limiting corruption. Gradually, he eroded the power of his barons. Seeing which way the military-political wind was blowing, Hugues de Lusignan acknowledged Louis IX as his feudal overlord and Louis ordered ex-queen Isabella to retire to the abbey of Fontevraud, where she took the veil shortly before dying in June of 1246 at the age of 58 after a life whose highs and lows read like the script of a Hollywood epic. All was not well with Louis after the short campaign in Poitou against Henry III. With what sounds like malaria and recurrent, debilitating high fevers, his health worried his courtiers so much that they forced Marguerite to swear an oath in the abbey church of St-Germain-des-Prés that she would not contest any conditions of Louis' last will and testament, which they might prevail on him to accept. This has been taken by historians as proof that the young queen – she was then only twenty-one or twenty-two – was a power to be reckoned with, whom they had to curb in this way.

Louis recovered but, while severely ill at Pontoise and feeling near death in December 1244, he made a vow that, should he recover, he would answer the call of the new pope Innocent IV, who wanted to mark his papacy with a crusade to liberate the Holy Land from Muslim control. This was to be the Seventh Crusade, out of which Blanche tried hard to talk her son until his sense of a religious mission won out over her sensible advice despite her persuading the bishop of Paris to release him from his crusader's vow. In 1248 the Holy Land erupted again when the sultan of Egypt defied the negotiations that had ended the Sixth Crusade and retook Jerusalem, massacring the Frankish defenders. This was all the justification that Louis needed.

At the time, Europe was far from at peace: Innocent IV and Holy Roman Emperor Friedrich II had continued the papal-imperial struggle in Italy, so Friedrich, although holding the title of 'king of Jerusalem', ignored the call for crusade, and actually sent messengers to warn the sultan of Egypt that the crusaders were coming to attack his country. The commercial republics of Venice and Pisa, having long since concluded that it was better to accept the Muslims as trading partners than to fight them, also tried to sabotage the enterprise, fearing a French crusade might damage their trading rights in the East.[2] King Béla IV in Hungary was struggling to restore his country's infrastructure ruined by the Mongol invasion of 1241; the Latin Kingdom of Constantinople was beset by enemies on all sides; and King Henry III of England had enough troubles of his own, so that ruled out any major other participation in Louis' *iter in Ierusalem* or 'journey to Jerusalem', as the crusade was euphemistically called. In any case, Henry III was hardly going to join any enterprise that included, let alone was promoted by, his wife's brother-in-law in Paris. Also, it has to be stated that, unlike the situation a century earlier, there was no widespread enthusiasm in Europe for another crusade, it being common knowledge by now that the prospect of rich plunder and fiefs to be won there which had attracted so many crusaders in the past was by this time largely illusory. As to saving the site of Christ's crucifixion, the educated but poor contemporary poet Ruteboeuf said it thus:

> One can serve God well without leaving one's own country, by doing harm to no-one. If I go [on crusade] what will become of my wife and my children? Time enough to fight the sultan [of Egypt] when he comes here.[2]

The devout Louis IX was, however, driven by a sense of divine calling that refused to take account of the lack of interest in his project. The only non-French contingent was a small one from England led by Henry II's illegitimate grandson Guillaume Longespée II, 4th earl of Salisbury. Thus, the full financial burden of the crusade would fall on France. Once restored to health, Louis assembled members of his court led by his brothers Robert d'Artois and Alphonse de Poitiers, and charged them to assemble a host of knights and men-at-arms. Meantime, he set about collecting, with the support of the Church, the enormous sum of 1.5 million *livres tournois*[3] by a special tithe of one-tenth of incomes, to which the Church, which collected another one-tenth of personal incomes as *la dime*, promised to add a tenth of its total income in France.

This took three years to raise, and permitted, among other costly preparations, the construction of the fortified port-city of Aigues-Mortes on French territory – now in Provence and far from the sea, but still impressive – where the main body of the crusading fleet was assembled, some other ships also leaving from Marseille, which was not Louis' territory, but lay within the German Empire. Many of his barons and knights had to mortgage their fiefs to raise the money for their expenses, and departed, leaving their lands protected by the Peace of God in the charge of their female relatives, as did Louis, having appointed his mother to act as regent in his absence. By this time, the sultan of Egypt had massacred the inadequate Latin garrisons in the Holy Land, making the Seventh Crusade a matter of urgency in Louis' eyes.

With Louis and his brother Charles d'Anjou aboard the *Montjoie* – a vessel thirty metres long and weighing about 500 tons – Marguerite and her sister-in-law the wife of Robert d'Artois, accompanied by their ladies-in-waiting and domestic servants, left in a fleet of some thirty ships bearing 3,000 knights with their docile palfreys and spirited *destriers* – the valuable warhorses – plus 5,000 crossbowmen and 7,000 sergeants-at-arms, smiths, armourers and other craftsmen necessary to keep an army in the field, plus provisions for all the horses and men. They overwintered on Cyprus – a Latin kingdom since Richard Lionheart conquered it during the Third Crusade – as guests of Henri de Lusignan, titling himself King Henry I of Cyprus, but popularly known as Henri le Gros. Not until 4 June 1249 did Louis' army land near Damietta in the Nile delta, Egypt's great river being at its annual lowest. Louis' twofold intention was to capture several Egyptian cities, which he could trade back to the sultan in exchange for Jerusalem and also to seize as much as possible of Egypt's rich stores of grain, to feed his army in the Holy Land. Two days after his landing, the inhabitants and garrison of Damietta fled, setting fire to the souks with their stocks of valuable spices, but neglecting to destroy a bridge spanning the Nile, which the crusaders used to access the far bank of the river and reach the city walls. On the evening of 6 June, the crusaders occupied the city, Marguerite made herself as comfortable as she could within the walls of Damietta, but rarely dared venture outside. Previous crusaders had taken a vow of celibacy for the duration of their journey, but Louis was plainly enjoying normal conjugal relations – as witness the children born to Marguerite during her time in the East.

When told that an organised brothel for his supposedly celibate soldiers existed in a tent within a stone's throw of his own, Louis said nothing.

Even for those quartered inside Damietta, safety was relative, as disease soon began causing fatalities – in particular the 'gippy tummy' that bedevilled later invaders in the land of the Nile, and could so easily develop into fatal dysentery. Taking heart after the arrival of his brother Alphonse de Poitiers with another fleet carrying reinforcements, Louis ordered the combined army to set out on the 150-mile march south towards Cairo. Left behind in Damietta were the three noblewomen and their attendants, Marguerite being in the final weeks of pregnancy. Whether she had accompanied Louis IX for this once-in-a-lifetime adventure – as Eleanor of Aquitaine had done with Louis VII on the Second Crusade – or because she did not want to be left in France dominated by Queen Blanche as regent without Louis' protection, was never clear. However, before departing from Damietta, Louis placed the city and the fleet moored nearby in the Nile estuary, under her command.[4] This was the only time a woman was given such power throughout the two centuries of the crusades.

En route towards Cairo, Louis' army was trapped by the annual floods of the Nile in August and September, suffering many casualties. Malaria, scurvy, dysentery and typhus also claimed many victims, but a worse disaster was awaiting them at the battle of al-Mansourah, where the Mameluk commander Baibars ordered a town gate to be left open as a trap. Pumping adrenalin, the French knights rushed inside, led by Robert d'Artois, Guillaume Longespée II and 280 Templars, followed by the foot-soldiers, and … found themselves ambushed in the narrow streets. Casualties were high. Among those killed were Louis' brother Robert and Guillaume Longespée, together with most of his English contingent and all the Templars. Louis attempted to make an orderly retreat to the safety of his rear base at Damietta, where Marguerite was about to give birth. Besieged en route within a makeshift camp under constant skirmishing by Egyptian cavalry, the crusaders grew desperate. News of the disaster reached Damietta where, according to the chronicler Jean de Joinville, Marguerite suffered nightmares that she and her baby were being captured by the Muslims, from which she awoke screaming. When a very elderly crusader was stationed in her bedchamber each night with drawn sword, to reassure the pregnant queen, it was said that she begged him to behead her, should the Muslims break in. Courteously, he agreed that he would do that.

Retreating again, down the Nile to Fariskur, Louis' diminished army – now mainly of foot-soldiers – was defeated yet again. He and his brothers Charles and Alphonse were captured and taken back to al-Mansourah, where they were confined in chains, but otherwise well treated with the surviving nobles who had surrendered. However, conditions for the rank-and-file in a tightly guarded camp outside the town were so bad that deaths from disease steadily reduced their numbers. Louis' capture turned out to be good fortune for him when he contracted dysentery and was cured by a Muslim doctor, without whose knowledge of medicine he would probably have died, as did many rank-and-file in the camp. Louis delegated to Marguerite command over the remains of his army from 7 April to 6 May 1250. If those dates are correct, she became 'commander in chief' one day before giving birth to another son, christened Jean Tristan by one of the many bishops in Damietta. More important than the holy water used was the presence as midwife of *magistra Hersend physica* – Doctor Hersend, the wife of the royal apothecary, rewarded by Louis with a lifetime pension of 12d per day for her services at the birth. After returning to France, Hersend and her husband bought a house on the Petit Pont in Paris and, presumably, lived there happily ever after.

Louis and his brothers were ransomed for 800,000 gold *bezants*, half to be paid before he left Egypt, after Marguerite raised the money from the Templars in their secondary capacity of international bankers. She also had to resolve a mutiny by the crews of the Pisan and Genoese ships in the harbour, which she accomplished by bribery and providing food for the starving crews. The chaos in Damietta is hard to reconstruct, but it seems that Marguerite took the infant Prince Jean Tristan on board the king's ship for safety before the city was handed back to the Egyptians, and set sail to leave the shattered dreams and inadequate generalship of the invasion behind her. The half-ransom having been handed over to the Egyptians, on 5 May Louis surrendered Damietta, the only Egyptian city actually conquered for all the lost lives, but the Genoese and Pisan vessels still moored in the port of Damietta were not allowed by the Egyptians to set sail until the ransom money had been weighed and its value calculated. Raising it had been a difficult task undertaken in France by Queen Blanche, threatening barons, the Church and the self-governing towns with dire consequences if they did not contribute.

The ransom was found on being counted to be 30,000 pounds short – the amount Marguerite had been forced to spend, to keep the Italian ships there. The Templars being unwilling to produce any more money, it was left to the Sire de Joinville to break into one of their locked treasure chests to 'borrow' the shortfall, after which Charles d'Anjou was released and Louis consented to the anchors being weighed. Louis and a small contingent then sailed away to Acre in the Holy Land, while most of the surviving crusaders released with him returned straight away home to France, totally disillusioned. Back in Egypt, thousands of other Christian prisoners were summarily executed, sold into slavery, or were freed after converting to Islam.

On the six-day voyage Louis showed a critical change of personality, caused by religious obsession compounded with guilt at the costly failure in money and lives of the whole pointless crusade. Although still weak from the attack of dysentery and hardly able to walk unsupported, but furious that his brother was gambling to pass the time instead of entertaining him, he threw the game board and the dice overboard in a tantrum of righteous indignation.[5] Louis spent the following four years in strengthening crusader castles and cities in the Holy Land and in pointless negotiations for truces with the several Muslim powers surrounding what was left of the Latin kingdom of Jerusalem. Two more pregnancies during this time saw Marguerite give birth to Prince Pierre in June 1251 at the Templar fortress of Château Pèlerin, a few miles south of Haifa, and Princess Blanche – she was given the name of Marguerite's first-born who had died in 1243 – while staying in the fortified city of Jaffa in the south of the Latin Kingdom during 1253. Convinced that he was doing God's will, although there was no longer even a pretence of being able to retake Jerusalem, Louis ignored several written warnings from Queen Blanche in Paris that he should give up the crusade which had proved as pointless as that of his grandfather Philippe Auguste and Richard Lionheart in 1189–92.[6]

To fill her days, Marguerite attended his court when Muslim ambassadors came to negotiate this or that truce, but she could no longer prevail upon Louis, whose overly devout upbringing and recent traumas left him unable to decide between his crusader's oath to liberate Jerusalem and his duty as monarch to return to France and put an end to the unrest caused by his long absence. If he had hopes of reinforcements from Europe, they were in vain. Isolating himself from Marguerite and his closest advisers, he learned in spring 1253 of his mother's death in Maubuisson abbey on 27 November 1252 at the age of 64. Typically, when the Cistercian nuns and monks were hesitating about whether to start the prayers for the dying, Blanche had herself placed on a pallet on the floor in nuns' robes and used her last strength to intone the prayer for the dying herself.[7]

The kingdom now devoid of both king and regent, Louis should have returned to France immediately, but was still in the East seventeen months later. Even the eventual departure nearly turned to tragedy, as it required Marguerite and the young children to be escorted clandestinely from Acre to Tyre in a period when there was no truce with either Damascus or Egypt to guarantee their safety.[8] On 24 April 1254, a mixed flotilla of thirteen galleys and some sailing ships departed from there for Cyprus, where there was a narrow escape from shipwreck in a gale. Louis refused the advice of his crew that he, Marguerite and the children should be put ashore for their safety, arguing with the sailors that, if it were God's will the ship should founder, he would share their fate. Louis left behind in the Holy Land a loyal vassal as seneschal supported by a token force of 100 other knights and 100 sergeants-at-arms, which was hardly going to keep the Muslims at bay.[9] His confusion and anger seems to have made him increasingly difficult even for Marguerite to deal with. At one point she was reduced to begging Joinville to ask a favour of Louis, saying that, if she asked, he would do the opposite of what she wanted. The king, she told Joinville, had become *divers*, meaning perverse, capricious, bad-tempered – unstable is perhaps the best single rendering into English.[10] Certainly his arrival in France six weeks after leaving Cyprus did nothing to improve his mood, for the administration of the country was in a bad state and corruption rampant after a year and a half with no effective ruler.

By mid-September the royal family was back in Paris, where Marguerite gave birth to a daughter who was given her mother's name. During the royal couple's 6-year absence a war had been launched in Aquitaine, where Henry III's seneschal Simon de Montfort had alienated most of the duchy's vassals by his heavy-handed government and provoked a violent uprising, supported by King Alfonso X of Castile in the hope of acquiring the rights he thought his family had been given by Henry II. Henry III held de Montfort responsible, but at the English court, Eleanor of Provence took de Montfort's side, showing little confidence in her husband who, perhaps because he had been manipulated by the regents from the moment he became king at the tender age of 9, had never acquired the firmness necessary to impose his will against resistance. In contrast, during his absence in 1253 she showed toughness and political good sense. Spending most of the funds he had amassed for a crusade, amounting to £27,000, the king led an army to Aquitaine and restored a semblance of order.

Travelling back to England, he was persuaded by Queen Eleanor, who had been in contact with her sister Marguerite, to stop in Paris and meet Louis face-to-face. It was the first time the two sisters had met since their weddings. At the start of the visit, Henry kept his household knights close, as though expecting treachery, which meant that sheer numbers obliged them to be accommodated in the Templars' halls outside the walls of the city because no building inside the walls was large enough. Eventually relaxing, he and Eleanor moved into the palace on the Ile de la Cité, Louis IX and Marguerite courteously moving out for the duration of their stay.

Chapter 17

The Provençal Sorority

This was not the only time that these two Provençal-born queens used their sisterly relationship to bring their husbands closer in the cause of peace. Eleanor had arrived in England in 1236, a girl of twelve married on 14 January 1237 in Canterbury cathedral to the 28-year-old king of England by Archbishop Edmund Rich. Her wedding dress was of shining gold material, tight at the waist and flaring out to wide pleats at her ankles, with long sleeves lined with ermine, the whole setting off, to good affect, her dark-haired Mediterranean beauty, inherited from her mother and grandmother. Riding to London shortly after the wedding in Canterbury, she was crowned queen consort in Westminster Abbey, following which a banquet attended by the great and good welcomed her formally into England.

Having just had to impose a tax of two marks of silver per hide – reckoned as roughly 120 acres – to raise the dowry of 30,000 marks for his sister Isabella on her marriage to German Emperor Friedrich II, King Henry III had wanted a similar dowry from Eleanor's father, who bargained him down to 20,000 marks and eventually only promised to leave her 10,000 marks when he died. Rather typically, Henry gave way, but got a bargain, all the same. He also gave way when asking for financial assistance from his vassals for his own and his sister's weddings. The problem Eleanor of Provence brought him was 170 or so of her Savoyard relatives, some of whom accompanied her to England and others who arrived subsequently. They slowly but surely procured lucrative positions and estates for themselves, earning for the young queen the hostility of the barons and the people of London, who already resented the Poitevin relatives of Henry III, whom he had settled in England. Eleanor's uncle Bishop William of Valence, who had shrewdly arranged this match as well as that of her sister Marguerite and Louis in Paris, became a trusted adviser of Henry III, which pleased the barons not at all. Another Savoyard uncle named Boniface actually became archbishop of Canterbury in 1241. The Savoy Hotel, on London's Strand – originally the beach along the north side of the Thames before the embankments were constructed – still marks the area which became known as Savoy, where Eleanor's relatives made their headquarters between the city and Westminster.

She was a passionate reader who adored Provençal poetry, and was very well-read by the standards of the age, with the intellect to match. On a more frivolous level, she imported expensive cloths to be made up for her, as well as the accessories to complement them, and became a leader of fashion for the noble ladies who could afford fine raiment. None of this endeared her to the citizens of London. On one occasion in the summer of 1263 when she was being rowed past the city, heading down-river in the royal barge, a hail of mud, stones and rotten food hurled at her showed her what they thought of her, forcing the mayor of London to intervene and conduct her to the relative safety of the bishop of London's house. The main cause of the incident was Eleanor's insistence on receiving the queen-geld, which was equal to one tenth of all fines paid to the Crown, and she also levied other taxes whenever she had the opportunity. That she was a tough lady is borne out by Henry III making her his regent at the age of 19 in 1253 when leaving England to re-impose his authority in Poitou. By then she was already known for her hard-headed, no-nonsense attitudes, quite unlike Henry's instinct for compromise.

She bore him five children. Four others have been mentioned in various sources, but may have died as infants and are not verifiable. Her first was Prince Edward, born in 1239, who became the warrior king Edward I after poor health as a child; on one occasion when he was severely ill aged 6 or 7 she insisted on staying with him at the abbey of Beaulieu in Hampshire for three weeks, although this was forbidden by the rules of the community. Three years later, she persuaded Henry III to make him duke of Gascony – hardly a trouble-free appointment. Her second child, born the year after Edward, was Princess Margaret, later betrothed to Alexander III of Scotland. Princess Beatrice came two years later and Edmund, later known as 'Crouchback' in 1245. The nickname did not refer to any deformity, but was seemingly a misconstruction of 'crossback', due to his wearing the crusader cross stitched on the back of his surcoat in the Ninth Crusade, where he fought alongside his brother Edward. The last child of Eleanor and Henry III was a daughter christened Katherine, who was deaf and never learned to speak, but her endearing character so touched her parents that her death at the age of 3 caused them great sadness.

For the next four years intermittent conflict between Henry and the barons failed to resolve the unrest in England. To settle his differences with Louis, Henry was persuaded by Eleanor of Provence to return to Paris at the end of 1259, to sign a peace treaty, under which he accepted the loss of title to the formerly Angevin possessions in the north and west of France in return for Louis confirming his title to Gascony and adjacent territory in the southwest. Many modern French people say, 'The Gascons stayed loyal to England long after the English had been thrown out of the rest of France.' They are amazed to be told that England was governed for centuries by French-speaking kings, from William the Conqueror onwards!

In 1256 Marguerite produced another son, christened Robert after his uncle who had died in Egypt; in 1260 her last child was another girl, the Princess Agnès. Louis, meanwhile, was assuaging his guilt at the failure of the Seventh Crusade by eschewing fine clothes and rich living. He regularly invited poor folk to share his spartan fare at table, insisted on serving them himself, and washed the feet of beggars, sending them away with handouts. Marguerite seems to have compensated for the king looking like a poor merchant by dressing herself sumptuously, to make the point that she was the queen of France. More lastingly, Louis set up hospices for returning crusaders injured in Egypt or the Holy Land. These included in Paris the Hôpital des Quinze-Vingts for those blinded on his crusade and other poor blind people. The curious name of the institution – hospital of the fifteen-twenties – recalls the medieval French custom of counting in twenties, still evident for example in the modern French words for 70 and 80, which are *soixante-dix* or sixty-ten and *quatre-vingts* or four-twenties.

The name effectively meant a hospital for 300 blind patients.[1] Seeking to explain the costly failure of his crusade to Egypt, Louis convinced himself that it was God's punishment for the lack of faith and the immorality of his subjects, to correct which he set about creating what he saw as a more god-fearing society, where blasphemy was a criminal offence, as was gambling, the lending of money at interest, and prostitution. To force the Jews in his kingdom to convert to Christianity, he ordered their religious books to be burned and, in 1269, the wearing of a yellow badge to distinguish them from Christians. Pope Innocent III had relaxed this rule for Jews while travelling because it made them the target of hostile treatment, but here – six and a half centuries before Nazi Germany – was the Christian king of France re-imposing it, on the advice of an embittered apostate Jew turned Dominican monk, who had taken the name Paul Chrétien.

In 1270, Louis IX set off to Tunis on the Eighth Crusade, ignoring the trust he had placed in Queen Marguerite at Damietta, and which she had so faithfully discharged, by appointing, not her but two members of his *curia* to rule as regents during his absence. As to, why Tunis? It seems that his brother Charles d'Anjou, who had become King of Sicily, convinced him that the emir of the city was prepared to convert to Christianity, but needed an excuse of *force majeure* to do so. Or possibly it was a desperate attempt to conclude a seemingly victorious crusade against a Muslim power, cost what it may. Left behind in France this time, Marguerite could only wait and pray. The first good news to reach her was that the city of Carthage had been taken by the French force; the first bad news was that her son Jean Tristan, the prince born in Damietta, had died aboard one of the ships from dysentery. Four days later, news reached her that, after a reign of forty-three years, Louis himself had succumbed to the plague on 25 August 1270 – although the cause of death could have been any of a dozen other diseases rampant in the siege camp outside the walls of Tunis and inside them.

Intent on saving his nephew Philippe from the same fate as his father and brother, Charles d'Anjou disengaged what remained of the crusading force and returned to France with him. The corpse of Louis IX, minus its entrails and packed in salt to delay putrefaction,[2] was transported back to France and buried with great ceremony in the presence of Marguerite at the royal cathedral of St-Denis, where she was to bury also her son, crowned as Philippe III, fifteen years later. Queen Marguerite's retirement from the world to the convent she had founded for the Cordelières de Sainte-Claire, or Poor Claires, at St Marcel outside Paris, where she was joined by her daughter Blanche, born in far-distant Jaffa during Louis

IX's first crusade, lasted for twenty-five years after Louis' death, but she was not idle there. Her insistence on the importance of Louis IX's life resulted in Jean de Joinville writing a biography entitled simply *La Vie de Saint Louis*, which, because he knew the king personally, brings Louis to life in a way that the chroniclers' customary summaries of kingly deeds never do.

Of the four daughters of Count Ramón Berenguer and Béatrice of Savoy, only she and Queen Eleanor, the widow of England's Henry III, were left. Attempting to resolve the troubled succession to the county of Provence – mainly over large debts outstanding – Marguerite solicited the support of her sister Eleanor's son King Edward I in London. After six years, Marguerite's persistence paid off when Pope Martin IV untied the Gordian knot by mediating between the various interested parties.

Apart from good works like making charitable donations, much of Marguerite's energy in her last years went into trying to persuade nine successive popes to canonise Louis for leading his two abortive crusades. These efforts were finally crowned with success in 1297, two years after her death at the age of 75. Marguerite had been the queen and later the dowager queen of France for thirty-six years, two months and twenty-nine days. Her tomb at St Denis was inscribed simply *Ici gît la noble reyne de France Marguerite, qui fut femme à monseigneur saint Loys, jadis roi de France, qui trépassa le mercredi devant Noël, l'an de l'Incarnation de Notre-Seigneur MCCXCV. Priez pour elle.* Here lies the noble queen of France Marguerite, who was the wife of Saint Louis, formerly king of France, and who died on the Wednesday before Christmas in the year of Our Lord 1295. Pray for her.

It would be nice to report that Queen Marguerite was kinder to King Philippe's young consort Isabelle d'Aragon than Queen Blanche had been to her. Alas, she behaved in exactly the same possessive and dominating manner.

The third of the Provençal sisters, Sancha, was born in 1225 or 1228. Her betrothal to Count Ramón VII of Toulouse was banned by Pope Celestine V on the grounds of consanguinity, enabling her sister Eleanor, already firmly ensconced in London and well able to manipulate her husband Henry III, to arrange Sancha's marriage to her brother-in-law Richard of Cornwall in 1243. When he became King of the Romans, i.e.

of Germany, in May 1257, although he only visited Germany four times, Sancha took the title of queen of the Romans, but was never crowned as such. It was nevertheless a giant step up for the youngest daughter of a count, who bore her royal husband three sons in addition to his four children by his first wife, Isabel Marshal.

The youngest Provençal sister, Béatrice, was born in 1234. On the death of Count Ramón Berenguer IV in August 1245, although only fourteen she was declared heiress to the counties of Provence and Fourcalquier, but her uncle Philippe of Savoy, who was archbishop of Lyons, negotiated her marriage to Louis IX's 20-year-old brother Charles. The wedding took place on 31 January 1246 at Aix-en-Provence, making Charles the new count of Provence. Knighted in May of that year, three months later he was given two other counties by Louis and was thereafter known as Charles d'Anjou, also as king of Sicily and Naples.

Count Ramón IV died in August 1245 with two daughters – the sisters-in-law Marguerite and Eleanor – already crowned queens. His wife, Countess Béatrice lived on for twenty-two more years, by which time her other two daughters – Sancha and Béatrice – were also titular queens. Even by the standards of medieval royal marriages, it was an amazing family.

Chapter 18

The Scottish Play

O f average height for the time, although short by modern standards, King John was rather plump and had dark reddish hair. His pleasures included the hunt and gambling, particularly at backgammon – like chess, a game brought back from the East by the crusaders. Literate in Latin and French, he was an avid reader, who had a mobile library constructed, so that he could take his reading matter with him on his travels. Opinions differ as to whether he was, or was not, an able military commander. If he was, the succession of defeats in the continental domains may be due to his unfortunate habit of alienating many of the vassals who might otherwise have supported him in the field. One of the ways in which he did this was by bedding their wives and daughters when the menfolk were not at home.

John's three legitimate daughters were Joan, born in 1210, who was married to Alexander II of Scotland at the age of 11 in 1221, and died on 4 March 1238; Isabella, born in 1214, married in 1235 to Emperor Friedrich II of the Holy Roman Empire, by whom she had four children before dying six years later; and Eleanor, born in 1215, who married William II Marshal in 1224. This was not, of course the William Marshal who had served Henry II, Richard and John, but his son. When they married she was only 9 years old and bore him no children before he died in April 1231. Whatever the reasons for the lack of children, her second marriage in 1238 to Simon V de Montfort produced seven children. She eventually died in April 1275 at the ripe old age for the time of sixty.

King John's first legitimate daughter Princess Joan – not to be confused with her illegitimate half-sister – was born on 22 July 1210, the third child of Queen Isabella. In 1214, the infant girl was betrothed to Hugues X de Lusignan, Count of La Marche with the city of Saintes, the county of Saintonge and the Ile d'Oléron as her dowry, in a very belated way to compensate the Lusignan family for King John stealing

Isabella of Angoulême away from Hugues X's father. The poor child was to be brought up in Hugues X's household until she became of age, but Hugues was an impetuous fellow, like most of the barons of Aquitaine, and attempted to claim her dowry long before her puberty and the commencement of conjugal relations entitled him to do so. On 14 May 1220, when she was not yet 10 years old, the arrangement was terminated by the intervention of Pope Honorius III, permitting Joan's mother Isabella d'Angoulême to marry Hugues X and Joan to be sent back to England.

What she made of this change in her destiny, is anyone's guess. Like all medieval princesses, she knew she was a pawn in the royal chess game, and this pawn was brought back into play two years later. In 1214 King John had knighted the son of Scottish King William I, Prince Alasdair mac Uillem at Clerkenwell Priory just a few months before Alasdair succeeded his father and became King Alexander II of Scotland at the end of that year. Once crowned by tradition at the village of Scone, across the River Tay from Perth, Alexander's knowledge of the dissatisfaction of the English barons incited him to join their rebellion, and swear fealty to Louis of France, earning himself excommunication by renouncing his allegiance to King John. After the treaty ending Louis' bid for the English throne on 12 September 1217, John's son Henry III offered Alexander the hand of his sister Joan.

Two years after her return to England, Joan was nearly eleven and Alexander twenty-three on the day of their marriage in York Minster on 25 June 1221, with Archbishop Walter de Grey – successor to Geoffrey the Bastard – officiating. Archbishop de Grey did more than just conduct the wedding service: he made it possible by lifting Alexander's excommunication for that oath of fealty to Prince Louis during the barons' revolt. The two kings at the wedding in the Minster had convened in York the previous year to iron out that problem and agree the dowry and other details. Gifting her with dower lands of Kinghorn, Hassendean, Crail and Jesmond, the Scottish king gained not just an under-age English wife, but also Joan's dowry of Northumberland, always coveted by the Scottish rulers as a buffer zone to keep the English at bay.

How Joan might have served as a go-between for Alexander and her brother will never be known because the Scottish court was totally dominated by his mother, the formidable dowager Queen Ermengarde de Beaumont, widow of Alexander's father, William the Lion. Only Joan's connection to the English court kept her mother-in-law in check once it became apparent that this new wife was unlikely to bear Alexander any children. The depth of Joan's frustration in Scotland may be gauged by the fact that in September 1236 and again in September 1237, when she accompanied Alexander to meetings with Henry III in England, which had been called to smooth out territorial disputes, she let it be clearly understood by her brother that she was desperate to escape Ermengarde's tyranny and return to live south of the border. With a rare sympathy for her position, Henry III granted his sister manors in Driffield, Yorkshire and Fen Stanton in Huntingdonshire to provide her with homes and an income. Once established in England, Joan befriended her sister-in-law Eleanor of Provence, and the two queens planned a holiday together in the form of a pilgrimage to Becket's shrine in Canterbury. Joan died the following year at the age of 28, enabling 40-year-old Alexander II, desperate to have an heir, to marry again. His choice naturally fell on a bride of childbearing age, the 21-year-old Marie de Coucy from Picardy in Northern France.

The loss of Normandy and the other continental possessions during his father's reign gave Henry III more time and money to concentrate on problems with the Welsh and Scots. His second child with Eleanor of Provence was born in Windsor Palace on 29 September 1240 and christened Margaret. When three years old she was placed on the marriage market when her father met Alexander II of Scotland in Newcastle during 1244 to repair relations between their two countries. As part of the negotiations Princess Margaret was betrothed to Alexander II's 2-year-old son by Marie de Coucy, who was named Alasdair mac Alasdair, but referred to in England as Alexander. Seven years later, on 25 December 1251 Margaret was married in York Minster by Archbishop Walter de Gray to the under-age king of Scotland Alexander III, his father having died on 8 July 1249, whereupon the boy became king at the age of 7. Medieval wedding feasts being conspicuous consumption carried to excess, it is useful that the library of York Minster has conserved a record of the preparations for this wedding.[1]

Henry III adored ceremonial and did not stint his daughter's nuptial ceremony. Already in July the king's steward commanded the wardens of the fairs at York, Pontefract and St Oswald to give every assistance to king's sergeant Richard de Shireburn, who was coming to purchase beasts for slaughter. In November the same officer was purchasing animals at Lincoln, Wakefield and Bradford. Commands issued to Geoffrey de Langley from 5 August onwards covered the important hunting of deer for venison: 100 *damos* or buck fallow deer were to be taken by him in the forest of Galtres, to the north of York, with local owners of deerhounds ordered to make these available to him in this operation. Another 100 *damos* were to be taken in forests south of the Trent. This order was only placed so early because the season for hunting male deer expired in mid-September. Once killed and butchered, the venison had, of course, to be salted for preservation. Nor were other deer spared, thirty to be taken in Sherwood forest for the court to consume at Nottingham on the journey north and, in late November, when the females could be hunted, de Langley was commanded to hunt down a significant number of hinds and boars in several forests, the butchered and salted carcases to be delivered to an upwardly mobile courtier in York named Sir Stephen de Bauzan. Even this was not judged sufficient when Henry III arrived in York, a week prior to the feast, with a bodyguard of thirty-eight *servientes regis ad armas* or men-at-arms, and commanded more venison and live he-goats for master Richard, the king's cook.

Also in August, wine was being procured in quantity. Roger Dacre, Henry III's wine buyer bought 132 *dolia* or tuns, each containing 252 gallons, from eleven different merchants at a total cost of £221 8s 8d, which he was required to deliver to the sheriff of York in October. Such was the state of the roads that merchandise of this weight had to be transported north by ship, each vessel carrying a maximum of sixty *dolia*. In October the sheriff was informed that the king would be sleeping on a specially made state bed *in camera archiepiscopi* – in the archbishop's bedroom of his palace adjacent to the Minster. There, a doorway was to be made between this room and the queen's bedroom, a room twenty feet long *cum fovea profunda* – with a deep privy. A similar bed was to be made for the young Scottish king and another for his bride. A constant stream of *nuncii* – royal messengers – must have been riding between the court and York and other destinations.

One week later, the sheriffs of York, Lincoln, Northumberland, Lancaster and Cumberland and the mayors and bailiffs of York and Lincoln were commanded between them to ensure a sufficiency of other meat and game for the tables. This amounted to the incredible quantity of 7,000 hens, 2,100 partridges, 125 swans, 115 cranes, 120 peacocks, 290 pheasants, 400 rabbits, 1,300 hares, 400 (apparently domestic) pigs and seventy boars. Fifty salmon from Cumberland and thirty from Newcastle were to be converted into fish paste. The sheriff of York was commanded to have constructed and held ready for the king's arrival *duas longas carettas cum toto atillio et harnasio* – two long carts complete with harness and fittings.

The only way the wedding guests could see what they were eating was by candle power. So, 3,000 pounds of wax was purchased in London, to make the necessary candles. Purchases of fine cloth from Italian merchants, to make festive garments for the king and family, totalled £328. The vestments and ritual plate for Margaret's private chapel in Scotland cost £87 13s 7d. Two expensive saddles, on which she could arrive in Edinburgh, were ordered for Margaret, one *cum sambuco de serico* – covered in silk. On 6 November the warden of Galtres forest was ordered to allow the considerable quantity of wood and charcoal necessary for the numerous cooking fires to be collected there and transported to York. The king's miller travelled to the city, where the bailiffs were to assist him in procuring sufficient corn for all the bread the guests would consume and the bailiffs of nine Yorshire towns were ordered to ensure the availablity on the day of 68,508 loaves at four loaves to the penny, costing a total of £71 13s 4d.

In addition to Alexander III, to be knighted on Christmas Day, several other dubbings were to take place, all the new knights so honoured to be given robes and tabards, or sleeveless tunics, made from costly material. Alexander was to be presented with a fine sword and silk-covered scabbard, which Henry III would buckle onto his young son-in-law at the ceremonial dubbing.

The Jews of York – sadly more famous for the massacre of the community they had suffered after taking refuge in the king's castle during 1190 – were not forgotten but taxed at the end of November to raise the sum of £100 for that busy man Sir Stephen de Bauzan to pay for provisions bought locally and the venison that was beginning to arrive in the city. He also had to supervise the construction of *unum furnum ad pastillos faciendos* – an oven for baking pastries, and another for cooking sauces. Why was a knight charged with this seemingly menial task? King Henry's personal cook, known as master Richard, did not arrive in York with a large team of underlings until near the end of the month. The keeper of the king's wines was commanded to release two *dolia* of the best red wine and one of good white wine to one Roberto de Monte Pessolano, a specialist in concocting spiced wines, one of which, *vina gariofilata* was mulled wine flavoured with cloves.[2]

Early in December the king's fisherman known as Guillelmus *pescator* arrived in York to catch fish in 'the king's pond on the Foss' – a small lake that had been made by damming the river Foss as part of the city's defences – and construct a stewpond, where the fish could be kept alive until the feast day. More salmon were ordered from Newcastle and Scarborough, as well as 10,000 haddocks, 500 conger eels and other fish. The frantic activity necessitated by all this late ordering hints at the guest list being even larger than had been initially calculated. To modern eyes, a significant omission in the long list of provisions for the wedding feast is cheese. Made in peasant homes, as it had been for hundreds of years from cow, sheep and goat milk, it was regarded as food fit for peasants, but not for the noble table, where some diners believed it to be harmful for their health. Most cheese that graced their tables was cooked in the form of tarts, although Henry III's son Prince Edward was once sent in person to Paris to buy 100 Brie cheeses at a cost of 35 shillings.[3]

Marine mammals were also missing from this menu, although whales and porpoises were prized and eaten as fish on Fridays and during Lent. Oysters and other shellfish were also a regular part of the diet, as they had been from Roman times. Although salads were common across the Channel, few uncooked vegetables were to be found on English tables. Henry III was partial to nuts, though, and commanded the sheriffs of London to purchase 2,000 chestnuts in autumn 1256.[4] To end a meal, indigenous and imported fruit, fresh or crystalised, were used to tempt the sated palate, the sugar coming from Italy, as did most rice, although the Moors also cultivated it in the Iberian peninsula. The spices so generously used in medieval cooking – often to disguise the taste of meat that was not fresh – came from much farther east, transiting into Europe via Alexandria, and had been introduced into England by returning crusaders.[5] Cornering the English spice market enriched several prosperous merchants in London, causing Henry III to undercut them by commanding the sheriffs at Sandwich to impound two large ships inbound from Bayonne bearing spices and other precious goods from the East until his agents first bought what he wanted direct from the ships' captains.[6]

Since accommodation at the time of the marriage was limited within the walls of York, it is not surprising that there were reports of nobles' servants coming to blows in securing their masters' accommodation, the damage they caused leading to pleas for compensation by the king after the celebrations. The warden of Galtres forest was informed on 15 December that the king wished 10-year-old Alexander III to be permitted to hunt there and take away all the game his party killed. Nor were the noble dead forgotten: Henry III commanded expensive gold and other offerings to be donated by him during the Christmas vigil at the shrine of St William, a Norman archbishop of York canonised in 1227. For distribution to the poor of the city, Henry's almoner Roger was supplied with 500 ells (about 625 yards) of cloth and 180 pairs of shoes, to be given them as charity. The list was long, in keeping with the feudal entitlement of the king to an *auxilium* or special tax for the wedding of the future queen of Scotland.

After the dubbings on Christmas Day and the wedding on 26 December, Henry III attempted to make Alexander III do homage for Scotland, but did not succeed. On the Twelfth Day of Christmas the party broke up after many presents had been exchanged and local purchases paid for. Alexander III headed north to Newcastle, his entourage expanded by Margaret's household. Henry III headed south via Pontefract and Doncaster, his household servants now frantically organising supplies of wine from York to stopping-places en route to Woodstock by 5 February, Windsor by 10 February and Westminster by 17 February, where another great festivity was to be prepared for Easter.

North of the border, all was not well. With an under-age king, Scotland at the time was ruled by a council of regency riven by a power struggle between the justiciar Alan Durward and Walter Comyn, the arrogant Earl of Menteith. Young Queen Margaret was not happy in Scotland and complained by letter to her family in England that she was not well treated by the Scottish regents. The language of the court was French, but she was very lonely and failed to comprehend why her husband – the only young person she knew in the whole country – was not allowed to live near her or even to see her frequently. She also disliked Edinburgh, its climate and the castle-palace perched on its volcanic outcrop, exposed to the wind and rain sweeping in from the North Sea. When Eleanor of Provence begged for her to be allowed a visit home, the request was rejected by the council of regency on the grounds that Alexander III's young queen might very well never return.

After Margaret had lived through four unhappy years, Eleanor of Provence sent her personal physician to check up on her daughter's health. On his return, he described her as looking pale and suffering depression. So Henry III sent an embassy to Edinburgh to enlist the support of some of the nobility in Margaret's cause. The diplomatic initiative in 1255 succeeded in gaining permission for the 14-year-old Alexander and 15-year-old Margaret to cohabit and be allowed to consummate their marriage, the members of the regency council being aware then that they would have to cede power to Alexander in seven years' time. Together the young couple travelled into Northumberland in September 1255 to meet Henry III and Eleanor of Provence. Two years later, when her brother Edward paid a visit to his sister and brother-in-law, life for Margaret was at last more normal after the awful early years in Scotland, but in 1257 Alexander and Margaret were taken prisoner and briefly held by the Comyn clan in a bid to overturn the regency council. They were eventually released after the intervention of her father and the regency council. Perhaps this is the reason why she went to England in 1260, to give birth to a daughter christened Margaret in Windsor castle in February 1261. She also bore Alexander III two more children: Alexander, born in January 1264; and David, born in March 1272.

When Alexander III came of age in 1262, he announced his intention to continue the work of his father in driving the Norwegian settlers out of Western Scotland and the Western Isles, long since colonised by raiders, traders and slavers from Scandinavia, especially Norway. After a truce of fourteen years since the death of his father, Alexander III gave King Haakon notice that he would buy the occupied Scottish islands or take them by force. Haakon objected and led a powerful fleet round the north of Scotland in the following year. Halting at the island of Arran, he began negotiations with Alexander, who prevaricated until the autumn gales drove some of the Norwegian ships ashore, leading to the indecisive Battle of Largs. After it, Haakon retreated to Orkney for the winter, but died there, after which Alexander was able to conclude a treaty with his successor Magnus VI, in which he gained the Western Isles and the Isle of Man, leaving only Orkney and Shetland to Norway.

In August 1274 Alexander III and Margaret travelled all the way south to Westminster abbey – where Henry III had been buried the previous November – for the coronation of Margaret's brother as King Edward I. Six months later, Alexander was a widower, Queen Margaret having died on 26 February 1275 at Cupar Castle, being buried in Dunfermline Abbey. Within eight years all three of her children were to die: 8-year-old David died at Stirling Castle at the end of June 1281, Margaret died in childbirth on 9th April 1283 and Alexander died at Lindores Abbey in January 1284, sometime around his 20th birthday. With all three of his legitimate children dead, Alexander decided to marry again in the hope of producing an heir. One year after the death of Prince Alexander, he despatched an embassy to France, which arranged the arrival in Scotland that summer of Yolande de Dreux, a member of a cadet branch of the French royal family. Alexander and Yolande were married at Jedburgh Abbey in Roxburghshire on 14 October 1285 before a large congregation of Scottish and French nobles. She was about 22 years of age, exactly half the age of her husband, and was to be Scotland's queen consort for only four and a half months.

Tragedy struck on 19 March 1286. After Alexander had spent the day attending a council meeting in Edinburgh, he set off on horseback to join Yolande at Kinghorn Castle in Fife. He had recently learned that she was pregnant and hoped the child would prove to be a son and heir. On crossing the Firth of Forth by ferry, the ferryman warning him that a storm was approaching. A few miles further on at Inverkeithing, with the daylight going, the bailie repeated the warning and suggested Alexander stay the night there and continue his journey after daybreak. Alexander shrugged off the advice and rode on with a small escort and a couple of local guides, with whom he lost contact in the darkness and foul weather. The next morning. his body was found on the foreshore of Pettycur, just a mile from his destination, presumably because his horse had stumbled in the darkness, throwing the king over a low cliff and breaking his neck.[7] On hearing the news, Yolande de Dreux miscarried.

Alexander's daughter Margaret had been married at the age of 20 to King Magnus VI's 15-year-old second son Eric Magnusson in 1281, to cement the alliance between the Norway and Scotland. Sadly, she died in childbirth two years later, leaving her husband a widower with a daughter named Margaret, who became heiress in 1284 to the throne of Scotland, being known as the Maid of Norway. Travelling across the North Sea at the age of 7 to claim her realm, this girl's fragile health gave way on board ship and she died on 26 September off Orkney, extinguishing that bloodline. The vessel returned to Bergen, where she was buried.

Chapter 19

An Imprisoned Empress and a Girl Called Gwenllian

Princess Isabella was the second daughter of King John and Isabella d'Angoulême. Her unfortunate marriage to Emperor Friedrich II of the Holy Roman Empire is thought to have been the result of an informal meeting between Friedrich and Pope Gregory IX, who argued that Emperor Friedrich, several times excommunicated, could save his soul by creating an English-German alliance to contain French expansionism and be a stabilising influence throughout Europe. This would increase the likelihood that thousands of the continent's knights and barons would feel it safe to answer a call for yet another crusade. The key to turn this complicated lock was 21-year-old Princess Isabella, who was formally betrothed to the 40-year-old twice-widowed Friedrich in London in February 1235, her brother Henry III agreeing to a dowry of 30,000 marks, which Friedrich stashed in his war-chest, being in a state of constant conflict in Italy. To raise this sum, Henry had to impose on his vassals another *auxilium* of two silver marks per hide.

Legend has it that, on her way to the wedding in July 1235 at Worms cathedral, Isabella unveiled her face and hair so that the townspeople of the cities she passed through could appreciate the beauty shortly to be enjoyed by their emperor. Unfortunately, Friedrich was not so impressed. In the cathedral, Isabella was crowned as Empress of the Holy Roman Empire, Queen of Germany and Queen of Sicily. The symbolic grandeur did not last long. After the July wedding, Friedrich conferred on his bride as her dower land the castle of Monte Sant'Angelo. This may have sounded to Isabella like a palace of her own but was a bleak and forbidding fortress in southern Italy. Her only loyal servants were two personal maids, who had accompanied her from England. All other members of her household were sent back home by Friedrich. Rather like William II, husband of Isabella's aunt Joanna in Sicily, Friedrich kept a harem of beautiful Muslim girls guarded by black eunuchs for his exclusive pleasure, but paid regular visits to Isabella in Noventa Padovana, now a suburb of Padua most noted for its Ikea store. There, she was kept in seclusion so complete that when her brother Richard of Cornwall paid a visit on his way back from crusade, she was not allowed to participate in the public ceremony of welcome.

There is doubt even about the number of children she produced for the Emperor. They seem to have been four in number, although some sources say five. Born in the year after the wedding, her first son named Jordanus was baptised with water brought back by crusaders from the river Jordan. Probably polluted, it did him little good, for he died shortly afterward. So did her next child, a daughter christened Agnes, born the following year. Also in 1237 Isabella produced a daughter named Marguerite, followed by a son in 1238, known as Heinrich. Survived by Marguerite and Heinrich, Isabella died aged 24, apparently in childbirth, and was buried in the cathedral of Andria, not far from Castello Sant'Angelo. Her grave in the cathedral was next to that of one of Friedrich's previous wives, Isabella of Jerusalem.

The last child of King John and Isabella of Angoulême was Princess Eleanor, known in her lifetime as Eleanor of Leicester. Her misfortunes began early. London being occupied at the time by the rebel barons and French forces under Prince Louis, her birth took place in Gloucester during 1215. It is probable that Isabella d'Angoulême's last child by John never met her father, since he died at Newark in October of the following year.

As she grew up, the most powerful man in England was William the Marshal, who had faithfully served Eleanor of Aquitaine, Henry II, Richard and John. So it was seen as an honour for Eleanor of Leicester that, before he died in 1219, she was betrothed to his eponymous son with a dowry of ten manors and an income of £200 per annum. They were married at the New Temple church in London on 23 April 1224, when she was nine and he thirty-four. Seven years later, she was a widow. Whether she had ever shared his bed, is unknown, but there was no issue. Under the law, she was entitled to one-third of the shared estates, but was still too young and inexperienced to prevent her brother-in-law Richard Marshal seizing the estate, allegedly to pay off the debts of her late husband. Whether he ever compensated her, is unknown. After forming an alliance with Llywelyn Fawr, he travelled on to Ireland, where his father had held land, and died of wounds received at the Battle of the Curragh.

After trying for several years to obtain justice, Eleanor swore an oath of chastity before Archbishop Edmund Rich of Canterbury.[8] This presumes that she was a virgin, but may have been a clever way of preventing her brother the king marrying her off again as one of his wards. After seven years of chaste life, at the age of twenty-three she met Simon de Montfort, 6th earl of Leicester, who married her in a private ceremony on 6 January 1238 in the royal chapel of Westminster Palace, the king himself giving away the bride. As so often in his reign, Henry III accepted the *fait accompli*,[9] and used the excuse that de Montfort had seduced Eleanor to account for his reluctant approval of the marriage, thus avoiding the scandal of having a pregnant unmarried sister. De Montfort having been in England only a few months, the marriage added fuel to the fire of hostility to 'foreigners' taking liberties. There remained the awkward business of annulling the oath of chastity, which obliged her husband to travel all the way to Rome, where Pope Gregory IX consented to do that, disregarding the disapproval of most English ecclesiastics. Matthew Paris acidly observed in the third person as 'the monk of St Albans' , 'The *curia* of Rome reasoned more subtly than it is given to us to comprehend.'[10] This seems to be an oblique reference to the considerable funds de Montfort had collected before his departure.

Given the circumstances, Eleanor's second marriage seems to have been a genuine love-match, which produced seven children, six of whom survived to adulthood. These years of apparent wellbeing came at a price. Her husband was playing for high stakes in the second barons' war, leading a faction that proposed creating a parliament elected by citizens in the independent towns. This progressive step alienated many of his allied barons, who changed sides in the hope of retaining all their privileges. At the Battle of Evesham on 4 August 1265 Eleanor's 27-year-old son Henry was killed near the body of his father, which was terribly mutilated for the crime of being before his time. Eleanor fled to Central France and sought asylum in the convent of Montargis Abbey, where a sister-in-law was abbess, and died there in 1275. Meantime, Henry III and his successor

Edward I seemingly forgave Eleanor for marrying without royal approval and permitted her representatives in England to claim for the restitution of her inheritance and to enact the provisions of her will.

But tragedy still stalked this bloodline. Shortly before his death at Evesham, Simon de Montfort had signed the Treaty of Pipton recognising his Welsh ally Llywelyn ap Gruffudd as the paramount prince of Wales, the title of Tywysog Cymru – *princeps wallie* in Latin – being formally conferred on him. For this, the widowed Llywelyn paid over a consideration of 30,000 marks and was betrothed to de Montfort's daughter, named Eleanor like her mother. She was at the time 6 years old, being born in 1258. Fleeing with her mother to France after Evesham, the girl was married to Llywelyn by proxy – *per verba de presenti* – in 1275 and set sail for Wales with her brother Amaury in two vessels, to avoid travelling through England. Intercepted by privateers or pirates from Bristol, who were afterwards well rewarded by Edward I, Llywelyn's betrothed was incarcerated in Windsor castle for three long years, during which Llywelyn was branded a rebel for refusing to perform homage to the English king. Negotiations through intermediaries that included two of the five popes elected during this time ended when Llywelyn was forced to sign the Treaty of Aberconwy with Edward I, his support from the other Welsh princes having radically weakened. With Eleanor then aged 19 or 20, Edward I paid for the formal wedding in Worcester cathedral, where he gave the bride away and also paid for the wedding feast. Eleanor thereafter styled herself *principessa wallie, domina snaudonie* – princess of Wales and lady of Snowdon.

In his new role as husband of the English king's cousin, Llywelyn set to work using this new status to re-impose his authority over the other princes and Eleanor stepped into the role of diplomatic negotiator with Edward. Shortly after the wedding, she petitioned him to pardon ten men of her household still kept in his prisons. Some months later she called herself *devota alienora principessa wallie*, asking Edward to show clemency to her brother Amaury, taken with her at sea and held at first in Corfe castle and later Sherborne castle. He had been a canon and treasurer of York Minster before fleeing to France in 1265. His sister's petition was backed by the pope and Archbishop John Pecham on the grounds that Amaury was currently a papal chaplain. Edward I acceded to the request, allowing Amaury to return to France in April 1282 after swearing an oath never to return to England, unless summoned by the king. He was never to see his sister again, for she died giving birth to her only child, a daughter christened Gwenllian, on 19 June 1282 in the royal palace at Abergwyngregyn.

It was indeed *annus horribilis* for Llywelyn, Eleanor and their daughter. Six months later, during King Edward I's brutal and bloody conquest of Wales, on 11 December 1282 Gwenllian's father Llywelyn was killed in battle after treacherously being separated from his followers. His brother assumed the guardianship of his infant niece, but was in turn betrayed, wounded and captured by the English with his family six months later. He was taken to Shrewsbury and executed. Gwenllian and the daughters of her uncle were all confined for life in remote priories in Lincolnshire.

Edward I took no chances with his infant second cousin Gwenllian ferch Llywelyn , who was both descended from the royal family of Aberffraw and, like himself, a great-grandchild of King John. To ensure she could never marry and have sons who might claim the principality of the no longer independent country of Wales, he had her confined in the Gilbertine priory at Sempringham. Why there? Gilbert of Sempringham, the crippled son of a Norman lord whose disability prevented him being raised as a warrior, travelled to study in the schools at Paris.[11] On his return, he founded in about 1131 the only English order of monks and nuns, of which the priory at Sempringham was the mother house, ruling over twenty-three others of the order, some for both sexes and others just for males. At Sempringham, nuns following the Cistercian rule and canons regular following the Augustinian rule coexisted but never saw each other.

Gilbert was reputed never to have touched a female person in his life, but was a charismatic preacher, who incited his first female followers from the local population to shut themselves away from the sinful of the world. When men also joined the community, male and female quarters were segregated. In the church for Mass, the women were separated from the men by a central wall running the length of the building. Outside the church, the female members of the community lived behind high walls, never to be seen again by outsiders and themselves never again to set eyes on the world. Each day, the food, clothing and other goods necessary for the nuns were passed by local women through a hatch in the outer wall with a shutter at both ends. When the outside shutter was closed, a lay sister opened the inner one and removed the goods, so no one could look either in or out at any time. Lay brothers and lay sisters recruited from the local peasantry acted as unpaid servants and the strictness of Gilbert's rule inflicted on a parishioner who cheated on the one-tenth tithe due to the Church – the Council of Westminster of 1175 listed as tithable all produce from grain, wine, fruit, new-born livestock, cheese, wool, lambs and more – the pain of seeing his year's production burned in the village street.[12] Not surprisingly, in the 1160s the lay brothers rebelled, complaining that they were overworked and underfed and, more seriously, that the presence of enclosed men and women in the same community provoked 'moral lapses'. After five bishops and Henry II wrote to Pope Alexander III, the order was cleared of these charges. Within ten years of Gilbert's death in 1189, he was canonised, but his foundation was not a happy place for adults, and a miserable one for a child.[13]

For fifty-three years, Gwenllian languished in Gilbert's priory 'at the pleasure' of Edward I, Edward II and Edward III. Never learning Welsh, she had no idea how to pronounce or spell her own name. Did she ever learn that her second cousin Eleanor of Brittany was kept locked up by the king in rather more luxurious conditions, but still confined for many of the same years? Having known no other life, Gwenllian died at Sempringham priory in June 1337, a few days before what would have been her fifty-fifth birthday.

After causing the death of all the Welsh lords who might reasonably have succeeded her father as Prince of Wales, Edward I conferred the title on his eponymous son, who became its first non-Welsh-speaking holder. From him it passed through the centuries all the way to Charles, son of Queen Elizabeth II.

Chapter 20

Enduring Love: Eleanor of Castile

After all the accounts of young girls sent into foreign lands to bear children to much older husbands, suffering bullying mothers-in-law and imprisonment, at last a love story!

Among the best-known monarchs of medieval England, Edward I is remembered today for the seven magnificent castles he built at Caernarfon, Flint, Rhuddlan, Conway, Criccieth, Aberystwyth and Cardigan to mark and confirm his conquest of Wales. It was said that every stone in these fortresses was the grave stone of a Welshman killed by Edward's troops. In contrast with his military career of violence and bloodshed, his married life was exceptionally affectionate after marrying a daughter of King Fernando III of Castile at the abbey of Las Huelgas outside Burgos in 1254. By then Fernando was dead, but the prior arrangements were honoured and executed by his son and successor, King Alfonso X, known for his erudition as *el sabio* – the wise.

Both spouses were descended from Eleanor of Aquitaine, who was Edward's great-great-grandmother and also the great-great-grandmother of his betrothed, Princess Leonor of Castile. When the couple married on 1 November 1254, the dowager queen of Castile, Jeanne de Dammartin, was not present, but already retired to Abbeville, the capital of her county of Ponthieu, which lay between Flanders and Normandy. Edward was fifteen and Leonor just 13 years old – a teenage bride gifted with dower lands in England: the towns of Stamford and Grantham, the Peak and the manor of Tickhill.[1] Henry III's political reason for the marriage was to settle the disputed Castilian claims on Gascony. Travelling with Prince Edward was Archbishop Boniface of Canterbury, whose negotiating skills were to be employed persuading Alfonso X renouncing any rights to Gascony as part of the marriage contract, also passing to Edward his rights from his mother to the French counties of Ponthieu and Montreuil. So, like all the others, it was a political match, but the close relationship between Edward and Leonor was to make this a love story that endured until and after her death in November 1290.

In the constant jockeying for position of the Christian kingdoms of Northern Spain, Leonor was first intended for marriage to King Theobald II of Navarre, but Theobald's mother Margaret of Bourbon, acting as his regent, chose to ally Navarre with neighbouring Aragon instead and backed out of the prior arrangement. Early in 1254 Henry III and Alfonso began negotiating the marriage of the young couple, Henry being so keen to extinguish the Castilian claims on Gascony that he cancelled elaborate preparations for dubbing Edward a knight in England and asked Alfonso X to knight Edward in Burgos before the wedding. The ceremony was set for 13 October, but Edward was detained in Aquitaine by business of state connected with his vague status as *dominus* or lord of Aquitaine, and did not arrive in Burgos until 18 October, when Alfonso knighted both the prince and several of his companions, 15-year-old Prince Edward standing head and shoulders above the others, his height earning him the sobriquet 'Longshanks'.

After the wedding, the young couple travelled north into Gascony, where the local inhabitants were *not* delighted to see them. Edward apparently had no funds and had to borrow money repeatedly, although whether to pay the troops left there to defend his territory or for his own expenses, is unclear. They were still there when Leonor gave birth before or just after her fourteenth birthday. Generally speaking, child marriages were not consummated before the bride was fifteen, as the risk of complications for younger girls was well known. This child was a daughter, who died shortly after the birth. Following her recovery, Leonor was despatched to England in the late summer of 1255. Landing at Dover, she was welcomed by the castellan Reginald of Cobham, who had been ordered by Henry III to escort her to London, with a visit to the shrine of Thomas Becket on the way. She dallied for a couple of days in Canterbury, where the bailiffs were ordered to supply all her needs at a cost of £29 11s 1½d. Another stop en route was in Rochester, staying in the castle adjacent to the impressive cathedral.

The first acquaintance of Eleanor – as Leonor became in England – with the city of London was its stink, wafted towards her approaching cortege on the prevailing westerly wind. As in Paris, there were no sewers in London. So, all the city's foul effluent floated slowly down the many open watercourses leading to the Thames, where the incoming tide would hold it for hours before it was carried away seawards on the ebb tide. The weather, chill and damp in mid-October, would have lessened the stench but, to a princess from Castile, the idea of a great city where no one could drink the water in the polluted wells must have seemed primitive. Otherwise, her welcome to the capital *bene cortinata* – streets dressed with bunting – was one of the impressive ceremonials for which Henry III had a taste. He came out to greet her, with a number of the great and good and the lord mayor of London, accompanied by the chanting choirs of St Paul's and Westminster Abbey.

Reaching the palace of Westminster, usually up-wind of the city's stench, Eleanor found her rooms thoughtfully redecorated at Henry's orders – fond of décor, he spent much energy and money on restoring and refurbishing a number of his palaces that had fallen on hard times. In Castilian style, he had the walls of Eleanor's quarters hung with tapestries and covered the stone floors with carpets. Elsewhere, the palace – and especially the gardens – fell a long way short of the elegance Eleanor had known in Burgos and the other castles and palaces where she had been brought up. She soon imported more tapestries, carpets and porcelain tableware from Spain, and even a number of the new-fangled forks for use at table – although whether used to lift food to the mouth or simply to steady the shared meat while one cut off a portion, is unknown. What was first thought of by the natives as the extravagance of a foreign queen became gradually fashion as she popularised the embellishment of noble living quarters with wall-hangings, carpets and artistic glazed tiles, rather as Eleanor of Aquitaine had done when she came to England with Henry II. It was disapprovingly observed by the natives that her Castilian retinue was numerous, but her wardrobe so scanty that Henry III commanded 100 marks to be given her, to buy some more suitable clothes and a handsome palfrey. Having grown up speaking her mother's native tongue as well as Castilian, she had no need to master a new language. Most unusually, Eleanor had also been taught to write. Her father prescribed instruction in the trivium, comprising rhetoric, grammar and logic, and the quadrivium, embracing arithmetic and geometry, music, astrology, physics and metaphysics, and made a point of ensuring that his daughters should be as well educated as the sons. In addition, Leonor had lessons in what the Victorians would call deportment: how to stand, sit, walk and talk elegantly, while the boys had to master the skills of the hunt, but also singing – Prince Enrique becoming a famous troubadour. After King Fernando died of dropsy two years before Leonor's marriage, her eldest brother Alfonso succeeded to the throne and continued the elegant lifestyle, interspersed with absences on campaign against the Moors holding out in the south of Spain.

The numerous relatives and dependents who had accompanied Eleanor to England were fed, accommodated and lavishly entertained at King Henry's expense, arousing more xenophobic resentment among his vassals. The chronicler Matthew Paris recorded it being said how people took an instant dislike to the habits and religious practices of the Spaniards 'who were the very refuse of mankind, contemptible in their dress, and detestable in their manners.'[2] It was widely considered that there were already too many foreigners sucking at the paps of the royal family; of the several waves of Savoyard relatives of Queen Eleanor of Provence, many served Henry III well, although his vassals felt these foreigners had usurped their privileges.

Prince Edward reached London on 29 November, in direct defiance of an order from his father to go instead to Ireland. The accusations of Eleanor being a spendthrift lessened when it was appreciated that she came with the expectation of the county of Ponthieu, inherited from the family of her mother Jeanne de Dammartin, second wife of Fernando III, but this only happened on the death of her brother Fernando, ten or more years later. However, from early on, she showed a talent for business that amassed a large fortune in the next few years. Her eyes accustomed to irrigation, topiary and Moorish horticulture in Spain, she personally designed elegant gardens for the royal castles with water features. Travelling from London to Canterbury, she visited Leeds castle in Kent, to be refused admission by Lady Baddlesmere on the grounds that her husband was not at home. The insult cost them the castle, which Eleanor took over, adding a *gloriette* joined to the main building by a vaulted bridge across the moat, which still stands.

As to her relationship with her mother-in-law Eleanor of Provence, the two women had little in common and conflict was soon made inevitable by Edward's mother not concealing her expectation that she would again control her son after his long absence from her and the years during which he had become accustomed to making his own decisions. This was not at all the way Eleanor of Castile saw things. Only once did the queen and the consort-in-waiting have a truce, when they travelled together in October 1257 to St Albans to give thanks for the older woman's recovery from a serious illness. Edward also had differences with his father, including a taste for tournaments, of which Henry III strongly disapproved, partly because he considered his son and heir should not put himself at risk of life and limb.

Widespread baronial resentment, principally of Henry III's taxation, shook the stability of his reign in 1258, when Eleanor of Castile was only a girl of sixteen. When the second barons' war ended in 1265, she was still in her early twenties. As political tension in England built up and the Welsh grew restive, Edward and his young wife spent several stays in Gascony and on French territory, earning criticism for the apparent frivolity of his life on the tournament circuit. Having spent her childhood at the Castilian court, the only girl surrounded by brothers and half-brothers, the older ones coming and going on campaign at first with Fernando and then with Alfonso after their father's death, and the younger ones being trained for a warrior's life, she took for granted that both Jeanne de Dammartin and Fernando's first wife Beatrix of Swabia had accompanied her father on campaign.[3] It thus seemed to Eleanor quite normal to travel with her husband.

On return to England, she continued to do this, supporting him and her father-in-law against the baronial party under Simon V de Montfort. Far from fleeing the now open conflict by crossing the Channel to the safety of Ponthieu, she took command of Windsor castle and the baronial hostages confined there. After the royalist defeat at the Battle of Lewes, Edward was a hostage of de Montfort, who considered Eleanor of Castile too dangerous to be left at liberty and had her confined in the palace of Westminster. Her lands had all been sold or mortgaged to provide money for Edward to hire mercenaries, but in 1265 the situation was reversed after the Battle of Evesham and the death of de Montfort and his son. By the evening of 4 August, the civil war was over. That morning, Eleanor had been a penniless prisoner; the next day, she was the consort of a proven warrior prince, and frequently appeared at his side on public occasions, with no longer the stigma of being 'just a foreign princess'.

In the spring of 1268, after producing three daughters, all of whom had died young, Eleanor gave birth to a healthy son christened John. He was followed by another son named Henry in 1268 and a daughter who survived in June 1269, named Eleanor after her mother. Two years later, the kingdom was relatively calm and Prince Edward decided it was time for him to embark on the great adventure of a crusade. Or did he? Eleanor's father was later to be canonised as a crusader, the *reconquista* of Spain from the Muslims being blessed by Pope Urban II as being equally important as a crusade to the Holy Land. So it may well have been Eleanor's discreet influence that played a part in Edward's decision in midsummer 1268 to join the Eighth Crusade declared by his uncle Louis IX of France. This must have seemed a heaven-sent chance to live up to the image of the father-in-law he had never known and his brothers-in-law in Spain. The problem was that he had no funds and crusading was an expensive luxury that required him to borrow money from all and sundry, even mortgaging Gascony to Louis for £17,500, to be repaid from the revenues of Gascony over twelve years.[4]

The domestic arrangements for a long absence from England included one give-away insight into Eleanor's relationship with her mother-in-law. Eleanor of Provence had an impeccable record as mother of Henry III's children and was also close to her grandchildren – as we shall see later – yet they were not entrusted to her. Instead, Richard of Cornwall was named as their guardian.

However, the best preparations in the world came to naught. King Louis and his son Jean Tristan died before the English princely couple arrived in North Africa and the siege of Tunis was abandoned. With the health of Henry III becoming precarious and discontent among the barons growing again, he wrote to Edward, telling him to return to England. Edward did not comply, spending the winter of 1270–71 on Sicily with Eleanor, initially as guests of Charles d'Anjou. But that winter was no Mediterranean holiday; after a storm that destroyed the allied fleet, Eleanor gave birth to another daughter which died before being named. She was already pregnant again before resuming the journey to the Holy Land in spring, arriving at the Templars' fortress-port of Acre in May 1271. Early in 1272 Eleanor gave birth to another daughter, later known as Joan of Acre, but also learned her son John had died in England.

As Edward was to discover, getting his fleet and army to the Holy Land was only the beginning of an impossible dream. Despite calling in loans and levying all the taxes his English and Gascon vassals and the Church could bear, the costs of the crusade mounted higher and higher, reaching an estimated £100,000 – an astronomical sum for the time that would cripple him financially for years to come.

There were many assassinations and attempted assassinations in the Latin Kingdom, riven by internecine struggles among the Christians and frequent outbursts of violence between them and the Muslims. In one such attack, Edward was wounded by an assailant's dagger, said to have been poisoned, but possibly just dirty. He might have lost the use of the injured and inflamed arm, had not a surgeon cut away much necrotised flesh before the inflammation had spread too far. Eleanor wanted to stay with her husband throughout the painful operation, but was forced to leave the room because her grief and lamentations were disturbing everyone. Later versions of the event described her sucking the poison out of Edward's wound to save his life, but this was probably poetic embellishment to illustrate the depth of their attachment to one another.

In September 1272, when Edward had partially recovered from both wound and operation, the crusade was abandoned. Edward, Eleanor and their household took ship for Sicily before the winter gales and just reached there in December, when they learned of the death of Henry III during the previous month. The country was being governed in the interim by a council of regency under Edmund of Almain, earl of Cornwall, but it seems curious that Edward did not head home to be crowned, dallying in Gascony to sort out an unruly vassal there, and even travelling to Châlons to take part in a tournament in summer 1273, where he narrowly avoided being taken hostage. Why do that, when he was, as all returning crusading kings were, no matter how little they accomplished, a hero of all Christendom for having actually been to the Holy Land? In June 1273 Edmund of Almain crossed the Channel to urge Edward's return, but the uncrowned king still did not hurry back to his island realm, choosing instead to spend part of the summer in Paris. Eleanor meanwhile was pursuing a slow journey into Aquitaine, pregnant again.

While there, at Bayonne, she gave birth on 24 November to a boy named Alphonse after her half-brother Alfonso X of Castile.

In June and July of 1274 Eleanor and Edward were in Ponthieu, not just for her to renew acquaintance with her mother Jeanne de Dammartin, but for the young couple to cast an eye over the county of which Eleanor had become heiress on the death of her brother Alfonso. For whatever reason, Joan of Acre, now approaching 3 years old, was given into her grandmother's care and left in Ponthieu when her parents departed. On 2 August 1274, they stepped ashore at Dover and met Eleanor of Provence, now dowager queen, at Canterbury. With her were the surviving children who had been left behind in England, to whom their parents were strangers: 6-year-old Prince Henry and 4-year-old Princess Eleanor. The joint coronation of Edward I and Eleanor of Castile took place immediately after their return to Westminster on 19 August 1274, nearly two years after the death of Henry III.

Little over two months after the coronation, Prince Henry died after a long illness. Neither parent was with him when he passed away in the care of the adult to whom he was closest: his grandmother Eleanor of Provence. The small body was transported to Westminster and there buried in the abbey beside Edward I's other dead children. This death, however, presented England's new king with the problem that he no longer had a son and heir. Having lived on borrowed funds since the marriage, he also had no money. By then, the kingdom was once again riven by dissent and both the Scots and the Welsh were taking advantage of this on the borders.

Edward's ruthless warfare against the Scots earned him the nickname *malleus scottorum* – the hammer of the Scots. To obtain the money needed to deal with these incursions, Eleanor of Castile was reduced to selling off some of her jewellery, while Edward mortgaged everything including her dower possessions and borrowed on a colossal scale from a consortium of Florentine bankers to build his chain of castles in Wales. Their terms were roughly 15 per cent per annum, but the accounts were adjusted – there's nothing new in banking – to conceal the fact that the king of England was involved in usury condemned by the Church. Turning into the worst kind of borrower, Edward refused to repay the loans, driving the

Ricciardi and Frescobaldi Florentine banking families into bankruptcy with him owing them the equivalent of £417 million in today's values.

It is not clear at what point Eleanor of Castile decided that she must provide herself with income independent of the king's purse but, between 1274 and her death in 1290 she acquired, by various financial manipulations, estates producing more than £2,500 per annum, many acquired by taking over debts to Jewish moneylenders, but all shrewdly chosen for manageability. In many cases the estates sold to her were compensated by other property in juggling acts that earned her a rebuke from John Pecham, who became Archbishop of Canterbury in February 1279. He criticised particularly her assuming of debts to Jews because of the implication of usury at one remove and also inveighed against the rapacious demands on her tenants made by Eleanor's bailiffs. Effectively, she built up in twenty years a nationwide property empire organised in seven regional departments. In addition to a highly mobile scout named John le Botiller, who presumably was paid finder's fees, there was the queen's steward Walter de Kancia, a chief bailiff in each region and many local bailiffs, all under the eagle eye of the queen's auditor John de Lovetot. In that time of primitive communications, the administration of her estates required eight full-time messengers, half of them described as *nuncii* and the others as *cursores* or runners.[5]

Although dearly loved by her husband, who showed no mercy to his enemies, Eleanor was not otherwise a popular queen because of a reputation for ruthless efficiency. The winding-up of her estate after her death in 1290 revealed many transgressions made in her name, which had to be corrected *post mortem*, whether she had known of them or not. Subsequent queens of England had her to thank for the precedent of creating a stable source of wealth for the royal consorts, although none seems to have been so successful as her in business. Throughout Edward's travel and bloodshed in Wales and later in Scotland, Eleanor went with him, controlling her 'head office team' wherever she was. She had no overt political role – indeed no official role except to provide another heir – but did not need one, since it was common enough in all ages for powerful women to influence their husbands in privacy and thus not be seen to affect their public decisions. She did, however, issue written instructions to the clerks of the royal household, which they obeyed, to stay on the right side of her. Like most medieval queens, she also arranged her children's betrothals and marriages, choosing not to bring her male cousins to England to marry English heiresses and acquire their wealth, which would have been seen in the xenophobic climate of the time as enriching foreigners, but betrothing her daughters preferably to English nobles in the hope of enlarging the power base of Edward's supporters in the country. Opinions differ as to whether she was a good mother to the children who survived infancy, or whether she was too attached to her husband to take much interest in their offspring, but it was normal in those days for royalty to make a stable and safe home for their young children, with reliable staff to look after them until they were of an age to travel from place to place with the court.

The notable exception was Joan of Acre. After being left with Eleanor's mother Jeanne de Dammartin in Ponthieu for four years, being given an education but also being terribly spoiled by her indulgent grandmother, she arrived in England a spirited and nearly uncontrollable girl, to be told that Edward I had betrothed her to a son of King Rudolf I of Germany. Her suitor dying in an accident before they could meet, Edward I arranged a second marriage almost immediately. Joan was so difficult that her imposed husband Earl Gilbert de Clare of Gloucester set out to seduce her with expensive gifts and clothes. He was almost thirty years older and recently divorced when they were married on 30 April 1290 in Westminster Abbey, the year when Joan's mother became increasingly ill. Joan dutifully bore him a son and three daughters before Earl Gilbert died in 1297.

The young widow, her spirit intact, fell in love soon afterwards with a humble squire in Edward's household named Ralph de Monthermer *and married him in secret*. In total ignorance of this scandalous behaviour, Edward I was negotiating her betrothal to Count Amadeus V of Savoy. Joan refusing to have anything to do with this project, her father attempted to force her into marrying the Savoyard by seizing her lands. She informed him that she was already married to her lover – and pregnant by him! De Monthermer was thrown into prison, but Edward had to give in when Joan argued that it was not disgraceful for a great earl to take a poor wife, nor for a countess to honour a gallant young knight. So why was it wrong for her to choose de Monthermer as her husband? Whether it was her advocacy of women's rights or the increasingly swollen belly of this rebel daughter that changed Edward's decision, to avoid the disgrace of an unmarried daughter of the king of England producing a bastard, we do not know. De Morthermer was released from prison at the end of July and paid homage to his father-in-law on 2 August 1297, being created earl of Gloucester and of Hertford to put the require gloss on the matter, and thereafter rose in the king's favour, while Joan produced two sons and two daughters by him.

Princess Joan was not the only rebellious daughter of Edward I and Eleanor of Castile. Elizabeth of Rhuddlan, their eighth-born, acquired her toponym because Queen Eleanor gave birth to her while accompanying her husband in the conquest of Wales. As her time approached, she was staying in the partly-built castle at Rhuddlan in North Wales, where her quarters had been modified to give her some peace in what was at the time Edward's military headquarters. To afford her some privacy, a garden was laid out with walks, seating and a fishpond, but the area was still a war zone. Born there on 7 August 1282, Princess Elizabeth was betrothed before her third birthday by her father to Jan, the newly born son of Count Floris V of Holland, who was sent to England at the age of 7 to be educated at King Edward's court. The reverse protocol of sending the boy to the girl's family could have been a device to protect Jan from the civil unrest that was to claim his father's life, but darker motives were in play.

In the summer of 1285 Princess Elizabeth and her younger brother Prince Edward spent most of the summer with their parents and siblings, including a stay at Leeds Castle and the obligatory visit to Becket's shrine in Canterbury. Their grandmother Eleanor of Provence was in retirement at Amesbury Priory in Wiltshire, where the whole family visited her, leaving there when they departed 6-year-old Princess Mary as an oblate, veiled as a nun. The whole family got together rarely: from the age of three, when her parents went to sort out the continental possessions and visit northern Spain, Elizabeth did not see them again until she was six and would hardly have recognised them. In addition, by then Eleanor of Castile was already weakening in her final illness.

In 1296 Count Floris was murdered in a conspiracy headed by Edward I, his title passing to the son who was in England, after which Edward invited a group of pro-English Dutch nobles to come to England, to ensure that Floris' 12-year-old son would be an ally for England, despite his father's fate. The wedding of Princess Elizabeth and Jan took place at Ipswich on 8 January 1297, with the king and Elizabeth's brother Prince Edward, to whom she was close, among the guests. This was before the bride's fifteenth birthday, and the bridegroom was two years younger. Princess Elizabeth was not in a good mood and seemingly lost her temper during the wedding preparations because some jewels she had ordered were not ready to be worn. Was that an excuse for her outburst, or was it caused by her not fancying her future husband after meeting him for the first time? Or, perhaps she resented being married off to become a mere countess, when other princesses became queens. Or was she simply aware that her life might also become forfeit in the machinations of the English wool trade with Holland?

Edward I had already married off his daughter Margaret, who was seven years older than Elizabeth, to Duke Jan II of Brabant, neighbouring Holland. So why was he trading a second daughter into a less than royal family in the same part of Europe? One reason was that this was another round in the Plantagenets' long-running feud with the Capetian kings of France, whose territory was bordered on the northeast by the Low Countries, where Edward had fought and lost a war against a French army fielded by King Philippe Auguste in 1297–8. The other reason was wool, of which the medieval importance is echoed still today in the symbolic woolsack serving as the seat of the Lord Speaker of the House of Lords.

The wool-clip from the millions of sheep in England financed a large part of Edward I's wars in Wales, including the construction of all those castles. So vital was it to protect the flocks from the wolves, that Edward ordered a complete eradication of these predators throughout England. Wool exports were rigidly controlled and the principal purchasers of the wool, sent abroad to be spun and woven into cloth, were in the Low Countries. In 1275 Edward imposed an export duty of 6 shillings and 8 pence – one third of a pound sterling – per standard bale of wool. In 1280 about 25,000 bales of wool were exported from England, and the trade later peaked at about 45,000 sacks per year, with the duty steadily increased to reach 46 shillings and 8 pence per bale in 1341.

The original plan had been for Elizabeth of Rhuddlan and her young husband to travel back together to Flanders after the wedding but, whether because of the continuing civil unrest there, or for more personal reasons, Elizabeth refused to go, obliging Jan to depart without her in the company of the two regents, to whom he had to swear obedience before they left. With Eleanor of Castile long dead, there was no one to intercede on the young princess' behalf. King Edward, whose short temper was well known,[6] was furious at her obstinate defiance, to the point of grabbing her bejewelled coronet soon after the wedding and hurling it into the fireplace, where two expensive gems broke away from their mounts, and were lost. The coronet was, rather embarrassingly, a present from King Philippe le Bel, so that the missing stones had to be replaced by a goldsmith at King Edward's expense.[7]

Still, Elizabeth – a girl of some spirit – refused to give way. So did her father. To keep his wilful daughter under strict control, King Edward made her spend most of the year after her wedding in travelling with the court in England. In the autumn, he accompanied her across the Channel, ending up at Ghent, where Elizabeth enjoyed meeting two of her sisters, Duchess Margaret of Brabant and Countess Eleanor, who was married to Henry III of Bar, in what is now the French province of Lorraine.

Jan I ceded control of the county of Holland up to his fifteenth birthday to one of the regents, who was murdered at Delft in August 1299, after which the still youthful count ceded power for five years to another noble. Two weeks after issuing that charter, the childless count of Holland conveniently died, allegedly of dysentery although it was widely believed that he had been murdered by poisoning. Not until the summer of the following year did Elizabeth return to England, and it took nine further years for an agreement to be reached over the repayment of her dowry.

A childless widow of seventeen, Elizabeth was back where she had started, both physically and legally as a *feme sole* requiring a powerful husband. Three years later, she married Humphrey de Bohun, 4th Earl of Hereford and Essex. By an unusual legal measure, he relinquished all his property to the Crown before the marriage and had it restored to the couple jointly afterwards – which hints that Elizabeth's strong will which had caused her youthful outbursts and outright defiance of father and first husband was still intact. Between 1303 and 1316 she bore de Bohun eleven children, eight of whom lived to adulthood. Her death on 5 May 1316 came during the birth of their last daughter, who died with her.

In one respect, Elizabeth's mother was probably unique. Her lifelong love of books caused her to have her own library with a scriptorium for the copying of books by scribes and at least one illuminator to embellish them. Before going on crusade in 1272 she commissioned a French translation from the original Latin of Vegetius' *de re militari* for Edward to read on the voyage. Now regarded as an inadequate work, it was at the time greatly respected. Archbishop Pecham, although no admirer of this strong-willed queen, did dictate and send to her a dissertation in French on angels and their functions. She commissioned other religious works herself, but also romances and other light reading for her personal pleasure.

In 1279 Edward and Eleanor of Castile travelled to France, formally taking possession of her counties of Ponthieu and Montreuil. Edward thus became count of Ponthieu as well as duke of Aquitaine and did homage for his French possessions to King Philippe the Bold of France. The northern French territories were inherited by Edward II and Edward III until confiscated by King Philippe VI de Valois in April 1369. This almost constant companionship of Eleanor and her husband could have been her way of ensuring his fidelity – rare among medieval English kings, he left no record of any extramarital affairs or bastard children by any mistresses. For fifteen months between May 1286 and August 1289 Eleanor and he left England in the care of his regents under Edmund of Almain. On Edward's return he launched an enquiry into corruption by judges and officers of the realm, some of whom were severely punished, but which earned Almain a pardon for some lesser transgressions, so that he continued in various offices for many years to come.

The perennial lack of funds for Edward's campaigns was partly solved by despoiling England's Jewish financiers, an activity in which Eleanor participated directly by seizing the assets of the wealthiest one, Jacob of Oxford. Because they did not fit anywhere else in feudal society, the Jews were directly subject to the king, without any other overlord intervening, who might have pleaded their cause. They were excluded from the provisions of Magna Carta and were taxable at the will of the sovereign without any recourse. In 1218 Henry III proclaimed his Edict of the Badge, obliging all Jews in England over the age of seven to wear a yellow felt patch sewn onto their outer garments, and reinforced this with his 1253 Statute of Jewry. In addition, increasingly harsh taxation screwed out of them an estimated 200,000 marks – more than a king's ransom. The confusion and bloodshed of the second baron's war saw many Jews dispossessed and killed by Gentiles who owed them money and sought thus to vitiate the debts *in personam*. In London alone some 500 Jews were murdered. Following in the footsteps of the King Louis IX, in 1275 Edward's new Statute of Jewry tightened the screw more, forbidding the lending of money at interest when there were few other ways of Jews earning a living in England.

Their lot was not much better in formerly tolerant Aquitaine, where medieval carved figures of Jews in twelfth-century churches are shown wearing the *pileum cornutum* – a conical hat – even on carvings of Christ's disciples. Edward expelled all his Jewish subjects from the duchy in 1287, so that he could seize their fixed assets and take over all the debts owing to them, dunning the debtors for repayment – a device also used in England, which came as a nasty surprise to murdering debtors who had thought that killing their moneylender would free them from payment of interest and repayment of principle. The mood in England was still very xenophobic. Returning north in 1289, Edward sought to cover his enormous debts by new taxes and sugared the pill for his vassals and vavasours by proclaiming the Edict of Expulsion on 18 July. To use the Nazi expression *judenfrei*, England was free of Jews and the Crown lacked their services as moneylenders until Oliver Cromwell's parliament invited them to come back in 1655.

Eleanor approved plans to marry two of her daughters – Joan of Acre, born in April 1272, and Margaret, born in March 1275 – and pressed for the betrothal of Prince Edward to Margaret, the Maid of Norway, which came to naught with that princess's untimely death. But her health was waning. In the summer of 1290, the royal couple took a leisurely tour of Eleanor's estates in Northern England, its pace dictated by a debilitating illness from which she was suffering. Since she had survived sixteen pregnancies and recovered after each birth without known complications, her general level of health must have been excellent until shortly after the birth of Prince Edward in 1284, when her household records show frequent purchases of medication. So her final illness was possibly an opportunistic infection due to attacks of malaria having weakened her. At the beginning of August in Silverstone she was not even well enough to attend Mass, obliging Edward to summon his autumn parliament to Clipstone in Nottinghamshire, since he did not want to leave her for long enough to travel to London and back. The parliament was not in those days a place, but simply a meeting of the Grand Council, and could take place wherever the king wished. Eleanor's last weeks saw the daily itinerary of the court reduced by her worsening health to eight miles a day until it reached the village of Harby in Nottinghamshire, which she was never to leave alive. With Edward by her side, she died in the evening of 28 November 1290, aged 49. Stunned by her loss, for three days he was incapable of any kingly action: no petitions were accepted; no charters sealed.

Following custom, Eleanor's body was embalmed after the heart and viscera had been removed, the latter for burial in a replica of her tomb at Lincoln cathedral. The rest of her body was slowly brought south to the capital. Distraught at the death of his almost constant companion of the last thirty-six years, Edward caused an elaborately carved stone cross bearing her likeness to be erected where her bier stopped at the end of each day's journey back to London. Three of these Eleanor crosses still exist, although damaged, at Waltham, Northampton and Geddington, but the most famous one at Charing in central London was later replaced by a statue of Charles I and a token monument erected in the forecourt of the nineteenth-century Charing Cross Hotel instead. Its position is the geographical point from which official distances from London are calculated.

Popular etymology had it that the place-name 'Charing' was a corruption of the French *chère reine*, meaning 'dear queen'. In fact, it is derived from an Old English word *cierring*, meaning a bend in the river Thames. Eleanor's body was buried on 17 December 1290 up-river in Westminster Abbey, where her gilt-bronze effigy is a masterpiece of the art. Her heart was claimed by the Dominicans, an order she had generously patronised, and buried at their priory of Blackfriars in London.

Edward's profound grief fought against remarriage, but counsellors who had his ear murmured that it was his duty to the realm to father more sons, since the only surviving son of Eleanor, the prince known as Edward of Caernarfon after his place of birth, might die and leave the kingdom prey to a power struggle between the husbands of his sisters. By 1293 Edward I accepted this argument, although he did not finally take a second wife until a decade after the death of Eleanor of Castile, when he was sixty and married 20-year-old Marguerite of France, daughter of Philippe III, after a long and tangled negotiation. She bore him two sons who reached adult age and a daughter christened Eleanor in memory of his first wife, but who died aged 5. The succession was as secure as it could be, but it was in fact Eleanor of Castile's last-born son who came to the throne as Edward II in 1307.

Chapter 21

Isabelle of France and Her Reluctant Husband

After the accounts of so many loveless marriages uniting young girls with much older men and some of which ripened into enduring respect between the spouses, with maybe a measure of affection, and one marriage between two young royals that did become a loving relationship, what of those royal betrothals where the girl found herself sent away to a foreign country to produce babies for a husband who was simply not interested in sleeping with her? One thinks immediately of Berengaria of Navarre. En route to the Holy Land on the Third Crusade Richard the Lionheart named as his heir, should he die on the crusade, his nephew Arthur of Brittany, a toddler who was a vassal of King Philippe Auguste. That would have been as good as handing to Philippe on a plate the entire Angevin Empire of England, Normandy and the other continental possessions. Determined to prevent what she saw as this appalling possibility, Richard's mother Eleanor of Aquitaine scanned the courts of Europe for a suitably submissive wife for her favourite son, who had no interest in women or matrimony, by whom he might just father a son before reaching the Holy Land.

Her eagle eye settled on Berengaria, daughter of King Sancho VI of Navarre, a princess who was universally described without the attribution of beauty and intelligence that was customarily accorded to the daughters of kings, but rather as being prudent, gentle, virtuous and docile. Although her exact date of birth in Tudela is unknown, she was well past her twentieth birthday and must by then have been regarded by her father as more suited to a convent than a marital bed. When Eleanor travelled all the way to Navarre in Northern Spain, Sancho the Wise was delighted to get this daughter off his hands, and consented to Eleanor's proposal without hesitation, in anticipation of becoming the father-in-law of Richard, king of England, duke of Normandy, duke of Aquitaine and count of Anjou.

Escorted by Eleanor on a 1,300-mile journey from Navarre northwards into Aquitaine, eastwards to Italy and south along the length of the Italian peninsula to Sicily, where her future husband had been overwintering and refitting his fleet on the way to the Holy Land, Berengaria was there abandoned by Eleanor, who hastened back to England, to foil the treachery of Richard's brother John Lackland during the king's absence on crusade. Sent away to virtual house arrest in a monastery on the mainland with her future sister-in-law, Richard's sister Joanna, Berengaria was later shipped off with her in a merchant vessel bound for a safe haven on Rhodes, the island fortress of the Ordo Hospitalis Sancti Johannis Hierosolymitani – famous as the Knights Hospitaller. The plan unravelled when they were shipwrecked on Cyprus and nearly taken hostage by the self-styled emperor of that island, Isaac I. When Richard made landfall there after the end of Lent, there ensued a violent conquest of the island, after which he had to marry the bride his mother had foisted on him. On 12 May 1192 in Limassol Berengaria became the virgin bride of a 33-year-old warrior fixated on the crusade and with a thousand cares more important to his way of thinking than begetting a child.[1]

Another princess with a similar problem a century later, following her marriage to a husband whose interests lay elsewhere, was Isabelle of France. Born in 1295 or early in 1296, she was the only surviving daughter of Philippe IV of France, known as Philippe le Bel, and his consort Jeanne de Champagne, who was confusingly also queen of Navarre. Although her parents originally had in mind for her a Spanish marriage, her role in the game of child betrothals was changed to cement the truce of 1298 between France and England and settle the long dispute over the remaining Plantagenet possessions on French soil and those that had been lost by King John. Betrothed when she was only 2 years old to Prince Edward of Caernarfon, heir apparent to the throne of England, she was raised in the palaces of the Louvre and on the Ile de la Cité, and grew into a beautiful young woman gifted with a keen intelligence and literate in French and Latin.

As to her future husband, never have a father and his son been less alike. Edward I more often had a bloodstained sword in hand than a book. Disdainful of comfort, he was always planning his next campaign. His son

Prince Edward, who came to the throne on 7 July 1307, four days after his father's death, was more interested in music, play-acting, costly clothes and verse than manly pursuits like the hunt, hawking, tournaments and warfare. He was, as the Edwardians would later say, 'very musical', although his creativity did express itself by a fascination with architecture and shipbuilding. At the sumptuous wedding in Boulogne on 25 January 1308 in the presence of five kings and three queens – not including the mother of the bride, who had died two years before – the groom was three months short of his twenty-fourth birthday. His bride was just 11 years old and cannot have had any idea of what lay ahead.

Her trousseau included dresses of silken brocade, velvet and taffeta, numerous furs, seventy-two headdresses, two gold crowns and one of gold and silver, plus 383 metres of linen, for purposes unknown.[2] Her fashionably pale skin, long blonde hair and slightly rounded face caused even the bridegroom to dub her 'Isabelle the Fair'. However, the young king Edward II was already in love with a handsome Gascon knight from Béarn named Piers Gaveston.[3] His father had banished Gaveston from court in an attempt to end their close relationship, but one of Edward II's first acts as king was to recall Gaveston and confer on him the earldom of Cornwall, together with lavish presents. He had already given him a wife in the person of his niece Marguerite, an heiress from the rich de Clare family, with whom Gaveston fathered two daughters.

It is said that, after Isabelle's arrival in London, her husband also gave to his lover some of her jewels as well as several of the wedding gifts. More seriously, Edward also perpetuated the unrest of his barons by relying on Gaveston's advice instead of respecting that of his official counsellors, the earls of Lincoln and Warwick and the future earl of Pembroke, who had been charged by Edward I on his deathbed with guiding his son and specifically to prevent the return of Gaveston.[4]

Among the advisors Isabelle brought with her from Paris for her coronation in February 1308 were her uncles Charles de Valois and Louis d'Evreux. The dowager queen of England was an aunt of hers, two of her brothers-in-law were her cousins and the most powerful baron, Count Thomas Plantagenet of Lancaster, was her uncle. This did not prevent Edward from throwing himself into the arms of Gaveston when they met, calling him 'my brother'.[5] Worse was to come: Edward had entrusted

Gaveston with organising the coronation in Westminster Abbey a month after the wedding in Boulogne. The royal couple – Isabelle aged 12 or 13 and Edward twice her age – walked from the palace of Westminster to the neighbouring abbey on a woollen carpet strewn with flowers under an embroidered canopy carried aloft on decorated poles by the barons of the Cinque Ports. Ahead of them, carrying the regalia for the coronation, walked the earls of Lancaster, Warwick, Lincoln and Hereford, but it was Gaveston, dressed even more sumptuously than the king in a robe of imperial purple silk embroidered with pearls, who hogged the limelight and insisted on carrying St Edward the Confessor's sacred crown. In her magnificent coronation dress, Isabelle was radiant, but Edward outraged those present, having eyes solely for his lover – to the point that one of the nobles present declared he only restrained himself from attacking Gaveston physically out of respect for the young queen and the sanctity of the abbey.[6] A century before, England had been ruled by Richard I, whose known sexual preferences did not diminish his reputation because he 'took the man's part' in coupling, but Edward II did not.[7]

The festive arrangements made by Gaveston were a disaster, culminating in the banquet being served late and poorly cooked, during which the final insult to Isabelle was the king choosing to sit with Gaveston instead of beside his young queen. Behind them hung tapestries depicting their personal arms, and not the arms of Edward and his queen. After the departure of her scandalised father and brother and other royal guests, Edward's teenaged queen was without political support at court, but was advised by her uncle Thomas of Lancaster to navigate a careful path between the courtiers who hated Gaveston and those who sought to curry favour with him in order to reach the king's ear. Very astutely for one so young, she played a waiting game, not confronting Edward and not associating herself with any baronial faction. She also managed in time to create a positive relationship with Gaveston, which must have been difficult, given his often criticised arrogance. Her letters to her father complaining that her dower possessions did not afford sufficient funds may have been intercepted. Conceding to pressure from Thomas of Lancaster, Edward was forced to exile his favourite once again, but chose to make him Lord of Ireland with handsome remuneration in June 1308. The Christmas court was held at Windsor without him. When he returned to court in June 1309, Edward II was more circumspect, spending time with Gaveston but also behaving in public more respectfully towards Isabelle, to deflect the hostility of his barons.

It seemed for a while that Gaveston, Edward and Isabelle were living in uneasy truce as she grew up, quietly building her own party at court, principally the Beaumont family, in which her closest friend was Isabelle de Vesci, a former confidante of Edward's mother, Eleanor of Castile. When she came of age, Edward was careful to sleep with her often enough for appearances. In the summer of 1311 Edward was manipulated into leading a campaign against the Scots under Robert the Bruce, during which he and Isabelle narrowly escaped capture. Returning to London, they found that the barons had constituted a committee of twenty-one 'ordainers' who composed a series of 'ordinances', which severely limited the powers of the king and royal household, exiling Gaveston, but also banning from court Queen Isabelle's supporters Isabelle de Vesci and Henri de Beaumont.

Political in-fighting was far from being the main problem for the people as a whole. There is much talk today of climate change and its effects. Dendrochronology and ice-core analysis show that temperatures plunged and precipitation increased early in the fourteenth century all over the Continent, but especially in the north. It is thought that this was caused by atmospheric pollution from several volcanic eruptions in the tropics, of which people in Europe knew nothing. The change favoured oak trees, which thrive in cool, wet weather, but caused crops to rot in the fields during what is called the Medieval Climate Anomaly and the subsequent Little Ice Age. Financial problems included a radical decline in wool production and consequently severe reduction in the wool exports so important to the economy of medieval England. All over Europe, starvation claimed thousands of lives, culminating in the great famine of 1315–21. Excavation of the medieval mass grave at Spitalfields Market outside London's city walls, which was previously thought to date from the Black Death, recently revealed that the Anomaly had earlier claimed 18,000 lives from London's population of 50,000 alone.[8] Poisoning by ergot, a mould growing on damp rye, was one cause. Although the Black Death is not supposed to have arrived in Western Europe before 1348, some form of plague was also reportedly raging in

England before then, but is difficult to separate an actual plague from series of outbreaks of dysentery, cholera and other diseases that claimed many lives of malnourished people when the crops rotted in the fields.

Perhaps that is part of the reason why, at Christmas 1311, the queen took pity on the exiled Gaveston's wife Marguerite de Clare and sent her generous presents. The absent husband possibly misunderstood the gesture, defying the barons' edict and the cold weather by returning to London early in 1312, causing Edward's cousin the furious Thomas of Lancaster to take arms against the king and his troublesome Gascon, who did not have the sense to stay away. Although now pregnant with her first child, Isabelle fled with Edward and his Gascon favourite northwards towards Newcastle.[9] Gaveston having been left in Scarborough, perhaps hoping to take ship to France, on arriving at Tynemouth Edward abandoned Isabelle in an unsuccessful endeavour to draw Lancaster's forces away from Scarborough. Gaveston was taken prisoner by a consort of nobles on 19 May, his captors being divided as to what should be done with him. Solving the problem, although not to everyone's liking, the Earl of Warwick Guy de Beauchamp took charge of this awkward prisoner on 19 May and had him executed at Blacklow Hill between Warwick and Kenilworth by two Welsh men-at-arms on 18 or 19 June. They accorded him the posthumous 'dignity' of beheading the corpse, as befitted an executed noble. Gaveston's death did little to calm the barons' unrest, but Edward was predictably distraught with grief.

Four months later, on 13 November 1312 Isabelle, aged probably 16, gave birth for the first time in Windsor castle – to a son named Edward, who would come to the throne as Edward III in January 1327. At last, in fathering an heir to the throne, Isabelle's husband had done something of which his barons approved. In May 1313 the royal couple journeyed to France for a state visit, marred only by a fire in Isabelle's tent which badly burned one arm and hand, but did not prevent her presenting expensively embroidered purses to her three brothers and their wives. In November she miscarried, but recovered in time for a reciprocal banquet in London, at which she saw two of the purses hanging from the belts of two Norman knights, and took this for proof of the infidelity of the sisters-in-law. Entrusted by Edward with a diplomatic mission to Paris the following year, Isabelle told her brother the king of her suspicions about the two knights who had worn the purses given to her sisters-in-law, resulting in the execution of the two supposed lovers and imprisonment of the sisters-in-law, during which they died. Some historians quite reasonably suspect that this was her attempt to block the succession of her brothers' offspring and clear the way for her son Edward to claim the French throne, but there is no supporting evidence.

Isabelle managed one way and another to get pregnant by her reluctant husband three more times, bearing John of Eltham on 15 August 1316, Eleanor of Woodstock on 18 June 1318, and another daughter, Joan of the Tower, in 1321. For a husband with little interest in women, Edward was extremely lucky to have four children. Instead of being grateful, when he chose a new favourite in Hugh Despenser the Younger, any intimacy between husband and wife ceased and Isabelle prudently set about cultivating support from chosen magnates and bishops, to create her own power base. Bishop Burghersh of Lincoln, who was thought to owe Isabelle gratitude for his nomination to the see, and Bishop Orleton of Hereford incurred Edward's wrath, but were protected by Pope John XXII, who exhorted both lay and ecclesiastical magnates to intercede for them. Bishop John Stratford of Winchester, who was in disgrace for accepting his see in defiance of the king's known wishes, had to pay a fine of £1,000 to Hugh the Younger and had no love for either him or his father. Among the magnates, Isabelle's uncle Henry of Lancaster was staunch in her support, as were several others who were repelled by the Despensers' arrogance. If one thinks about it, arrogance was a requirement in the medieval nobility, but there were obviously limits to what was acceptable behaviour, and the Despensers exceeded those by far.

After a defeat early in the campaign against the Scots in autumn 1322, Edward II rode south, ostensibly to raise more troops, leaving Isabelle in Tynemouth Priory. As the Scots drew nearer, Isabelle demanded he return to rescue her. This was not the first time he acted as though indifferent to her safety, offering instead to send the Despensers, whose aid she rejected, and who, anyway, were heading south with Edward. Left to face the invaders with only her household servants, she ordered some to fight a rearguard action, keeping the Scots at bay while she requisitioned a ship at the cost of some lives, having decided that risking interception at sea by Flemish privateer allies of the Scots, who were blockading the northern coast, was better than staying still and waiting to be captured by Scottish land forces. Fortunately the skipper of her ship was a good sailor, carrying her far enough south to land and head for the security of York's strong walls.

Meeting Edward afterwards, Isabelle was understandably furious with him and the Despensers, who had counselled him to save himself rather than ride to her rescue. Accusations and counter-accusations flew in all directions, but the Despensers' hold over Edward isolated Isabelle from him even more than during Gaveston's time of influence. By November 1322, Isabelle was being kept without revenues and deprived of contact with her children, while Edward lived with Hugh the Younger, whose avarice enabled him to deposit at interest with the Florentine bankers Bardi and Peruzzi the sum of £6,000 in autumn 1324 and a further £5,735 two years later. Some of this fortune came from his own estates, but some was the product of bribery and payments to him for release from wrongful imprisonment. His wife Marguerite was made housekeeper of the queen, charged with reading all her incoming and outgoing mail to prevent any treasonous negotiations with her brother, King Charles IV of France. There were rumours that the younger Despenser attempted to have Edward's marriage to Isabelle annulled.[10] However, rumour was one thing and the sequestration of Isabelle's estates near the south coast in 1324 on the purported grounds that they *might* be used as bases by the enemy in a French invasion, was fact. This, for her, was the final straw that decided her to sail her own course from then on and leave Edward to drown with the Despensers.

With an English embassy in Paris attempting unsuccessfully to resolve the knotty issue of Gascony, papal nuncios proposed that Isabelle travel to Paris and mediate between her brother and her husband. With the help of bishops Orleton and Burghersh and the ambassadors in Paris, Isabelle persuaded Edward to let her go. On 9 March 1325 she crossed the Channel with a large retinue – and succeeded where the embassy had failed: Charles IV's *curia* conceded that most of the English possessions be returned to Edward as soon as he came and personally swore fealty for Gascony and Ponthieu. The Despensers refused to let him out of their sight, so Edward pleaded on 24 August 1325 that he was too ill to travel. Overcoming Edward's suspicions with the help of her bishops,

Isabelle persuaded the king to transfer title to the duchy of Aquitaine and the county of Ponthieu to their teenage son, who could perform homage for him, releasing Edward from this feudal obligation to Charles IV. Escorted by Bishop Walter Stapleton, Prince Edward travelled to France and, on 21 September, performed homage to his uncle Charles at Bois-de-Vincennes.

When it was obvious that Isabelle intended keeping Prince Edward in France, Bishop Stapleton left Paris surreptitiously and crossed the Channel with the bad news, causing Edward II to agitate for the return of Isabelle and the boy. In return, he was informed via an intermediary that she refused to return to London until he had sent away the younger Despenser, which he could not bring himself to do. Telling Charles IV that she must live as a widow until the Despensers had been removed from the English court, Isabelle donned widow's weeds.[11]

Among the English émigrés in Paris was Roger Mortimer, who had been Lord Lieutenant of Ireland for a while, but was sent to the Tower in 1322 for raising the Marcher territories against Edward II. He escaped – some said by drugging his guard, while others believed he had made a hole in the wall of his cell to slide down a rope to a boat waiting below the walls of the Tower – either of which methods raised the question of who made the arrangements and smuggled him in the means to do that. The answer is Bishop Orleton and Richard de Bettoyne, a goldsmith who had been mayor of London, both great enemies of the Despensers.[12] Fleeing down-river and across the Channel to France, Mortimer sought asylum at Charles IV's court in Paris, offering to assist in Charles' war against Edward II in Gascony.

Isabelle decided that – to reverse the old saying – what was sauce for the gander was also sauce for the goose. Although Mortimer was married with a wife and twelve children in England, Isabelle took him as her lover some time about Christmas 1325. The scandal of this adultery reached the Pope, who, unimpressed by Isabelle's dressing as a widow, informed Charles IV that he must not countenance his sister's illicit relationship. Clad in her widow's clothing to make the point that her marriage was over, Isabella removed herself to Flanders with a number of other English exiles who had their own reasons to hate Edward II and the Despensers – plus inevitably an assortment of adventurers hoping to profit from the enterprise. These volunteers formed the nub of a small army, expanded by Flemish mercenaries.

In March 1326, alarmed by reports of Isabelle's growing army in Flanders, Pope John XXII attempted a reconciliation between the royal spouses, but Edward II refused to send away the Despensers, which was a pre-condition of the Pope's settlement, and they in turn persuaded the king to declare his wife and son outlaws! It was not only princesses who could be bartered, and on 27 August 1326 Isabelle betrothed her 13-year-old son Edward to Count Guillaume I of Haimault's 12-year-old daughter Philippa[13] in return for the count's hospitality and, more importantly, his provision of 132 merchant ships and six warships for an invasion of England. The young couple being second cousins, a dispensation from consanguinity was required from Pope John XXII, which was given at Avignon in September 1326. On 23 September, Isabelle's fleet set sail from Doordrecht. The voyage passed without incident, ending on the following day at the mouth of the river Orwell, seventy miles northeast of London, the roundabout route having been chosen in order to avoid the patrolling English flotilla and the south coast defences put in place to prevent a French invasion. Although the initial landing force was small, totalling around 1,500 men, enemies of the Despensers swiftly rallied to them once ashore, including nobles and powerful churchmen, who chose to overlook the discreet adultery between Mortimer and Isabelle, who continued to wear widow's clothing for effect.[14] Hearing of their progress to Bury St Edmunds and Cambridge, the king took refuge in the Tower, but on 2 October was forced to leave by the citizens of London, who had had enough of him and his cronies. As they rode out, desperate to get away before it was too late, the capital was left in a state of anarchy with the bishop of Exeter and a courtier assassinated and beheaded, as well as widespread looting, violence in the streets and liberation of the prisoners in the Tower.

Through Oxford, Isabelle and Mortimer pursued the fleeing king westwards, with Henry of Lancaster in command of the troops. The elder Despenser barricaded himself inside Bristol castle, where, after a brief siege, he surrendered and was informed by his noble captors that he was to be 'drawn for treason, hanged for robbery, beheaded for misdeeds against the Church.' His head was sent for display in Winchester, of which he had been named earl, and his body cut up and fed to dogs. Isabelle's two children who had been sent away to live in his household were returned to their mother after years of separation. Seeking shelter in Wales, Edward II there took ship for Ireland[15] with the young Hugh Despenser, but was forced back to Cardiff by foul weather in the Irish Sea. Fleeing again from Caerphilly on 2 December, they were so closely pursued that that had to leave behind all their jewels, food and the king's treasury totalling £13,000, of which Isabelle took charge, to use as she pleased.

Her dual prey was captured in Neath Abbey on 16 November, Hugh the Younger being summarily judged for high treason and castrated, disembowelled and quartered on 24 November, apparently while tied to a high ladder so that the large crowd assembled for the spectacle could see all the gory details of his dying,[16] after which his head was taken to London for display, impaled on a pike at London Bridge. Other leading supporters of Edward II were beheaded or imprisoned. The remaining problem was what to do with Isabelle's husband, to prevent any possibility of rescue by his remaining partisans in the country. His demise was the only sure way, but there had not been a precedent of legal execution of a monarch in England since the Norman Conquest in 1066.

The death of William the Conqueror's son King William Rufus may have been a deliberate killing to rid the country of a dissolute ruler who died without issue, having neither married nor taken mistresses and whose licentious court was a scandal of the time. The official story was that he died on 2 August 1100 while hunting in the New Forest, being slain with an arrow through the lung fired by Sir Walter Tyrrel, a member of the hunting party. It was said that the arrow was shot at a stag, but missed and bounced off an oak tree before hitting William Rufus. Accidents while hunting were numerous because the huntsmen were riding spirited horses at speed through difficult country when loosing their arrows at the quarry, but the circumstances were suspicious. Tyrrel, reputed to be an excellent shot, departed precipitately and crossed to France, but that could have been merely prudent. No one else in the group of nobles apparently tried to see whether the king was actually dead, but rode away, leaving the body where it lay on the ground; later some local peasants collected the corpse and transported it on a cart to

Winchester cathedral for burial. Only one member of the hunt, William Rufus' landless younger brother Henry, acted fast and with clear self-interest. He rode off straight away to Winchester to secure the royal treasury, not without a measure of violence, then hastened to London, to get himself crowned. Archbishop Anselm of Canterbury had been exiled by the late king and Archbishop Thomas of York was in the north, so he persuaded Bishop Maurice of London to crown him as King Henry I in Westminster abbey just three days after William Rufus' death.

However, that was hardly a precedent for the barons mulling over what to do with Edward II because, although William Rufus had been unpopular, his death *could* have been an accident. With Edward II already a prisoner after a minor war against him led by his wife Queen Isabelle and Mortimer, who had harried him across half the country, nobody would believe that his death was an accident.

Chapter 22

Three Queens in One Castle

During January 1327 at Westminster Parliament debated the future of this king who refused to plead before it, even to save his life. A few miles down-river in London, the citizens were declaring that Isabelle's younger son John of Eltham was the true lord of the capital and that his elder brother Prince Edward must replace his father on the throne of England, with the deposed king incarcerated for life. On 12 January, although there was no legal precedent, the lords temporal and spiritual drew up a long list of reasons why the king must abdicate in favour of his son. At Kenilworth castle he was visited by two bishops, who had already interviewed him previously and now urged him to renounce the crown, promising that he would be well treated, if he did so. The alternative, they said, was that the people would otherwise repudiate him *and his sons*, ending the Plantagenet dynasty by choosing a new king elsewhere. Reduced to copious tears, Edward was then led out, distraught and half-fainting, before the main deputation. When Bishop Orleton repeated the ultimatum, Edward replied that he was grieved that his people should repudiate him, but that he would accept his fate if one of his sons were chosen to succeed him.

A week later, the deed was done, leaving the way clear for 14-year-old Prince Edward to be crowned as King Edward III in Westminster cathedral on 1 February by Archbishop of Canterbury Walter Reynolds. With power being held temporarily in the hands of his mother as guardian of the under-age king, and Mortimer constantly at her side, not everyone who had been against Edward II was happy with this arrangement. Mortimer was not popular and Isabelle was guilty in the citizens' eyes of being a foreigner, like all the other princesses traded young. People also held it against her that she had enriched herself excessively and continued to do so. Compensating herself for the sequestrations of her dower estates, Isabelle had them restored and more, the global value increasing from the original annual value of £4,400 to £13,333.[1]

A council of regency, which did not include Mortimer, was later constituted under Henry of Lancaster. As at every regime change, some nobles who had not taken sides previously opposed the coronation and planned to free Edward II from imprisonment. In early April Mortimer had him moved to Berkeley castle in Gloucestershire, a fortress held by one of his sons-in-law, but a group of rescuers under a Dominican named Thomas Dunheved and his brother Stephen broke into Edward's quarters and rode away with him. The news was deeply alarming to Isabelle and Mortimer. Although Edward was swiftly recaptured and Thomas Dunheved was hauled before Isabelle, imprisoned and died in a dungeon without trial, she and Mortimer feared that a better organised attempt to liberate the ex-king might succeed. So, towards the end of August, he was brought back to Berkeley, his days numbered, whether he knew it or not. Learning in September 1327 that a conspiracy of Welsh lords planned to rescue the king – more from hatred of Mortimer, as a Marcher lord, than for love of Edward – Isabelle and her lover discreetly arranged the ex-king's demise. Two weeks later the death of the 43-year-old prisoner, probably on 21 September, was announced. The three knights who had rid the country of a useless monarch were tried for his murder three years later, but allowed to escape to France, one of them later having his estates quietly restored after his return and sitting in Parliament for more than two decades.

Exactly when the theory first surfaced that Edward was held down by his killers, a pierced horn inserted into his anus to prevent any superficial scarring and a red-hot poker thrust deeply through it as fitting punishment for sodomy, is not clear. Whatever people had really thought about Edward II during his lifetime, his tomb in Gloucester Abbey rapidly became a pilgrimage site with reports of miraculous cures engineered by the abbey's community to attract the donations of thousands of pilgrims.

All this manoeuvring having done little to quell the unrest among the English nobility, and Edward III's fifteenth birthday approaching, Isabelle and Mortimer knew their guardianship of him had just over three years to run. Their recent conduct having alienated her uncle Henry of Lancaster and many others, by October 1328 the country was again in a state approaching civil war. In command of the royal forces, Mortimer took the fortresses of Lancaster, Leicester and Bedford with Isabelle appearing on horseback wearing armour at his side, to show that Edward II's widow was now a warrior queen. Like that later, more famous, Frenchwoman Joan of Arc, who also adopted male armour, this was not because she might be in physical danger in combat. Rather, it was because this specifically masculine medieval costume was the perfect mode of cross-dressing for women wishing to switch genders in the social sphere because the armour, by completely concealing the form of the female body, made her to medieval eyes an, albeit temporary, male leader of men.[2]

Isabelle and Mortimer managed to cling to power in an increasingly unstable political landscape for two further years. From whom, and how, Isabelle's still teenaged son on the throne learned about his father's death is a mystery, but he certainly blamed Mortimer for it. The young king had plenty of other problems on his mind, so it was his mother who took the next step in getting him married. The bishop of Coventry was sent to France during October 1327 to marry Philippa of Hainault as Edward's proxy in Valenciennes during October 1327. On 24 January 1328 the marriage of England's new king was celebrated in person at York Minster. The new queen was swiftly taken to their hearts by the people of England, so different was Philippa's gentle character and generous nature to that of her unapologetic and acquisitive predecessor, most people soon forgetting the ample cause Edward II had given Queen Isabelle 'to make her own bed and lie on it'. Philippa, in contrast, seemed the embodiment of the passive virtues of humility, obedience, modesty, piety and chastity. In the medieval work *speculum dominarum* – the mirror for princesses – which was written for Jeanne de Navarre by her confessor Durand de Champagne early in the fourteenth century, the role of a queen is expressed almost entirely in terms of charitable acts. It reads, in part, 'her reputation for mercy should make her visits a welcome solace to the poor, the oppressed, and the unfortunate' epitomising the queen's 'virtuous love of God, relatives, neighbours, fellow Christians, husband, and children.' Philippa personified all these medieval feminine virtues.

In contrast, Isabelle was determined to pursue Edward I's wars against the Scots, but levying the necessary taxes made her even more unpopular.

Indeed, many of the proceeds stayed in her household and Mortimer also enriched himself greatly, with expenditure to match. After the Scottish invasion of County Durham in 1327, Isabella decided that the only solution was to negotiate a peace treaty to end the warfare that had continued since 1296 in the form of raids, skirmishes and cattle-rustling – a traditional activity on the borders, for which the author's ancestors would eventually be expelled from Scotland in the nineteenth century. The peace treaty was signed by Robert the Bruce in Edinburgh on 17 March 1328 and ratified by the Parliament sitting at Nottingham on 1 May. A betrothal and marriage being the conventional way of sealing this sort of alliance, in accordance with the Treaty of Northampton, Isabelle's daughter Joan of the Tower was married on 17 July 1328 to Robert Bruce's son David. She was 7 years old and her groom even younger. One year later, after the death of his father, on 7 June 1329 5-year-old David Bruce became king of Scotland, although not formally crowned at Scone Abbey until November 1331.

In autumn 1330, when their days as guardians of Isabelle's son were drawing to an end, the king having been born in December of 1312, the queen and Mortimer retired to Nottingham castle, where William Montagu, a noble friend of Edward III, led a score of men into the keep through a secret passage on 19 October. Isabelle and Mortimer had been planning to arrest him, so when the intruders burst in, there was a brief and bloody fight, which ended with Mortimer under arrest and Isabelle reputedly throwing herself at the feet of her son and begging him to show mercy 'to gentle Mortimer'. Henry of Lancaster's troops rapidly took control of the whole castle, blocking any chance of Mortimer's escape or rescue.

The coup d'état so efficiently accomplished, he was tried in the following month and found guilty on fourteen charges of treason, including the murder of Edward II. This covered most of the long-term political grievances against Isabelle as regent, all now blamed on her 'partner in crime'. Sentenced by Parliament to be drawn and hanged as a traitor, Mortimer was hanged at Tyburn on 29 November but, by the clemency of Edward III, not subjected to the tortures and indignities often imposed on executed traitors before death. Although confined in Windsor castle for several months until transferred to her own property at Castle Rising in Norfolk, Isabelle was never accused of any wrongdoing during the regency. Her immense riches accumulated during that period had to be returned to the state, but she was given the generous allowance of £3,000 per annum by Edward III,[3] which made her appropriately rich for England's dowager queen.

Although Isabelle never regained political power in England, she continued to play a part in France, agreeing with Charles IV a settlement of the quarrel in Gascony. The French king upped a previous offer for the territory of £60,000 by a further 50,000 marks with an amnesty for the Gascon rebels, except for eight named knights who were banished and their castles destroyed. When Charles IV died in February 1328 without a male heir, Isabelle slightly bent the rules of feudal succession with the argument that, since her son Edward III was a nephew of the dead French king and his closest male relative, being a descendant in direct line through her of Philippe IV, he should therefore inherit the throne of France. The claim did not succeed, but launched the 100 Years War, in which her adored grandson Edward of Woodstock, Prince of Wales, would distinguish himself, becoming known in Aquitaine as *lo princi neguer*[4] or the Black Prince.

At the beginning of 1333 open warfare with Scotland saw the Scots occupying Berwick-on-Tweed and an English force besieging the city. Edward III travelled north with an army to block any attempt by the Scots to lift the siege. Philippa travelled with him, but was left safely in Bamburgh castle, twenty miles to the south, while he took up a position on Halidon Hill, a commanding site two miles to the southwest of the besieged port-city. To confirm a truce, Edward took hostages including the son of Sir Alexander Seton, the Scottish commander of Berwick. Considering that Seton was tricking him, Edward announced that he would hang two of the hostages each day the town held out. One of the first two hanged in sight of the walls was Thomas, Seton's own son. Whether or not this weighed on Philippa's mind as tarnishing her husband's soul, she is best remembered as the queen who pleaded successfully with Edward III to spare the lives of the burghers of Calais in 1346. Although only recorded by chronicler Jean Froissart, the story goes that, after the Battle of Crécy, the walled town of Calais was ordered by Philippe VI of France not to surrender to the victorious English. When, after an 11-month siege by

Edward III, starvation forced the population to yield, Edward undertook to spare the citizens if six of their leaders would walk out and surrender themselves to him. Six of them did, wearing nooses around their necks as a sign that they expected to be hanged. And so they would have been, had she not intervened with the king – according to Froissart.

With the Scottish relieving force resoundingly defeated by Edward at Halidon Hill in July 1332, the under-age Scottish King David II and Joan of the Tower were sent for their safety to France, where they were favourably received by Philippe VI. During their absence from Britain, David's cause attracted more support in Scotland, so that he and Joan were able to return home in June 1341, when, aged 17, he could rule in his own right. The cross-border warfare continuing, he was taken prisoner in County Durham in October 1346, and remained in captivity for eleven years, during which Edward III allowed his sister Joan to visit her husband in the Tower of London. If Edward's purpose was to get Joan pregnant – perhaps to keep hostage a child of David by her – it failed, despite a number of conjugal visits.

After David II's release in 1357, he returned to Scotland. Never having been accepted in Scotland, Joan had had enough of her husband's infidelities there, and decided to remain in England with her mother at Castle Rising in Norfolk, midway between Kings Lynn and Sandringham. Queen Philippa managed to effect a reconciliation between the dowager queen and Edward III, who blamed Isabelle for the invasion of England and Mortimer for the murder of his father. When Edward and Philippa came to visit England's dowager queen and the king's sister, and be entertained with falconry, feasting and music, there were thus three queens in residence at Castle Rising.

The rest of the time, Isabelle occupied herself with charitable works that did little to correct her public reputation. Among these, following the custom of Queen Marguerite, second wife of Edward I, she made gifts to the Greyfriars church in Newgate, enabling its construction to be finished. Well past her sixtieth birthday – a good age for the time – the dowager queen died on 22 August 1358 in Hertford castle. Being in good health until nearly the end of her life, she had allegedly appeared on St George's Day in April wearing a silk dress embroidered with 300 rubies and 1,800 pearls. The body was embalmed, transported to

London and buried in the Greyfriars church at the end of November with the Archbishop of Canterbury officiating. Her expressed desire was to be buried in her bridal dress, made when she was about 12 years old. It seems unlikely that this was carried out, but a casket containing the heart of Edward II was placed in the tomb with her, on her instructions. Aged only 41, Joan too died at Hertford castle in 1362 and was buried in the same church. If not the archbishop, someone else must have pronounced the words *requiescat in pace* over their coffins at the time, but neither queen's remains were to be left in peace there. Converted into a parish church known as Christ Church, Newgate, after Henry VIII's dissolution of the monasteries, the building was destroyed in the Great Fire of 1666. Rebuilt by Sir Christopher Wren, it was destroyed again in the Blitz of 1940 with all trace of human remains vaporised. The roofless shell of the church is now a public garden.

In Philippa's 40-year marriage to Edward III, she bore him thirteen children. Three died in the Black Death of 1348, a year memorable for armed outlaws trespassing in the royal forests, risking the severe forest laws by burning hedges and enclosures in their desperate search for food. By the time she died in August 1369 from what appears to have been dropsy, an excessive retention of fluid in the tissues, she had outlived eight of her children and was survived by four sons and one daughter. It was in her memory that Queen's College, Oxford, was founded after she was buried with great pomp on 9 January 1370 in Westminster abbey. Eight years later, Edward III was laid to rest beside her.

Epilogue

Given the high numbers of pregnancies endured by noble and royal women in this period, one may wonder why there was not a population explosion in Europe. Various explanations exist. One argument is that the continent was overpopulated, not for the available space, but for the amount of land already cleared for agriculture and the methods used in crop-growing, with ratios of grain harvested to seed sown as low as 2:1. In the event the serfs did ever produce a surplus, this was requisitioned by the unproductive knightly families they served, so there was no incentive for those who ploughed and sowed to improve farming methods. Add to that the consequences of climate change – or even one cold, wet summer – and the already subsistence-level nourishment of the serf classes reduced them to near-starvation level with consequent disease and epidemics actually sending populations into decline. In addition, feudal warfare was total war, in which the first step was to burn the enemy's crops, cut down his orchards and vines and slaughter or drive off his livestock. The knightly classes could survive this to some extent by retaliation or consuming stockpiled provisions, but the poor were left with serious shortages in the next winter.

This reduced resistance to disease, so that, even if children were born to the peasants, they mostly died young. In addition, the poor diet resulted in anaemia in adults of both sexes and and amenorrhea in the women. Serfs being tied to the land they occupied, there was no way they could seek a better life elsewhere without risking harsh punishment. In Imperial Russia, where serfdom continued into the nineteenth century, with the size of an estate being described as having so many 'souls', both men and women were flogged with the *knout* or cat o' nine tails for any slight disobedience or indiscipline. At least in medieval France serfs could risk trying to reach a Church-founded *bastide*. There, incomers would be protected from their owners, enfranchised and given a plot to cultivate for themselves, subject to taxation.

Medieval demography is not an easy subject, because few accurate contemporary records exist for analysis, but there was great disparity between the countries of Europe. In the German Empire population is estimated at 6.4 million in 1100, rising to 7.3 million in 1200 and possibly 9 million in 1300. In France, only two-thirds its modern size, the comparable figures are 11 million in 1100, rising to 13 million in 1200 and 17 million in 1300 – not an explosion, but a slow and steady progress. By contrast, in England, Wales, Scotland and Ireland grouped together the total population was 2.7 million in 1100, 3.2 million in 1200 and 4.1 million in 1300. These low figures are reflected also in the Low Countries and Scandinavia.

As we have seen, the better diet of the nobility theoretically permitted large families, but the effect was often countered by infant and child mortality. In addition, the appallingly high number of noble and royal women who died in childbirth poses the question why nothing was done about this. A root cause was that illness and death were seen as God's will, to counter which nothing could, or should, be done. Yet, there were some enlightened medical practitioners in southern Europe.

Jews and Muslims being banned from the rigidly Christian north of France, the Albigensian crusaders under Simon de Montfort were appalled to find imams and rabbis teaching alongside Christians when they reached Montpellier. In the more tolerant Occitan-speaking south of the country, the word *convivença*, meaning pagan tolerance which allowed interchange of ideas with non-Christians, considerably improved knowledge and practice of medicine and surgery. Jewish doctors and surgeons trained in Montpellier and Salerno in Italy. The statutes of the University of Montpellier in 1239 required any person practising medicine or surgery to have studied there and obtained a licence from the bishop and a *licentia docendi* or teaching diploma from the university. In the county of Provence the Constitutions of 1306 relating to the Jews permitted them to practise medicine and surgery, providing they were properly qualified, and allowed them to visit Christian patients who had previously confessed themselves and taken the sacrament, so were ready to face their God![1]

Medical knowledge in Europe was based chiefly on Greek and Latin texts that had survived the Dark Ages in monasteries. Greek knowledge of anatomy, necessary for surgery, came largely from contact with Egyptians at Alexandria. However, understanding of infection was scarce, leading, for example, to the death of Richard Lionheart from gangrene probably introduced into the wound he received at Châlus castle by the knife or hands of the man trying to cut the head of the fatal crossbow bolt out of his shoulder to save his life. Central to much Greek medicine was the theory of the four humours, which needed to be in balance for health, so illness might be treated with dietary advice to restore the balance. Greek knowledge of herbal medicine was often mixed with folk remedies prescribed by 'wise women', many abhorred by the Church as witches. Physic gardens, where medicinal herbs were cultivated, existed in many monasteries, where leaves and roots of the plants were used to make infusions and ointments until the second Lateran Council in 1139 discouraged the religious from practising medicine.

The German Benedictine abbess Hildegard of Bingen (1098–1179) believed that illness was a symptom of a bad relationship with the Christian God, but also codified in her book *causae et curae* the use of herbal medicine, based on the Biblical teaching that all things on Earth had been put there by God for the use of mankind. *Kitab al-Qanûn fi al-Tibb* or the book of the Canon of Medicine by the Persian philosopher Ibn Sīnā, known as Avicenna in Europe, was written even earlier, about 1030, and drew on the considerable knowledge of medicine available in works by previous Greek, Indian and Muslim writers. The theory and practice of surgery owed much to the second-century Greek philosopher known as Galen, who had learned anatomy by treating gladiators suffering from hideous injuries received in the games at Pergamon. Yet, some of his ideas were wildly wrong, because based on animal, and not human, anatomy.

The only medical intervention most sick people would get in the Middle Ages was bleeding, by incision into a vein or by the application of leeches, or cupping. The latter practice, known to have been used since 1,500 BCE, was the application of heated glass or metal cups to the skin. When the air inside the cups cooled and exerted a suction effect on the skin, it was thought to 'draw out' the cause of internal problems. Cupping is still favoured today by some Olympic athletes to relieve stressed muscles.

As far as obstetrics went, the Anglo–Saxon term 'midwife' from Germanic *mit* and *Weib* simply means a female companion for the woman giving birth, and implies no anatomical knowledge, which helps to explain why so many women died during and after a difficult birth. There was, however, in eleventh-century Italy the *schola medica salernitana* – less of a formal school and more of an association of doctors founded at Salerno in the ninth century, where medical texts translated from Greek and Arabic at the monastery of Monte Cassino provided the basis of what became known as *ars medicinae* – the art of medicine. Some of the diagrams produced there illustrated various dangerous malpresentations of a foetus that may have originated in Greek-Egyptian Alexandria – where there was no taboo, thanks to the centuries of mummification, on postmortem dissection.

The Salernitan doctors were all men, who drew on Greek and Arab sources and the Latin writings of Soranus of Ephesus and Muscio in North Africa to propose treatment, by herbal pessaries and other means, of menstrual problems, tumours, prolapse and fertility issues concerned with 'the female testicles'. Uterine suffocation was a hypothetical physical condition believed in the Hippocratic corpus to crush the lungs when women's wombs moved around the body, producing also hysteria – directly composed from *hysterika*, the Greek word for uterus. Galen's contemporary Aretaeus seems to have been responsible for the theory of the uterus moving about in the body. The 'wandering womb' was thought to be cured by burning a feather beneath the woman's nostrils to make an unpleasant smell and drive the uterus away from her head while some sweet-smelling thing was placed near her vagina, to attract the uterus back to its proper place. Some people held that menstruation, all sexual activity and pregnancy were harmful for women, in direct contradiction of Hippocratic teaching that these were normal, and indeed essential for healthy females. There was also the Judeo-Christian misogynistic belief that women were rendered unclean and dangerous to men by their normal functions of menstruation and childbirth.

Some of the 'cures' of folk medicine are simply bizarre. One was that a husband unable to impregnate his wife should procure the uterus of a hare, dry it and reduce it to powder, which was to be mixed with wine and drunk. The woman was to do the same with the testicles of a hare. This was said to produce a male child when the couple lay together after the woman's next period. For headaches and pains in the joints, healers took equal quantities of helenium and radish, wormwood and bishopswort, cropleek and garlic and hollow leek. Pounded together and boiled in butter with celandine and red nettle, then left in a brass vessel until dark brown in colour and strained through a cloth to remove solid particles, the resulting greasy mess was rubbed on the painful part.[2] Presumably, the massage had some effect, as when modern mothers 'rub away' a child's pain.

The doctors of the *schola*, being all male, did not intervene in childbirth. Whereas women healers could palpate a patient's breasts and belly, male doctors did not touch female patients' bodies. This could have been a good thing when one thinks about the high risk of puerperal fever in nineteenth-century lying-in hospitals due to male doctors going from patient to patient without even washing their hands. Fortunately, also practising in Salerno were some female obstetricians, who were considerably more knowledgeable than most midwives of the time and had acquired hands-on knowledge of caring for women giving birth and the complications which could arise.

One of these, named Trota or Trocta and sometimes called Tortola de Ruggiero, was referred to in the book attributed to her as *magistra* – or 'female master', indicating that it was dictated to a clerk, women not then being literate in southern Italy. The body of learning loosely called *Trotula* – meaning, more or less, 'the little book of Trota' – was written in Latin, copied and circulated among the top levels of European nobility, and may have saved many women's lives. Entitled *De curis mulierum ante, in et post partum*[3] – the care of women before, during and after childbirth – it was a handbook for midwives, based on practical experience of these women in Salerno and their pupils in Montpellier. The cardinal recommendation was for basic hygiene at the time of birth, the avoidance of noise, stress and worry for the mother and the administration of opium to relieve pain. But some of the advice was specific.

> Using great caution, the patient should be induced to sneeze, holding her nostrils and mouth tightly, so that the greater part of the energy and force be directed toward the uterus ... Above all,

she should be protected from chill, and suffumigations of aromatic substances should be placed far from her nostrils, but near the orifice of the vagina, since the uterus has a propension for sweet smells and shrinks from the fetid ... Musk, amber and aloe wood and similar substances are suitable for the rich, while aromatic plants such as mint and origano will do for the poor.[4]

Such was the fame of the women in Salerno that the twelfth-century poetess Marie de France wrote in her tragic poem of two ill-fated lovers entitled *Le lai des deus amanz:*

> *En Salerne ai une parente, riche femme mut ad grant rente;*
> *Plus de trente anz i ad esté. L'art de phisike ad tant usé*
> *Que mut est saives de mescines, tant cunust herbes e racines,*
> *Si vus a li volez aler e mes lettres od vus porter*
> *E mustrer li vostre aventure, ele en prendra cunseil e cure;*
> *Teus lettuaires vus durat e teus beivres vus baillerat*
> *Que tut vus recunforterunt e bone vertu vus dufrunt.*

I know a woman in Salerno who is rich and highly paid. For more than thirty years she has practised medicine there and is an expert who knows all about herbs and roots. If you want to go there with a letter from me, and tell her your problem, she will look after you. She will give you potions to cure you and fortifying drinks to make you strong.

While in provincial France many midwives were disparagingly labelled *accoucheuses* or *ventrières* – birth-women or belly-women – in thirteenth-century Paris a corps of women was trained with male doctors at the college of St Côme et St Damien.[5] Hildegard of Bingen, who had served as a nursing nun before becoming abbess, wrote two medical treatises; one was *causae et curae*, which was a blend of sound common sense and folk medicine. Every convent, of course, needed at least one nurse among the sisters, to avoid the need to bring in a male doctor to cope with illness or injury.

Being a midwife in England was somewhat less dangerous than in France because English universities had no schools of medicine. In France, however, accredited doctors kept a wary eye on female practitioners who might be usurping their function and thus depriving them of fees. The Church too, was a danger: midwives were instructed to baptise a baby about to die, in order for its soul to go straight to heaven, but if they baptised a baby that did not die, the local priest could denounce them for stealing his baptismal fee. Yet, women who had the knowledge and skills were in such demand that some travelled many miles to assist a noble birth: a Parisian woman named Asseline Alexandre attended the duchess of Burgundy in childbed while Jeanne Goutière attended Queen Isabeau of Bavaria, consort of the French King Charles VI who bore him eleven live children.[6]

Since there were some trained midwives, why were they not employed by *all* the Plantagenet princesses? The appalling answer seems to be that they were usually regarded as common women, who had no place in a noblewoman's bedchamber at such a time. Such prejudice would later be called snobbery. How sad that this should cause so many unnecessary and agonising deaths.

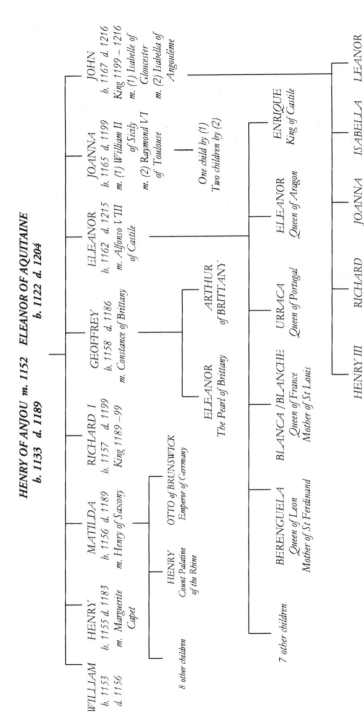

HENRY OF ANJOU *m. 1152*   **ELEANOR OF AQUITAINE**
b. 1133 d. 1189   *b. 1122 d. 1204*

WILLIAM
b. 1153
d. 1156

HENRY
b. 1155 d. 1183
m. Marguerite
Capet

MATILDA
b. 1156 d. 1189
m. Henry of Saxony

RICHARD I
b. 1157 d. 1199
King 1189–99

GEOFFREY
b. 1158 d. 1186
m. Constance of Brittany

ELEANOR
b. 1162 d. 1215
m. Alfonso VIII
of Castile

JOANNA
b. 1165 d. 1199
m. (1) William II
of Sicily
m. (2) Raymond VI
of Toulouse

JOHN
b. 1167 d. 1216
King 1199 – 1216
m. (1) Isabelle of
Gloucester
m. (2) Isabella of
Angoulême

HENRY
Count Palatine
of the Rhine

OTTO of BRUNSWICK
Emperor of Germany

8 other children

ELEANOR
The Pearl of Brittany

ARTHUR
of BRITTANY

One child by (1)
Two children by (2)

BERENGUELA
Queen of Leon
Mother of St Ferdinand

BLANCA /BLANCHE
Queen of France
Mother of St Louis

URRACA
Queen of Portugal

ELEANOR
Queen of Aragon

ENRIQUE
King of Castile

7 other children

HENRY III
King of England
1216 – 1272

RICHARD
Emperor of Germany

JOANNA

ISABELLA

LEANOR

Appendix I: The legitimate children and grandchildren of Eleanor by Henry of Anjou

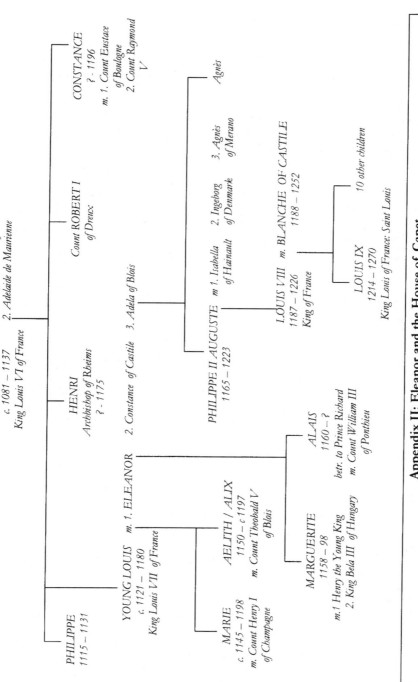

Appendix II: Eleanor and the House of Capet,

including her marriage to Young Louis and that of her Castilian granddaughter Blanca / Blanche to Prince Louis, later Louis VIII of France

PHILIPPE
1115 – 1131

FAT LOUIS   *m.* 1. *Lucienne de Rochefort*
c. 1081 – 1137   2. *Adelaide de Maurienne*
King Louis VI of France

HENRI
Archbishop of Rheims
? – 1175

Count ROBERT I
of Dreux

CONSTANCE
? – 1196
m. 1. *Count Eustace
of Boulogne*
2. *Count Raymond
V*

YOUNG LOUIS   *m.* 1. ELEANOR
c. 1121 – 1180
King Louis VII of France

2. *Constance of Castile*   3. *Adela of Blois*

MARIE
c. 1145 – 1198
*m. Count Henry I
of Champagne*

AELITH / ALIX
1150 – *c* 1197
*m. Count Theobald V
of Blois*

PHILIPPE II AUGUSTE   *m.* 1. *Isabella
1165 – 1223   of Hainault*

2. *Ingeborg
of Denmark*

3. *Agnès
of Merano*

Agnès

MARGUERITE
1158 – 98
*m.*1 *Henry the Young King*
2. *King Bela III of Hungary*

ALAIS
1160 – ?
betr. to Prince Richard
*m. Count William III
of Ponthieu*

LOUIS VIII   *m.* BLANCHE OF CASTILE
1187 – 1226   1188 – 1252
King of France

LOUIS IX
1214 – 1270
King Louis of France: Saint Louis

10 other children

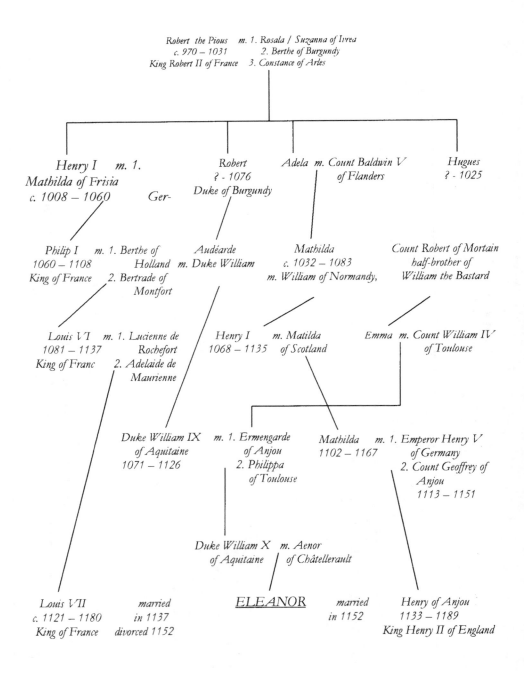

Robert the Pious m. 1. Rosala / Suzanna of Ivrea
c. 970 – 1031   2. Berthe of Burgundy
King Robert II of France   3. Constance of Arles

Henry I   m. 1.
Mathilda of Frisia
c. 1008 – 1060   Ger-

Robert
? - 1076
Duke of Burgundy

Adela m. Count Baldwin V
of Flanders

Hugues
? - 1025

Philip I   m. 1. Berthe of
1060 – 1108   Holland
King of France   2. Bertrade of
Montfort

Audéarde
m. Duke William

Mathilda
c. 1032 – 1083
m. William of Normandy,

Count Robert of Mortain
half-brother of
William the Bastard

Louis VI   m. 1. Lucienne de
1081 – 1137   Rochefort
King of Franc   2. Adelaide de
Maurienne

Henry I   m. Matilda
1068 – 1135   of Scotland

Emma m. Count William IV
of Toulouse

Duke William IX   m. 1. Ermengarde
of Aquitaine   of Anjou
1071 – 1126   2. Philippa
of Toulouse

Mathilda   m. 1. Emperor Henry V
1102 – 1167   of Germany
2. Count Geoffrey of
Anjou
1113 – 1151

Duke William X   m. Aenor
of Aquitaine   of Châtellerault

Louis VII
c. 1121 – 1180
King of France

married
in 1137
divorced 1152

ELEANOR

married
in 1152

Henry of Anjou
1133 – 1189
King Henry II of England

**Appendix III:
Eleanor's relatedness to Young Louis and Henry of Anjou**

Acknowledgements

Professor Friedrich Heer of Vienna opened my eyes to the distortion of history caused by the Victorian divines' belief that it should always show God's will directing mankind's actions. Gascon-speakers Natalie and Eric Roulet opened wide to me the Occitan civilisation and its beautiful language. Amy Ruth Kelly taught me much about medieval Aquitaine and its duchess Eleanor, the progenitrix of the Plantagenet line. Horsewoman Ann Hyland always spared time to educate me about medieval horses. Eric Chaplain, managing director of the Occitan publishing house Princi Neguer in Pau leant precious source material that saved much travel and sitting in libraries. That doyen of translators Miguel Castro Mata dug up some hidden gems that I might have missed. Valérie de Reignac at the Bordeaux Musée des Arts Décoratifs showed me many exhibits not normally seen by the public. My former comrade-in-arms John Digby Anderson delved into the archives of York Minster to find Kay Staniland's impressive account of the wedding there of Princess Margaret and Alexander of Scotland in 1251. Les Amis du Vieux Chinon gave permission for me to photograph the contemporary fresco in the Chapelle Ste Radegonde showing Henry II leading Eleanor away into captivity. My series editor Dr Danna Messer generously shared the fruits of her scholarship on more than one occasion.

To them all go my heartfelt thanks. With all that help, any errors remain mine alone.

For the production of this book at Pen and Sword Publications, my sincere thanks go to commissioning editor Claire Hopkins and production coordinator Laura Hirst.

Notes

All translations are by the author, unless otherwise attributed
All illustrations are from the author's collection. If any copyright has been infringed, please communicate with the author, care of the publisher, for correction in any subsequent edition.

Chapter 1

1. *Letters of Arnulf of Lisieux*, ed. F. Barlow, London: Camden Society Third Series 1939, No. 10, p. 14.
2. Meaning, from the county of Anjou.
3. Original spelling, Alianor.
4. *L'Histoire de Guillaume le Maréchal*, ed. and trans. P. Meyer, Paris 1901, Vol. III, p. 28.
5. *Bernard Epistolae*, No. cxiii in *Patrologia Latina* 182.
6. William of Newburgh, *Historia Rerum Anglicanum*, ed. R. Howlett, London: Rolls Series 82, 1884, Vol. I, p. 93.
7. See D. Boyd, *April Queen, Eleanor of Aquitaine*, Stroud: The History Press 2011, pp. 51–61.
8. At the time, this word was not used. Crusaders spoke of going on pilgrimage to Jerusalem or the Holy Sepulchre.
9. Except for 'decent washerwomen'.
10. The complicated proceedings are covered in Boyd, *April Queen*, pp. 117–23.

Chapter 2

1. Quoted in R. Bartlett, *England under the Norman and Angevin Kings*, Oxford: Clarendon Press 2000, p. 140.
2. *Arnulf of Lisieux*, p.14.
3. Walter Map, *De Nugis Curialium*, (eds) F. Tupper and M. B. Ogle, London: Chatto & Windus 1924, p. 278.
4. A. Richard, *Histoire des Comtes de Poitou*, Paris: Picard et Fils 1903, p. 115.
5. There is no single accepted method of Occitan spelling, although the associates of the nineteenth-century Provençal poet known as Frédéric Mistral tried to impose one. In any case the various dialects, such as Gascon, Avergnat and Provençal very widely in vocabulary and pronunciation.

6. Spelled *trobador* in Occitan, the word is derived from the verb *trobar* meaning 'to find, invent or create'.

7. *De amore* simply means 'about love', but the work is often referred to as 'The Art of Courtly Love'.

8. In referring to the object of his adoration by a masculine pronoun the troubadour emphasises his vassalage, much as a medieval Arabic poet addressed his lady as *sayiddi*, or 'lord'.

9. The present castle dates back only to the seventeenth century.

10. Richard, *Histoire des Comtes de Poitou*, p. 115.

11. Ibid., p. 116.

12. A. R. Kelly, *Eleanor of Aquitaine and the Four Kings*, Cambridge: Harvard University Press 1981, p. 87.

13. For a full account of the life of Eleanor of Aquitaine, see Boyd *April Queen*.

Chapter 3

1. Boyd, *April Queen*, pp. 146–50.

2. Richard, *Histoire des Comtes de Poitou*, p. 121.

3. Some sources say the birth was at Windsor castle.

4. The construction lasted forty-three years.

5. *Silvae majoris abbatiae chartularium majus*, Vol II (no page numbers).

6. He had been abbot of Bec Abbey in Normandy and was succeeded by Roger de Bailleul, who was elected to the see of Canterbury, but declined the honour and the office.

7. Cited in Kelly, *Eleanor of Aquitaine*, p. 110

8. *Chronicle of Melrose*, (eds) A. O. and M. Anderson, London: Perry, Lund, Humphries & Co. 1936, p. 79.

9. After the deaths of Henry II and Richard, King John hanged his Welsh hostages during the hostilities of 1211–12. See Barnwell Chronicle, p. 207.

Chapter 4

1. William of Malmesbury, *De regung gestis anglorum*, ed. W. Stubbs, London: Rolls Series 90, 1887, Vol. 2, p. 494.

2. F. Vercauteren, *Les médécins dans les principautés de le Belgique ... du viiie au xiiie siècle* in *Moyen Age*, No. 57 of 1951, pp. 72–3.

Chapter 5

1. Also spelled Alix.

2. From the French *nappe*, a cloth.

3. Bartlett, *England under the Norman and Angevin Kings*, pp. 131–4.

4. A practice known as syneisaktism.

5. Boyd, *April Queen*, pp. 163–80.

6. The original source of the name 'Lorraine', now a French region.

7. Bartlett, *England under the Norman and Angevin Kings*, p. 118.
8. D. Boyd, *Lionheart: The True Story of England's Crusader King*, Stroud: The History Press 2014, pp. 173–93.

Chapter 6

1. Some sources say Dover.
2. J. Carmi Parsons and B. Wheeler (eds), *Medieval Mothering*, New York: Garland 1996, pp. 13–15.
3. M. W. Labarge, *Women in Medieval Life*, London: Hamish Hamilton 1986, p. 77.
4. When bought by subscription for the library at Sotheby's in December 1983 at the price of £8.14 million, it was the most valuable book in the world.
5. *Diese goldene Seite bezeugt dem Leser, dass der fromme Herzog Heinrich und seine Gemahlin von ganzem Herzen die Liebe zu Christus über alles andere stellten.*
6. Also spelled Rikenzam according to Arnold von Lübeck's *Chronica Slavorum*.
7. See, at greater length, Boyd, *Lionheart*, pp. 205–20.
8. The term was first used by Victorian historian Kate Norgate. It still seems the most appropriate word to cover the kingdom of England, the duchies of Normandy and Aquitaine and the several counties on French soil.
9. Details of Matilda's early life in Saxony are taken from the study by Professor Dr Wolfgang Leschorn of Brunswick Technical University, downloadable from www.dom-minden.de/aktuelles/festrede_Minden 1168.pdf.
10. Kelly, *Eleanor of Aquitaine*, p. 209.
11. Ibid., p. 207.
12. Richard, *Histoire des Comtes de Poitou*, p. 206.
13. *Gesta Henrici Secundi Benedicti Abbatis: The Chronicle of the Reigns of Henry II and Richard I A.D. 1169–1192; Known Commonly under the Name of Benedict of Peterborough, Edited from the Cotton MSS.*, ed. W. Stubbs, London: Longmans 1867, Vol. 2, p. 72.

Chapter 7

1. Galicia is called *Jackobsland* in the Nordic sagas.
2. Still an impressive ruin, this was where papal legates tried to reconcile Henry II and Becket in 1169.
3. Some sources say, by the Cistercian abbot Henry of Marcy.
4. Sometimes spelled Torigny or Thorigny; in Latin, Robertus de Torigneio.
5. In the Asturias region of NW Spain.
6. The kingdom of Navarre lay mostly south of the Pyrenees and partly to the north in modern France.
7. Some sources say fifty-four.

8. In *Chronica latina regum Castellae*.
9. Boyd, *April Queen*, pp. 231–8.
10. The long papacy of Innocent III, born Lothar of Segni, began at the relatively early age of 37.
11. Which had been split by King Alfonso VII at his death, to provide a kingdom each for his sons Sancho and Fernando.
12. Neatly put in one on-line biography as: *Con él volvieron a unirse ambas Coronas, al heredar el reíno de Castilla por la muerte de su tío Enrique I (1217) y el de León por la muerte de su padre Alfonso IX (1230). Las dos herencias plantearon problemas y resistencias, salvadas gracias a la habilidad diplomática de la reina madre Berenguela.*
13. Meaning, the Catholic king and queen.

Chapter 8
1. According to Alberic des Trois-Fontaines in *Obituaires de Sens Tomei*.
2. J. V. A. Fine, *The Late Medieval Balkans: A Critical Survey from the Late Twelfth Century to the Ottoman Conquest*, University of Michigan Press 1987, p. 130.
3. Alberic des Trois-Fontaines, *Obituaires*.
4. R. L. Wolff, *Mortgage and Redemption of an Emperor's Son: Castile and the Latin Empire of Constantinople* in *Speculum* 29 of 1954, p. 60.
5. Name in Old Norse, Hrólf Rögnvaldrsson.
6. There does exist a miniature portraying together Richard, Joanna and Philippe Auguste, which may imply that the handover took place in Paris, not Poitiers.
7. Boyd, *April Queen*, pp. 227–8.
8. Roger of Howden, *The Annals of Roger de Hoveden: Comprising the History of England and of other Countries of Europe from A.D. 732 to A.D. 1201*, trans. H. T .Riley, London: Bohn 1853, Vol. II, p. 413.
9. Boyd, *Lionheart*, pp. 126–7.
10. *Gesta Henrici Secundi* ,Vol. II, p. 126.
11. Ibid., pp. 133, 158.
12. Roger of Howden, *Chronica*, ed. W. Stubbs, London: Rolls Series No. 51, 1870, Vol. III, p. 99; *Gerald of Wales, De Principiis*, ed. G. F. *Warner*, London: Rolls Series No. 21, 1861, Vol. VIII, p. 282.
13. Stubbs *Rolls Series No 47*, Vol II, p. 49.
14. Born in Tikrit, birthplace eight centuries later of Saddam Hussein.
15. Roger of Howden, *Chronica*, Vol. IV, p. 96.

Chapter 9
1. Boyd, *April Queen*, pp. 324–6.
2. Often rendered as 30,000 marks, equivalent to the 20,000 pounds recorded in the *Annals of Margam*, although historian F. M. Powicke held that both copies of the treaty specified 20,000 marks.

3. From Latin *carruca*. In classical Latin, it was a four-wheeled waggon; in medieval Latin, a heavy plough with iron ploughshare, pulled by a team of eight oxen. A carucate might be as large as 120 acres.
4. G. Sivéry, *Blanche de Castile*, Paris: Fayard 1990, p. 11.
5. Ibid., Note 3 on p. 259.
6. Ibid., p. 7.
7. M. Salcedo Tapia, *Noticias y Documentos de Itero de la Vega*, Palencia: Institución Tello Téllez de Meneses 1992, pp. 514–5.
8. Roger of Howden, *Chronica*, Vol. IV, p. 114.
9. Matthew Paris, *Grandes Chroniques*, trans. A. Huillard-Bréholles, Paris: Ecole des Chartes 1841, Vol. II, p. 317.
10. *Magna Vita Sancti Hugonis*, ed. D-L. Douie & H. Farmer, London: Thomas Nelson 1961, Vol. II, p. 14.

Chapter 10
1. Also known as Hawise and by other names.
2. Some sources say she was only nine at the time, but this seems unlikely, given the birth of Henry II in 1204.
3. Roger of Wendover, *Flores Historiarum*, ed. H. G. Howlett, London: Rolls Series 1886–9, Vol. I, p. 316.
4. Richard, *Histoire des Comtes de Poitou*, p. 407.
5. S. McGlynn, *Blood Cries Afar*, Stoud: Spellmount 2011, pp. 139–40.
6. http://plume-dhistoire.fr/isabelle-dangouleme-epouse-de-jean-sans-terre.

Chapter 11
1. The larger one, similar to the White Tower in London, was built by the Conqueror; the smaller, adjacent one by Henry II.
2. Guillaume le Breton, *Gesta Philippi Augusti* in *Recueil des historiens des Gaules et de la France (RHF)*, Vol. XVII, p. 170.
3. *Recueil des historiens des Gaules et de la France*, Vol. XVII, pp. 682–3; Richard, *Histoire des Comtes de Poitou*, pp. 424–5; Powicke *Loss of Normandy*, p. 468.
4. W. L. Warren, *King John*, London: Methuen 1991, p. 184.
5. *The Chronicle of Florence of Worcester with the Two Continuations; Comprising Annals of English History, from the Departure of the Romans to the Reign of Edward I*, trans. T. Forester, London: Bohn 1854, p. 314.
6. Ibid., p. 185.
7. Ibid.
8. S. Painter, *The Reign of King John*, Baltimore: Johns Hopkins University Press 1966, p. 231.
9. Anonymous of Béthune in *Recueil des historiens des Gaules et de la France*, Vol. XXIV, p. 105.
10. McGlynn, *Blood Cries Afar*, pp. 127–9.

11. Also as the Fair Maid of Brittany.
12. Sometimes written as 'Vipont'.
13. W. Page, *A History of the County of York, North Riding*, London: Constable 1914, Vol. 1, pp. 42–9.
14. G. Seabourne, *Eleanor of Brittany and her Treatment by King John and Henry III*, in Nottingham Medieval Studies 2007, Vol. LI, pp. 73–110; also essay by A. P. Parkes in *Feud, Violence, and Practice: Essays in Medieval Studies in Honor of Stephen D. White*, (eds) B. S. Tuten and T. Billado, Fareham: Ashgate Publishing 2013, pp. 280–5.
15. Seabourne, *Eleanor of Brittany*, pp. 73–110.
16. Excommunicated for the sin of imprisoning a fellow crusader.
17. Seabourne, *Eleanor of Brittany*, pp. 73–110.

Chapter 12
1. Bartlett, *England under the Norman and Angevin Kings*, p. 268.
2. *Brut y Tywysogion*, ed. J.W. ab Ithel, Cambridge: Cambridge University Press 2012, p. 258.
3. Ibid., p. 251.
4. Boyd, *April Queen*, pp. 246–8.
5. The main source for this chapter has been the entry under Siwan's name by Dr Danna Messer in the Dictionary of Welsh Biography, Aberystwyth, National Library of Wales 2018.
6. *Brut y Tywysogion*, p. 269.
7. Derived from Welsh *cant*, a hundred and *tref*, a town – roughly equivalent to the territory of a hundred in an English county.
8. *Brut y Tywysogion*, pp. 268–9.
9. Mathew Paris, *Historia maior* Vol II, p. 534.
10. Unpublished Register of Honorius III (Reg. Vat. 13, fol. 122) .
11. The land tax due on her English possessions, the name originally due to the practice of recording payments on identical notched sticks, one held by the Exchequer and the other by the vassal.
12. *Annales Monastici*, ed. H. B. Luard, London: Rolls Series No. 36, 1864–69.

Chapter 13
1. Sivéry, *Marguerite de Provence* Paris: Fayard 1987, p. 166.
2. Guillaume Le Breton, *Gesta Philippi Augusti*, pp. 83–4.
3. Roger of Wendover, *Flores Historiarum*, Vol. II, p. 180.
4. McGlynn, *Blood Cries Afar*, note on p. 300.
5. L. Delisle, *Etienne de Gaillardon*, Paris: B.E.C 1899, p. 21.
6. M. Powicke, *The Thirteenth Century 1216–1307*, Oxford: Clarendon Press 1988, p. 1.

7. C. Petit-Dutaillis, *La Vie de Louis VIII*, Paris: Bouillon 1894, p. 208.
8. *Le Breton in Recueil des historiens des Gaules et de la France*, Vol. XVII, p. 91.
9. Powicke, *Thirteenth Century*, p. 16.
10. Ibid., p. 32.
11. Ibid., p. 19.

Chapter 14

1. Also called Waldensianism.
2. Essay by Michael Camille in *Constructing Medieval Sexuality*, *Minnepolis:* University of Minnesota Press 1997, p.73.
3. The present ruins, while still very impressive, are of the castle later rebuilt to guard the Spanish frontier.
4. M. A Teulet, *Layettes du Trésor des Chartes*, Paris: Plon 1866, Vol. II, doc. 1813. *Layette* was the name given to the chests in which state documents were stored.
5. F. Lot and E. Fawtier, *Le Premier Budget de la Monarchie française*, Paris: Champion 1932, pp. cc-cci.
6. G. Sivéry, *Saint Louis et son siècle*, Paris: Tallander 1983, Chapter V, note 6.
7. Rigord, *Gesta Philippi Augusti* in *Recueil des historiens des Gaules et de la France*, Vol. XVII, pp. 30–1.
8. A term that did not then exist, but is used to show her power.
9. *Layettes du Trésor des Chartes*, Vol. II, documents 2264, 2265.
10. It is a slur still used. In 1997, Christine Deviers-Goncourt was sent to prison for her part in concealing the bribes paid in the affair of six frigates built in France for Taiwan. Her lover, Foreign Minister Roland Dumas, was found innocent, but she was openly branded *la putain de le République* – the whore of the Republic.
11. Matthew Paris, *Chronica majora*, ed. Huillard-Bréholles, Vol. III, pp. 399, 402.
12. Labarge, *Women in Medieval Life*, p. 54.

Chapter 15

1. N. M. De Wailly, *Jean, Sire de Joinville*, Paris: Renouard 1868, quoted in Sivéry, *Blanche*, p. 124.
2. J. Le Goff, *Saint Louis*, Paris: Gallimard 1996, p. 95.
3. Ibid., p. 154.
4. G. Sivéry, *Marguerite de Provence*, Paris: Fayard 1987, p. 33.
5. Ibid., p. 39–40.
6. Guillaume de St-Pathus, *Vie de Saint-Louis*, ed. F. Laborde, Paris: Picard 1899, p. 129 (available on line from Bibliothèque Natonale de France Gallica).

7. Sivéry, *Marguerite*, p. 43 citing *Recueil des Historiens des Gaules et de France*, Vol. XXI, p. 245.
8. Camille in *Constructing Medieval Sexuality*, pp. 70–1.
9. Ibid.
10. Sivéry, *Marguerite*, pp. 69–70, quoting Jean de Joinville in *RHF*, Vol. XXI, pp. 406–7.
11. Inaugurated in 2018, the new Palais de Justice is situated in the seventeenth arrondissement of Paris.

Chapter 16

1. P. Coss, *The Lady in Medieval England*, Thrupp: Sutton Publishing 1999, p. 87.
2. Rutebeuf was a *jongleur* or minstrel by all accounts, yet who wrote many poems, songs and even plays. He broke with the two schools of troubadour composition by composing long works exposing life's problems and commenting on social mores. His poems have been used as text for songs by Léo Ferrer and Joan Baez among many others.
3. With the absorption of the Touraine into the royal domain in 1203, there were two principal currencies in circulation: the *livre parisi* or Parisian pound and the *livre tournoise* minted in Tours. 1.25 *livres tournoises* = 1 *livre parisi*. On the model of late Roman currency, where 1 *libra* = 20 *solidi* and 1 *solidus* = 12 *denarii*, the French pounds were divided into *sols* and *deniers*, keeping the Latin signs: £, s and d. This continued in Britain, meaning pounds, shillings and pence until the introduction of decimal currency in 1971.
4. Sivéry, *Marguerite*, p. 97.
5. *Joinville Pléiade*, ed. N de Wailly, Paris: Bibliothèque de l'Ecole des Chartes 1867, pp. 283, 290.
6. Boyd, *Lionheart*, pp. 120–74.
7. Labarge, *Women in Medieval Life*, p. 55.
8. Sivéry, *Marguerite*, pp. 108–9.
9. Grousset, pp. 534–5.
10. See Sivéry, *Marguerite*, pp. 111–12 for a discussion of this incident in the original sources.

Chapter 17

1. Although transferred to a different address, France's most important ophthalmic hospital still bears the name given to it by Louis IX.
2. It may have been treated by *mos teutonicus* – the separation of flesh and bones, the bones alone being returned for burial.

Chapter 18

1. K. Staniland, *The Nuptials of Alexander III of Scotland and Margaret Plantagenet*, Nottingham Medieval Studies, Vol. 30, 1986.
2. Ibid., quoting Claus 39 Hen III, m. 2.
3. Ibid., quoting Rot. Miscell. in Torre, p. 34.
4. Ibid., quoting Claus. 40 Hen III, m.4.
5. A useful catalogue of early medieval foodstuffs may be found in B. Botfield (ed.), *Manners and Household Expenses of England in the 13th and 15th Centuries*, London: Shakespeare Press 1841, pp. 57–67.
6. Staniland, *The Nuptials of Alexander III* , quoting Claus. 10 Hen III, m.3.
7. *Chronicle of Lanercost*, pp. 40–2.
8. Later canonised as St Edmund of Abingdon.
9. Powicke, *Thirteenth Century*, p. 76.
10. *Matthew Paris*, p. 398.
11. Canonised at the request of Archbishop Hubert Walter by Pope Innocent III. Sources: *Catholic Encyclopaedia*, Oxford Dictionary of National Biography, Oxford: Oxford University Press 2004.
12. Bartlett, *England under the Norman and Angevin Kings*, p. 379.
13. E. Hallam (ed.), *The Plantagenet Chronicles*, London: Salamander Books 2002, p. 106.

Chapter 19

1. S. Cockerill, *Eleanor of Castile: The Shadow Queen*, Stroud: Amberley 2014, p. 81.
2. *Matthew Paris*, p. 765.
3. Cockerill, *Eleanor of Castile*, pp. 49–50.
4. Ibid., p. 157
5. A comprehensive account of Eleanor of Castile's property empire and its administration may be found in Cockerill, *Eleanor of Castile*, pp. 206–19.
6. At the wedding of his daughter Margaret, he had struck an esquire without cause, injuring him so badly as to require a substantial compensation.
7. *Manners and Household Expenses*, pp. lxxvi-ii (note) quoting *Rot. Miscell*, No. 71.

Chapter 20

1. Boyd, *Lionheart*, pp. 132–9, 142, 148, 174–5, 179, 189, 192, 195, 204, 208–9, 215.
2. A. Weir, *Queen Eleanor: She-wolf of France, Queen of England*, London: Pimlico 2006, p. 13.
3. Also spelled Gabaston and Gavaston.
4. M. Prestwich, *Edward I*, New Haven: Yale University Press 1997, p. 557.
5. Weir, *Queen Eleanor*, p. 37.

6. J. S. Hamilton, *Piers Gaveston, Earl of Cornwall, 1307–1312*, Detroit and London: Wayne State University Press 1988, p. 48.
7. Essay by James A. Schultz in *Constructing Medieval Sexuality, Minneapolis:* University of Minnesota Press 1997, p. 99.
8. W. C. Jordan, *The Great Famine*, Princeton: Princeton University Press 1996, p. 171; S. Phillips, *Edward II*, New Haven and London: Yale University Press 2011, p. 253.
9. Weir, *Queen Eleanor*, p. 58.
10. M. McKisack, *The Fourteenth Century*, in *The Oxford History of England*, Oxford: Clarendon Press 1997, p. 81.
11. *Vita Edwardi Secundi*, ed. N. Denholm-Young, London: Nelson 1957, p. 143.
12. McKisack, *The Fourteenth Century*, p. 81.
13. Phillips, *Edward II*, pp. 493–4, 500–1.
14. Weir, *Queen Eleanor*, p. 225.
15. Some said they aimed to hide on Lundy Island, but there would have been little point in that.
16. An illustration in Froissart's *Chronicles* depicts the scene.

Chapter 21
1. Weir, *Queen Eleanor*, p. 259.
2. Essay by *E. Jane Burns* in *Constructing Medieval Sexuality, Minnepolis:* University of Minnesota Press 1997, p. 114.
3. Eventually increased to £4,000.
4. Later known as the Black Prince, he inherited Isabelle's estate at Castle Rising, and is buried in Canterbury cathedral, where his impressive effigy continues to attract a stream of visitors.

Chapter 22
1. Arnaud, *Essai sur la condition des juifs en Provence au moyen age*, pub. Forcalquier, 1879, p. 36, quoted in article by C. Roth, *The Qualification of Jewish Physicians in the Middle Ages*, pp. 838–9 published in *Speculum*, Vol. 28, No. 4 of October.
2. Hallam, *The Plantagenet Chronicles*, p. 285.
3. The earliest copy in Britain is at Oxford in the Bodleian Library, MS Digby 79. See also *The Trotula: A Compendium of Women's Medicine*, ed. and trans. Monica H. Green, Philadelphia: University of Pennsylvania Press 2001.
4. *Sulle malatie delle donne*, ed. Pina Boggi Cavallo, Palermo: Piero Cantalupo 1994, p. 83.
5. *Naissance et petite enfance à la cour de France (moyen Age – xixe siècle)*, ed. P. Mormiche & S. Perez, Lille: Presses Universitaires du Septentrion 2016, p. 28.
6. Labarge, *Women in Medieval Life*, p. 181 quoting E. Wichersheimer and D. Jacquart in *Hautes Etudes mediévales et modernes No 35*, Geneva 1979, pp. 33, 191.

Index